Case Marking &
Grammatical Relations
in Polynesian

# Case Marking & Grammatical Relations in Polynesian

by Sandra Chung

University of Texas Press
Austin

For reasons of economy and speed this volume has been printed from camera-ready copy furnished by the author, who assumes full responsibility for its contents.

ISBN 978-0-292-76854-3

utpress.utexas.edu/index.php/rp-form

Library of Congress Catalog Card Number 78-56993
Copyright © 1978 by the University of Texas Press
All rights reserved
Printed in the United States of America

For my parents and grandparents

Contents

Preface ix

Abbreviations & Symbols xiii

0. Introduction 3
    0.1. The Polynesian Languages 7
    0.2. Phonological & Morphological Features 10

1. An Overview of Surface Syntax 12
    1.1. Structure of the Clause 12
    1.2. Structure of the Verb Complex 20
    1.3. Structure of the NP 23
    1.4. Rules Affecting Pronouns 30
    Notes 44

2. The Morphology of Case & Voice 46
    2.1. Case Marking 46
    2.2. The *-Cia* Suffix: Passive, Transitive, or Perfective? 65
    Notes 93

3. Case Marking & Grammatical Relations 95
    3.1. Two Positions on Case Marking & Syntax 96
    3.2. Subject-Referring Rules: Equi 106
    3.3. Subject-Referring Rules: Raising 132
    3.4. Direct Object–Referring Rules 169
    3.5. Other Major Rules 197
    3.6. Conclusion 202
    Notes 204

4. Case Assignment in the Ergative Languages 211
    4.1. Two Proposals for Case Assignment 211
    4.2. Case Assignment in Middle Clauses 216
    4.3. Some Rules That Are Sensitive to Case Marking 234
    4.4. On the Role of Case Marking in Syntax 240
    Notes 242

5. **Previous Approaches to the History of the Case System** 244
    5.1. Proto-Polynesian as an Accusative Language 245
    5.2. Proto-Polynesian as an Ergative Language 248
    5.3. Summary 259
       Notes 260

6. **The Passive-to-Ergative Reanalysis** 261
    6.1. A New Proposal 261
    6.2. On Reconstruction 266
    6.3. Proto-Polynesian *-Cia 268
    6.4. Proto-Polynesian *i 287
    6.5. Proto-Polynesian *e 297
    6.6. The Proto-Polynesian Case System 311
    6.7. The Rise of Ergative Case Marking 312
    6.8. Conclusion 314
       Notes 315

7. **Reanalysis & Pukapukan Syntax** 319
    7.1. The Passive-to-Ergative Reanalysis 320
    7.2. Pukapukan 322
    7.3. Testing the Prediction 325
    7.4. An Account of the Facts 352
    7.5. Two Further Examples 364
    7.6. Conclusion 375
       Notes 377

Appendix A. Orthography 383

Appendix B. Sources 384

Bibliography 385

Index 397

Preface

This book, a revision of my doctoral dissertation, is based on field research on four Polynesian languages --Maori, Tongan, Samoan, and Pukapukan-- conducted at various times over the years 1969-76 and supplemented by material from secondary sources.

Many of the Maori facts discussed here were gathered during a course on the structure of Maori taught at MIT in Fall 1969 by Kenneth Hale and Patrick W. Hohepa. Research on Pukapukan was conducted in Auckland, New Zealand, in 1970-71. Research on Tongan was conducted in Los Angeles and San Diego, California, in 1972-73 and 1975-76. Research on Samoan was conducted in Boston, Massachusetts, and Los Angeles and San Diego, California, during the period 1971-76.

The facts provided by native speakers have been supplemented by material from grammars of Polynesian languages --notably C.M. Churchward (1953), S. Churchward (1951), Williams and Williams (1950[1862]), Biggs (1969), and Elbert (1948)-- as well as data from nineteenth and twentieth century texts (see Appendix B). With few exceptions, the texts record traditional narratives and other stories from oral literature, and so can be taken to reflect spoken rather than written language.

I am indebted to the native speakers of Polynesian languages who contributed heavily to this work from the beginning. They are: Patrick W. Hohepa (Maori); Parepano T. Tukia and Atawua Rōbati (Pukapukan); Siō Mangisi, Vila Fonua, 'Ana Lindsay, and Sela Talakai (Tongan); Eteuati Reupena, Ali'itama Sōtoa, 'Ati Pālata, Palafu Tili, Felita 'Ava, Peka

Fo'isia, Ioane Faumuinā, Tupu Samuela, Lucy Feaver, La'auli Filoiali'i, Misaalifua Mo'otafao, Nelesoni Tu'ua, and So'otaga Lolofie (Samoan). I would like to thank Tamati Reedy and S.M. Mead for answering a number of questions about Maori by mail; also Reverend Fo'isia of the Samoan Congregational Christian Church of Carson, and Reverend Suitonu of the Samoan Congregational Christian Church of San Diego, for furthering my work on Samoan.

The Indonesian facts discussed in Chapter 7 were provided by Arief Budiman, Robert Item, Lisa Siregar, Ibrahim Hasan, Iwan Hirsan, and Johnny Basuki, to whom I owe thanks.

A number of other people helped this book to reach its final form. Criticism of an early draft, and a good deal of moral support, were provided by Stephen Anderson, Jorge Hankamer, and Susumu Kuno. Extensive comments on later versions were offered by Bruce Biggs, Kenneth Cook, Andrew Pawley, David Perlmutter, Tamati Reedy, and Alan Timberlake. Aspects of the Polynesian material were discussed with me at various times by Paul Chapin, Ross Clark, Georgia Green, William Seiter, Peter Sharples, and Calvert Watkins. I am grateful to all of these people, and in a more general way to David Perlmutter; also to Kenneth Hale and Patrick Hohepa, whose lectures on Maori syntax in Fall 1969 led, directly and indirectly, to much of what is reported here.

This research was supported at various times by an Alice F. Palmer Travelling Fellowship (Wellesley College), an Isobel Briggs Travelling Fellowship (Radcliffe College), a NDEA Title IV Fellowship, and a Whiting Fellowship in the Humanities (Harvard University); by the Language Research Foundation; by the Department of Linguistics, Harvard University (funds from the David and Lucille Packard Foundation), and research grants from the Academic Senate, UCSD. Preparation of the final version of this book was made possible by a Mellon Faculty Fellowship in the Humanities from Harvard University. Thanks to all.

Abbreviations & Symbols

a	nonspecific article	prog	progressive
Abs	absolutive	Prog	progressive auxiliary
Acc	accusative	prop	proper article
Agt	passive agent	Puk	Pukapukan
Ben	benefactive	Q	question
Caus	cause	Sam	Samoan
Comp	complementizer	sbj	subjunctive
compar	comparative	Subj	subject
DO	direct object	SubjPro	subject pronoun
du	dual	Suff	derivational suffix
Emp	emphatic	the	specific article
Erg	ergative	tns	(unidentified) tense
fut	future	Ton	Tongan
impv	imperative	Trans	transitive
Intr	intransitive	uns	unspecified tense-aspect-mood
Kap	Kapingamarangi		
lg	language	=	joins words of a gloss
Mao	Maori	-	morpheme boundary
Nmlz	nominalization	*	ungrammatical in the reading indicated; reconstructed
Nom	nominative		
ObjPro	object pronoun		
opt	optative	*( )	ungrammatical if the parenthesized material is omitted
Pass	passive		
pl	plural		
Pred	predicate	†	usually acceptable
prf	perfect	?	marginal; unidentified morpheme
pro	pronominal article		
Pro	pronominal copy		

Case Marking &
Grammatical Relations
in Polynesian

0. Introduction

This book investigates case marking and grammatical relations in Polynesian from three related perspectives. First, it describes the surface syntax of Polynesian languages, concentrating on case marking and other features which exhibit typological variation. Second, it identifies the grammatical relations of Polynesian languages, examines their role in syntax, and their relationship to case marking. Because grammatical relations are traditionally believed to be reflected transparently by case marking, and because the Polynesian languages exhibit great diversity in their case systems, the investigation has some theoretical interest. Third, it reconstructs the case system of Proto-Polynesian and accounts for its historical development into the systems of the attested languages. The reconstruction follows the guidelines of the comparative method; the account of subsequent changes in Polynesian contributes to a theory of syntactic change.

Chapter 1 gives an overview of surface syntax in Polynesian, focusing on the structure of the clause and its parts. This chapter presents background material assumed in later chapters; it is also intended as an introduction to Polynesian for general readers interested in these languages, either as members of a closely related language family or as instances of non-Indo-European languages. Topics discussed include basic word order, the structure of the verb complex, and the existence of a Relativization rule.

Chapter 2 describes the morphology of case and voice in five languages representative of the Polynesian family as a whole: Maori, Tongan, Samoan, Kapingamarangi, and Pukapukan.

4   Introduction

The description deals primarily with the case markers for subjects and direct objects, which recur throughout the family but are put to several different uses; they are organized in an accusative system in some languages, an ergative system in others, and a mixed accusative-ergative system in others. In addition, the function of a controversial voice suffix is examined for Maori and Samoan. It is argued that the Maori suffix indicates Passive, while the Samoan suffix serves primarily to indicate that a transitive subject has been removed by certain superficial rules.

Chapter 3 lays out two positions on the relationship between case marking and grammatical relations and evaluates them for Polynesian languages. The first of these claims that the categories picked out by the case marking of a language _are_ its grammatical relations: they are precisely the categories that syntactic rules will refer to if they pick out any subtypes of NPs. On this view, languages with an accusative case system should have an accusative syntax; those with an ergative case system should have an ergative syntax; and so forth. The second position, put forth by Anderson (1976) and Perlmutter and Postal (1974, 1977), among others, claims that grammatical relations may differ from the categories picked out by case marking. This position claims further that the relations _subject_ and _direct object_ are central to the syntax of all languages.

In order to evaluate these positions, it is necessary to understand the syntax of Polynesian languages and its organization. Accordingly, Chapter 3 develops a rule typology and then surveys the rules identified as deeper or more central in three Polynesian languages: Maori, an accusative language, and Tongan and Samoan, two ergative languages. It is argued that the rules in question in all three languages re-

5   Introduction

fer to subject or direct object if they mention any subtypes of NPs. This result supports the second of the positions outlined above. At the same time, it could be taken to support a theory of grammar, such as relational grammar, in which grammatical relations are basic terms of syntactic description.

Chapter 4 formulates case assignment rules for the ergative languages Tongan and Samoan. First, a general proposal for case assignment is defended which is phrased partially in terms of grammatical relations. It is then argued that a special case assignment rule is required to account for one transitive clause type in Tongan and Samoan. Finally, it is observed that several superficial rules in these languages appear to refer to case marking. The import of these observations is that case marking does play a role in syntax, although a relatively superficial one.

Chapters 5 and 6 deal with the historical question of how the Proto-Polynesian case system was organized. Since this question is controversial, Chapter 5 reviews some of the approaches taken previously to it. Chapter 6 uses data from a number of languages to reconstruct the functions of the case markers in Proto-Polynesian. It is argued that the Proto-Polynesian case system was accusative, and a scenario is proposed for the rise of ergative case marking in various daughter languages. Although the reconstruction is conducted within the framework of the comparative method and offers no new theoretical insights, the proposal for the rise of ergativity suggests one general route by which ergative languages may be created. This proposal claims that the ergative Polynesian languages acquired their case systems through a reanalysis of passive clauses as active transitive clauses.

Chapter 7, finally, investigates the syntax of Pukapukan,

a Polynesian language that appears to be in the process of actualizing the passive-to-ergative reanalysis. It is argued that the Pukapukan facts are not susceptible to one single synchronic analysis, but instead result from competition between two alternative grammars, one representing the pre-reanalysis, and the other the post-reanalysis, stage. The competition between these --and the progress of change-- cannot be accounted for within the early generative view of historical linguistics, which treats syntactic change as entirely discrete. It is then proposed that the nondiscrete aspects of the competition are governed by a substantive principle of syntactic change. This principle states that a new analysis is actualized earlier in clauses that are less distorted by syntactic rules, where superficial rules cause less distortion of the clause than do major or deeper rules. After discussing the consequences of this for Pukapukan syntax, the chapter proceeds to examples of change in other languages which support the principle and suggest refinements of it.

The various chapters of this book are united by their concern with case marking, grammatical relations, and their interaction in Polynesian syntax. They are also united by their approach, which deserves some brief remarks.

First, the approach of the synchronic chapters of this book is typological, in the sense that it deals primarily with five Polynesian languages, emphasizes their similarities and differences, and implies that many of its results will generalize to other languages of the Polynesian family. The approach has the advantage of enabling much syntactic ground to be covered in languages that are closely related and similar in many respects. Its disadvantages are obvious: no one language is analyzed exhaustively, and some effort is required on the part of the reader to associate particular rules with the languages in which they occur. Although such an approach seemed best for the topics dealt with here, it needs to be supplemented by more detailed work. Hopefully the material on Maori, Tongan, Samoan, Kapingamarangi, and Pukapukan which is discussed here (sometimes rather programmatically) will lead to deeper syntactic analyses of these languages.

Second, the approach of this book is deliberately aformal. Although various chapters are clearly indebted to transformational grammar and/or relational grammar, formalism and theory-internal statements have been avoided where possible. The absence of formalism may have led to some (unintentional) lack of precision in the description of facts or the statement of rules. However, I believe that this situation is more than compensated for by the advantages gained by taking a noncommittal position toward current linguistic frameworks. Although many particular analyses or proposals are argued for here, all of them can be formulated easily in several imaginable frameworks. I have resisted adopting any particular framework in large part because the facts do not uniquely select one over the others.

The rest of the introduction briefly describes the classification of the Polynesian languages and sketches some of their phonological and morphological features. See Biggs (1971) and Clark (1976) for more detailed treatment of these topics.

0.1. THE POLYNESIAN LANGUAGES

The Polynesian languages are a closely related family of languages spoken in the South Pacific. They form the easternmost subfamily of the Austronesian (or Malayo-Polynesian) family, whose members span the Pacific and include languages

8   Introduction

such as Malagasy, Tagalog, and Indonesian. Although the internal relationships of Austronesian are still being debated, it is now usual to recognize one branch of the family consisting of Polynesian plus most of the languages of Micronesia and east Melanesia (Pawley 1974). The Polynesian languages are among the best known and most extensively documented members of this Eastern Oceanic branch.

Because of unresolved questions of language versus dialect, the exact number of Polynesian languages is uncertain, but is usually placed at around thirty. Biggs (1971), whose list is followed here with minor emendations, recognizes twenty-six distinct languages.

The languages are now widely assumed to fall into the subgrouping proposed by Pawley (1966, 1967) and given in Table 1. The Tongic subgroup consists of two languages, Tongan and Niuean. The Samoic-Outlier subgroup includes four languages spoken in the same geographical area as Tongan and Niuean (namely Samoan, East Futunan, Ellicean, and Pukapukan), plus ten Outlier languages, so-called because they are spoken outside the triangle defined by New Zealand, Hawaii, and Easter Island. The East Polynesian subgroup contains the remaining ten languages.

In terms of overall linguistic features, the Samoic-Outlier languages are the most diverse --a situation caused partly by the Outlier languages' having long been in contact with other Eastern Oceanic languages. The Tongic and East Polynesian subgroups exhibit less internal diversity.

Given the number of these languages and their varying degrees of documentation, it would be unrealistic to attempt to deal with all of them here. The conclusions reached in this book are supported primarily by data from five representative languages, chosen because of their subgrouping, typological

Pawley's Subgrouping of the Polynesian Languages:

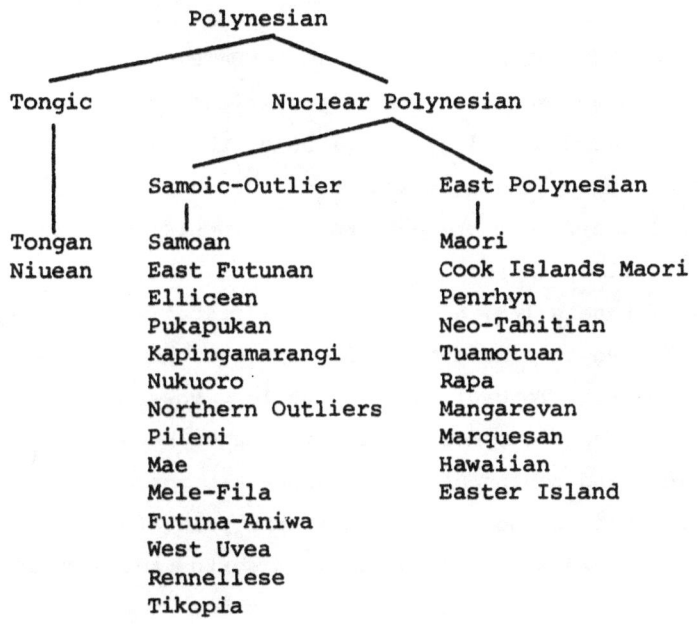

Table 1

10   Introduction

features, and degree of documentation. These are Maori, an East Polynesian language spoken in New Zealand; Tongan, a Tongic language spoken in the Kingdom of Tonga; and three Samoic-Outlier languages: Samoan, spoken in American Samoa and Western Samoa; Pukapukan, spoken in the northern Cook Islands (Pukapuka Island); and Kapingamarangi, spoken in the U.S. Trust Territory of the Pacific (Kapingamarangi Atoll).

0.2. PHONOLOGICAL AND MORPHOLOGICAL FEATURES
The Polynesian languages are characterized by an extremely straightforward phonology. Typically, the segment inventory of one of these languages includes five short vowels (/a, e, i, o, u/) and five corresponding long vowels; a series of voiceless stops chosen from /p, t, k, ?/; the corresponding series of nasals (/m, n, ŋ/); several fricatives, and a liquid. All vowel combinations are allowed, and a number of languages (e.g. Tongan) distinguish long vowels from rearticulated like vowels. Most of the languages permit only open syllables, and consonant combinations are not allowed. The most common phonological processes are palatalization (of /t/), vowel assimilations of various sorts, and fast speech phenomena such as devoicing of final short vowels.

The morphophonemics and morphology of these languages are also straightforward. Morphophonemically, one of the few processes of interest is the definitive accent, which marks specific NPs as definite by shifting the stress of their last constituent from its normal position (on the penultimate mora) to the final mora. The definitive accent affects NPs referred to in previous discourse as well as ones known more generally to speaker and hearer (e.g. Tongan 'a e la'á 'the sun'; Samoan i falé 'at home'), but does not affect pronouns or proper nouns. It occurs in Tongan and is attested sporadically in Samoan and Pukapukan. Morphologically, there are few general processes of inflection, and nouns and verbs are usually invariant. Pronouns probably rate some interest morphologically, since they distinguish singular, dual, and plural number and exclusive and inclusive first persons; they also occur in independent as well as clitic forms. Independent pronouns have the status of ordinary NPs; clitics occur in possessive pronouns or in second position within the clause (see 1.4.2).

As noticed by Biggs (1961) for Maori, the morphological glue of these languages is provided by particles: stressless, typically monosyllabic elements which precede or follow the head constituent of a phrase and indicate notions such as specificity, tense-aspect-mood, and deixis. Some of the particles most relevant to this book are discussed in Chapter 1.

1. An Overview of Surface Syntax

This chapter gives a brief description of the surface syntax of Polynesian languages, focusing on the structure of the clause and its parts. The description is intended to set the stage for the discussion of case and voice morphology in Chapter 2, as well as to give a sense of the typology of Polynesian languages, both as members of a closely related family and as languages unfamiliar to most general linguists. The discussion has been made as brief and general as possible and as a result is not particularly comprehensive. Those interested in a fuller account should refer to Biggs (1971) as well as the excellent grammars of C.M. Churchward (1953), S. Churchward (1951), and Williams and Williams (1950[1862]).

1.1 describes the basic word order of Polynesian languages and raises the question of whether the Outlier languages are SVO. 1.2 describes the structure of the verb complex; 1.3, the structure of the NP; and 1.4, several rules affecting pronouns.

1.1. STRUCTURE OF THE CLAUSE

1.1.1. Basic Word Order

By <u>basic word order</u> is meant the surface word order from which all other surface word orders can be derived (not necessarily the most frequent word order). This term is chosen to sidestep the issue of whether word order is present in underlying structure.

The basic word order of most if not all Polynesian languages is verb-initial:

13 An Overview of Surface Syntax

Mao (1)a. Ka whakawhaiāipo   rāua.
          uns become=sweethearts they=du
          'They became sweethearts.' (Waititi 1969: 72)

Sam b. Sā sola 'oia 'i le fale.
         past run he to the house
         'He ran to the house.'

Puk c. Yā pēwea koe i te ayó?
         past how? you at the day
         'How were you yesterday?'

Although the relative order of NPs following the verb is theoretically free, in practice it is influenced by several factors.

Pronouns tend to be attracted to the verb, regardless of their syntactic function:

Mao (2)a. Ka waha-a   e rāua   ngā kōkōwai.
          uns carry-Pass Agt them=du the=pl red=ochre
          'They carried home the red ochre.' (Orbell 10)

Mao b. Kua moe-a   au e te nanakia.
         prf sleep-Pass I Agt the monster
         'A monster has taken me as his wife (lit. I
         have been slept with by a monster).' (Orbell
         38)

Sam c. Ta'u mai 'i-āte a'u le tala 'i-ā   Ioane.
         tell here to-pro me the story to-prop John
         'Tell me the story about John.'

Semantic agents tend to precede nonagents:

Mao (3)a. Ka tuku-a   e Paowa te waka.
          uns leave-Pass Agt Paowa the canoe
          'Paowa left the canoe.' (Orbell 74)

Sam b. 'Ua galo   i   tagata 'uma lou igoa.
         prf forgotten Caus person all your name
         'Everyone has forgotten your name.'

Puk c. Lomilomi ai e   tana wawine ma na   tama
         massage Pro Erg his woman and the=pl boy
         'His two knees were massaged by his wife and

14   An Overview of Surface Syntax

        lua tulivae ia.
        two knee   that
        the children.' (Beaglehole and Beaglehole 1089)

Otherwise the most frequent word order is Verb Subject Object Obliques, where Subject and Object refer to surface grammatical relations:

Ton (4)a.   Na'e muimui 'a 'Ālani 'i-ate au 'aneafi.
           past follow Abs Alan at-pro me yesterday
           'Alan followed me yesterday.'

Ton   b.   'Oku va'inga'aki 'e he'eku tamasi'i ha fo'i
           prog play   Erg my   child   a one
           'My child is playing with a

           pulu 'i mu'i.
           ball at back
           ball in the yard.'

Puk   c.   Na wano i a-na   ki te uwi.
           past go Nom pro-he to the swamp
           'He went to the taro swamp.'

Puk   d.   Ko velevele i a Palaoa i ona   mataava
           prog clear   Nom prop Palaoa Acc pl=his channel
           'Palaoa was clearing his large channel

           i tona alai.
           in his coral
           in his coral barrier.' (Beaglehole and Beaglehole 1133)

   The fact that VSO is the basic word order is established not only by frequency but also by restrictions on the other possible word orders (notably VOS). In Tongan, for instance, declarative sentences allow VOS only if the direct object is definite --either referred to in previous discourse or else known independently to speaker and hearer. Compare the definite direct objects of (5) with the indefinite ones of (6):

Ton (5)a.   'Oku fa'u 'a e tēpilé 'e hoku tokouá.
           prog make Abs the table Erg my   sibling
           'My brother is making the table.'

15   An Overview of Surface Syntax

      b.   Na'e taa'i 'a Sione 'e Mele.
           past hit   Abs John Erg Mary
           'Mary hit John.'

(6)a.   *'Oku fa'u 'a e   tēpile 'e hoku tokouá.
       prog make Abs the table Erg my   sibling
       (My brother is making a table.)

   b.   *Na'e 'ikai ke kai ha ika 'e he tangatá.
       past not   sbj eat a fish Erg the man
       (The man didn't eat any fish.)

On the basis of evidence of this sort it is assumed that VSO is the basic word order, an assumption which to my knowledge requires only two qualifications. First, in Samoan and Pukapukan the frequency of VSO varies with the morphology of transitive clause types: VSO is no more frequent than VOS for clauses containing the transitive suffix in Samoan (see 2.1.4) and clauses with 'passive' case marking in Pukapukan (see 2.1.6). This suggests that the rule scrambling subject and direct object may have to be sensitive to morphology. Second, it may be that some Outlier languages have SVO as their basic word order, a possibility examined immediately below.

1.1.2. Are the Outlier Languages SVO?

In a number of Outlier languages (see 0.1) SVO is the most frequent surface word order, a fact which raises the question of whether it is their basic word order as well. This subsection provides the beginnings of an answer to this by examining the word order properties of one Outlier language, Kapingamarangi. It is argued that the basic word order of Kapingamarangi is actually VSO; the high frequency of SVO may reflect an incipient word order change.

The most frequent word order of Kapingamarangi clauses is SVO. Consider the transitive and intransitive clauses of:

16   An Overview of Surface Syntax

(7) a.   Keiokō ti ahina ku hakarongo nherekhai   ti
         then   the woman prf hear   the=pl=word the
         'The woman listened to the instructions of the

         kē.
         turtle
         turtle.' (Elbert 71)

   b.   Kei koe takahi-a   rā   tau   turuturu.
         and you kick-Trans that your post
         'Then you kick a post.' (Elbert 91)

(8) a.   Nau   tara rā   ku woti.
         their taro that prf done
         'Their taro was finished.' (Elbert 103)

   b.   Kei Ia ku ihepu ki roto   o ti monowai.
         and he prf jump to inside of the well
         'Then he jumped into the well.' (Elbert 64)

Although clauses with verb-initial word order do occur, they are infrequent and syntactically somewhat restricted. For instance, verb-initial transitive clauses are attested only when the subject is a pronoun, and they are always VSO, never VOS:

(9) a.   Ka kitē Ia ti moua e   takitaki tana
         uns see he the bird nonpast carry   his
         'He saw a frigate bird carrying a

         atu   parepare.
         bonito parepare
         parepare bonito (in his beak).' (Elbert 62)

   b.   Ka hī-na   rā   e koe tana rikau ki kai.
         uns wrap-Trans that Nom you his pack sbj eat
         'You will then wrap his taro package to eat.'
         (Elbert 138)

Verb-initial intransitive clauses always show the subject preceding any oblique NPs:

(10)   Ka rere mai ei mē i ono   nua o ti ariki.
         uns fly here Pro it at pl=his top of the priest
         'It flew over the priest.' (Elbert 73)

17   An Overview of Surface Syntax

By themselves these facts might seem to suggest that Kapingamarangi was basically SVO, and clauses like (9-10) were derived by a rule postposing the subject to the right of the verb. But the situation is more complicated.

To begin with, Kapingamarangi allows NPs other than subjects to precede the verb. Direct objects sometimes occur in this position, giving the word order OVS:

(11)a. Ni   korō nei ku hakarakiraki ko   au ki
        the=pl thing this prf dry   Nom   I to
        'I dried these things outside

        ti   maraerae.
        the   outside=house
        the house.' (Elbert 70)

   b.   Tērā rā   ti paipai   r'e   takatakahi
        therefore the flounder that=nonpast step=on
        'That's why people step on

        ko   ni   tāngata.
        Nom the=pl   people
        the flounder.' (Elbert 125)

OVS word order is most frequent when the subject is overt, but is also possible when it is unknown or has been deleted by zero-pronominalization (see 1.4.1) or imperative deletion:

(12)a. Tuku huku ne   kae ki he?
        my   tail past take to where?
        'Where are (you) taking my tail?' (Elbert 129)

   b.   Tou ripoko riu-a   ki rara, ou   wae
        your head   turn-Trans   to below pl=your foot
        'Turn your head downward, turn your

        riu-a   ki nua.
        turn-Trans   to above
        feet upward!' (Elbert 63)

In addition, it is the normal word order when conjunction reduction has applied to coordinate clauses sharing the same direct object:

18   An Overview of Surface Syntax

(13) a.   Nia   koro-mata i ti mūri ripoko ka khape
          the=pl eye   at the back head   uns pry
          '(He) gouged out the eyes behind his head and

          ki taha, ka hā i roto   ti ipu.
          to side uns put at inside the cup
          put (them) inside a coconut-shell cup.' (Elbert 79)

     b.   Thakahitinana   rā   ku raha mai, ku tuku
          mother=and=child   that prf fetch here prf leave
          'Mother and child were taken and put

          i pāhi ti imu.
          in side the oven
          into the side of the oven.' (Elbert 92)

NPs that are instruments, time phrases, locatives, goals, causes, or possessors can also precede the verb. In such cases the subject and direct object are typically postverbal, producing the word order Oblique VSO:

(14)   Uku   rima e   khumi e   au ti niu.
         pl=my hand nonpast hold   Nom I the tree
         'I'm holding the tree with my hands.' (Elbert 65)

Finally, all oblique NPs preceding the verb except for instruments and time phrases are copied by a postverbal pronoun. The copy for locatives, goals, and causes cliticizes to the right of the verb; that for possessors takes the form of a possessive pronoun:

(15) a. Ti rongorongo   e   tū   i ai thangata
         the casting=stand nonpast stand at Pro the=man
         'A man stands up inside

         i ono roto.
         at its inside
         the casting stand.' (Elbert 218)

     b. Thenua   nei e   hani moi kinei tangata
         the=land this nonpast come here Pro   person
         'Are people coming soon to this

         māria?
         soon
         land?' (Elbert 115)

19   An Overview of Surface Syntax

    c.   Koe tēai tau mē   e   hai taiā...
           you not your thing nonpast do   tomorrow
           'If you have nothing to do tomorrow (lit. If
           your thing that (you) were going to do does not
           exist)...' (Elbert 36)

A grammar which treated SVO as the basic word order would require several separate devices to describe these facts: one rule postposing the subject, for (9-10); another rule preposing nonsubjects to the left of the verb, for (11-14); and a copying strategy for nonsubject preposing that would affect certain oblique NPs, for (15). Further, it would be necessary to state nonsubject preposing to apply to the output of subject postposing, or take other steps to insure that no more than one NP would end up to the left of the verb. But in a grammar that treats VSO as the basic word order, all that is needed is a rule preposing any NP to the left of the verb, plus a copying strategy for the rule that affects certain obliques. The VSO proposal is thus to be preferred to the SVO proposal on the grounds of greater generality.

    The argument is strengthened by the fact that transitive subjects preceding the verb are sometimes copied by a postverbal pronoun, as in:

(16)a. Keiokō ti ahina ku penepene īa tana mē.
       then the woman prf prepare she her thing
       'Then the woman prepared the things.' (Elbert 73)

    b. Kōrua e   tē roā e kōrua.
       you=du nonpast not able Nom you=du
       'The two of you can't (carry it).' (Elbert 87)

Within the SVO proposal, examples of this type would dictate that a separate copying strategy should be attached to subject postposing, bringing the total number of devices to four. But within the VSO proposal, they can be dealt with simply by extending the existing copying strategy of NP preposing so that it optionally affects subjects. The simplicity of this provides further evidence for the VSO proposal.[1]

It appears, then, that Kapingamarangi has VSO as its basic word order, a conclusion which puts it in line with the other Polynesian languages of 1.1.1. However, it has the curious consequence that the basic word order and the most frequent word order of that language are not the same. It is tempting to suggest that this discrepancy reflects an incipient word order change, and Kapingamarangi may eventually reanalyze its most frequent word order --SVO-- as the basic word order. Similar changes may well have occurred in other Outlier languages, which according to Clark (1976) have SVO as their only surface word order.

1.2. STRUCTURE OF THE VERB COMPLEX

The verb complex consists of the verb plus its surrounding modifiers, where 'verb' is understood to include predicates describing states and adjectival properties as well as activities. This section describes the structure of the verb complex and two types of verbless predicates.

1.2.1. Tense-Aspect-Mood Particles

The verb is preceded by a particle which indicates tense, aspect, and mood, or else serves as a complementizer (see Chapter 3). In most Polynesian languages the tense-aspect-mood particle distinguishes past versus nonpast tense, progressive and perfect aspects, and indicative versus imperative versus subjunctive mood:

Mao (17)a. I   oma.
             past run
             '(She) ran.'

Ton   b. Kuo mohe.
              prf sleep
              '(He) has fallen asleep.'

21   An Overview of Surface Syntax

Sam   c.   'Ia sau.
              sbj come
              '(May you) come!' (S. Churchward 1951: 88)

Puk   d.   Ko   pēwea koe?
              prog how? you
              'How are you?'

In almost all languages imperative verbs do not have an overt tense-aspect-mood particle, and in some languages, e.g. Pukapukan, matrix verbs in narratives do not have one either. A number of East Polynesian languages have particles for embedded clauses which differ slightly from those found in matrix clauses. In Maori, for instance, the embedded clause particles do not distinguish perfect aspect (matrix clause kua) and indicate nonpast tense (embedded clause e) rather than unspecified tense-aspect (matrix clause ka). In other respects they resemble the particles found in matrix clauses.

1.2.2. Verbal Modifiers

The verb is followed by adverbs, directional particles, and other verbal modifiers:

Mao (18)a.   Ka tata noa mai hoki.
                 uns near just here also
                 '(They) just came closer.' (Orbell 30)

Ton   b.   Na'e hola mama'o.
              past run far
              '(He) ran away.'

Kap   c.   Ka noho rā   ki-nae e   au.
              uns stay that to-Pro Nom I
              'I will marry him.' (Elbert 16)

The most important of these for our purposes is the pronominal copy ai, an anaphor for several types of oblique NPs (Chapin 1974).

1.2.3. Verbless Predicates

Instead of a verb complex the clause may contain a verbless predicate --either a predicate nominal or a predicate PP-- which occupies the usual predicate position preceding the subject and other NPs.

Predicate nominals differ from true verbs in not being introduced by a tense-aspect-mood particle. Instead, if specific, they are introduced by the predicate particle ko (>'o by regular phonological change in Samoan), which does not allow tense, aspect, or mood to be specified:

Mao (19)a. Ko   te kauri te rākau nui.
            Pred the kauri the tree big
            'The kauri is the (really) big tree.' (Biggs 1969: 25)

Ton   b.   Ko   e   ta'ahine fakaaoli.
            Pred the girl   funny
            '(She) is a funny girl.'

Puk   c.   Ko   tana manatu-nga mua...
            Pred her think-Nmlz before
            '(It) was her first thought...'

The treatment of nonspecific predicate nominals varies somewhat throughout the family. Note that there is no copula.

Predicate PPs are preceded by a special set of tense particles (in East Polynesian languages) or else by the same tense-aspect-mood particles used for true verbs (in Tongic and Samoic-Outlier). They differ from true verbs in their failure to cooccur with directional particles, the pronominal copy ai, and certain other verbal modifiers:

Ton (20)a. Ka ne   i heni 'a Sione, 'e kata.
            if past at here Abs John   uns laugh
            'If John were here, (he) would laugh.' (C.M. Churchward 1953: 41)

23   An Overview of Surface Syntax

Sam   b.   'O   ananafi   sā   'ou i   le   umukuka (*ai).
           Pred yesterday past I   in the kitchen   Pro
           'Yesterday I was in the kitchen.'

Puk   c.   Na i te tāone oki   au.
           past at the town also I
           'I had already been in town.'

Although verbless predicates do not figure prominently in this book, the predicate particle ko does, since it is also used to mark NPs that have been clefted. As might be expected, all verbless predicates count as intransitive for the purposes of case assignment.

1.3. STRUCTURE OF THE NP
This section describes the internal structure of the NP and several oblique prepositions that can precede it. Discussion of the case marking of subjects and direct objects is postponed to Chapter 2.

1.3.1. Specificity-Number Articles
Common nouns are preceded by an article indicating specificity and number (or, in Tongan, by one article indicating specificity and another indicating dual or plural number). The specific articles indicate that the speaker can pick out the referent of the NP, while the nonspecific articles do not indicate this. The distinction resembles the specific versus nonspecific distinction discussed in the general linguistic literature, except that in Polynesian nonspecific NPs are not restricted to occurring under the scope of what Jackendoff (1972) calls 'modal operators' (see C.M. Churchward 1953):

Mao (21)a.   ngā   manuhiri
              the=pl guests
              'the guests'

Ton   b.   e   kau   polisi
             the pl   police
             'the police'

Sam   c.   se   aso
             a   day
             'any day'

Ton   d.   Na'a ku fa'o ia ki ha puha.
             past I put it to a box
             'I put it into a box (some box or other).'
             (C.M. Churchward 1953: 271)

For convenience, the specific article is everywhere glossed 'the', and the nonspecific article 'a'. Articles with no overt realization, namely the Samoan specific plural, are not indicated in the morpheme-by-morpheme glosses.

1.3.2. Pronominal-Proper Article

Proper nouns and independent pronouns are marked with the pronominal-proper article a, under conditions varying slightly throughout Polynesian. In general, a is required when the prepositions i or ki precede the NP (see 1.3.4 and 1.3.5). In Samoan and Tongan, a has the form ate before pronouns in these circumstances:

Sam   (22)   'i-āte 'outou
               to-pro you=pl
               'to you all'

In several languages a is also allowed when the NP is in the unmarked (i.e. nominative or absolutive) case. Maori, for instance, requires a for unmarked proper nouns and occasionally allows it for unmarked pronouns:

Mao   (23)   a   Pipo
               prop Pipo
               'Pipo (nominative)'

1.3.3. Nominal Modifiers

Demonstratives, adjectives, possessors, and relative clauses follow the head noun:

Mao (24)a. te tangata rā
            the person that
            'that man'

Ton   b.   e uma 'o e pēpē
            the arm of the baby
            'the baby's arm'

Sam   c.   le teine lea 'ua sola
            the girl that prf run
            'the girl who ran away'

Puk   d.   te manu totolo
            the bird crawl
            'the animal'

However, most languages allow demonstratives and pronominal possessors to combine with the specific/nonspecific article, in which case they precede:

Sam (25)a. le fānau a Fo'isia
            the children of Fo'isia
            'Fo'isia's children'

Sam   b.   l-a-na fānau
            the-of-him children
            'his children'

Possessors are preceded by one of the two particles a 'dominant' and o 'subordinate'. As the terms suggest, a is used for possessors who actively control the possessed noun; o is used for other possessor-possessed relationships, including that of the whole to its parts, of animate beings to their body parts, of individuals to immutable elements of culture or environment, and so on (see, e.g., C.M. Churchward 1953).

26   An Overview of Surface Syntax

Relative clauses are formed by deletion or pronominalization of the noun coreferential to the head; there is no separate morphological category 'relative pronoun'. For discussion of whether relative clauses involve a distinct Relativization rule, see 1.4.3.

1.3.4. Case Particles: i and ki
Noun phrases are either unmarked for case or else preceded by a case particle which indicates their syntactic function. I will arbitrarily refer to case particles serving exclusively to mark subjects or direct objects as case markers, and ones with oblique functions as prepositions. This subsection outlines the functions of two ubiquitous prepositions, i 'at' and ki 'to'.

Throughout Polynesian, i 'at' is used to indicate locatives, time expressions, sources, and objects of comparison:

Locatives

Mao   (26)a.   E   mau   ana i te ringa.
                uns carry prog in the hand
                '(She) was carrying (it) in her hand.' (Orbell 18)

Sam   b.   'Olo'o lātou nonofo   i se motu   i le
                prog   they stay=pl at a   island in the
                'They are living on an island in the

                Pasefika.
                Pacific
                Pacific.'

Time Expressions

Ton   (27)a.   Te mau ō   atu   'apō   'i he hongofulu.
                uns we   go=pl away tonight at the ten
                'We're coming tonight at ten.'

Puk   b.   I nā   vāia   na   topa ki muri...
                at the=pl   season past pass to back
                'Some years back...'

Sources

Mao (28)a. Ka haere mai a   Hōne i   te whare.
            uns go here prop John from the house
            'John came from the house.'

Sam   b.   'Ou te sau i   Hawai'i.
            I   uns come from Hawaii
            'I come from Hawaii.'

Objects of Comparison

Sam (29)a. 'Ua sili atu le fiafia o a'u 'i le American
            prf best away the like of me to the American
            'I like American Airlines better than

            Airlines i   lō   le Pan Am.
            Airlines than compar the Pan Am
            Pan Am (lit. My liking for American Airlines is
            greater than...).'

Puk   b.   ...tūkē   i   te taime mua   oki na i
            different than the time before also past at
            '...different from the time when I was there

            kiai au.
            Pro I
            before.'

In addition, it indicates causes or indirect agents, a function described separately in 1.3.5.

Ki 'to' is used to mark goals, far locations, and indirect objects:

Goals

Mao (30)a. Ka mau-ria   e   ia ki tana kāinga.
            uns carry-Pass Agt him to his house
            'He would take (the body) to his home.' (Orbell 14)

Sam   b.   E   to'atele tagata Sāmoa e ō   'i
            uns many   person Samoan uns go=pl to
            'Many are the Samoan people who go to

            Disneyland.
            Disneyland
            Disneyland.'

Far Locations

Ton (31)a. Na'e tō   mai ha 'uha ki he   motu.
            past fall here a rain to the island
            'Some rain fell on the island.'

Kap   b.   Ni   korō nei ku hakarakiraki ko   au ki
            the=pl thing this prf dry   Nom   I to
            'I dried these things outside

            ti   maraerae.
            the outside=house
            the house.' (Elbert 70)

Indirect Objects

Mao (32)a. Hōmai hoki ki a   au.
            give also to pro me
            'Give (it) to me!' (Biggs 1969: 116)

Puk   b.   Mea loa i   a   Uyo ki tona taina...
            say Emp Nom prop Uyo to his sibling
            'Uyo said to his brother...'

Although these uses of _i_ and _ki_ are fairly uniform throughout Polynesian, there is some variation in the marking of instruments and descriptive phrases meaning 'about NP'. Most Polynesian languages use _ki_ to mark instruments, but Samoan uses _i_ for this purpose and the Tongic languages have a separate preposition, _'aki_ 'with', which optionally cliticizes to the verb (see Seiter 1977). The Tongic and Samoic-Outlier languages use _ki_ to mark descriptive phrases meaning 'about NP', but Maori (and perhaps other East Polynesian languages) employs _i_ instead.

Note finally that Samoan _'i_ 'to' is derived from Proto-Polynesian *_ki_ by regular phonological change; Tongan _'i_ 'at' is optionally deleted before common nouns.

1.3.5. Stative Agents

One use of the oblique _i_ which will prove useful in Chapter 3 is that of marking indirect agents or causes (glossed 'Caus'

in the examples). These NPs may be animate or inanimate and
are typically associated with stative intransitive verbs --
verbs describing properties or the state resulting from an
action:

Mao (33)a. Ka mate te hoariri i   te toa.
            uns die the enemy Caus the warrior
            'The enemy died because of the warrior.'

Ton   b.   Na'e ngalo   'i-ate   au e pēpē.
           past forgotten Caus-pro me the baby
           'The baby was forgotten because of me.'
           'I forgot the baby.'

Sam   c.   Na   lavea le tamāloa i   le masini.
           past hurt the man   Caus the machine
           'The man was hurt by the machine.'

The animate i NPs of this sort will be referred to as <u>stative
agents</u>.

Although stative agents can cause the state described by
the verb in a direct or indirect fashion, in practice they
are often interpreted as direct causes. For instance, the
stative agent accompanying Samoan <u>galo</u> 'forgotten' is typically the person who does the forgetting.

In most Polynesian languages stative agents cannot be
freely associated with active verbs. For some speakers of
Maori, for instance, they cannot surface in the same clause
as an underlying active verb, though they can originate in
such clauses and subsequently be extracted (see Chapter 3, n.
11). For other speakers, however, they can apparently surface in almost any clause containing a verb. In Tongan,
stative agents cannot cooccur with active verbs, although inanimate causes can:

Ton (34)a. Na'a ne fakamālō 'i   he'ene ngāué.
            past he thank   Caus his   work
            'He thanked (him) because of his work.'

b. *Na'a ne 'alu mama'o 'i   he'ene fa'ē.
    past he go   far   Caus his   mother
    (He went away because of his mother.)

What is important about stative agents is that they are semantically agentive but syntactically oblique; as such, they can be used to determine whether a rule refers to semantic agency or syntactic subjecthood. They will be appealed to a number of times in Chapter 3.

1.4. RULES AFFECTING PRONOUNS

This section discusses two rules affecting pronouns and a third operating on the noun of a relative clause coreferential to the head. 1.4.1 describes zero-pronominalization, an extremely free deletion rule; 1.4.2 deals with Clitic Placement, a rule which moves or copies pronominal subjects; and 1.4.3 describes the fate of the coreferential nouns within relative clauses and argues that a distinct Relativization rule is required to account for them.

1.4.1. Zero-Pronominalization

All Polynesian languages have a rule of zero-pronominalization which operates with particular freedom in narratives and other stretches of connected discourse. This rule, also known as pronominalization-by-deletion or pronoun drop, deletes a pronoun coreferential with an antecedent in previous discourse. Zero-pronominalization is optional, unbounded, has no lexical exceptions, and in most languages affects pronouns of any syntactic function, though it applies most commonly to subjects or direct objects (see 1.4.3 for a curious exception). Throughout this book, pronouns deleted by this rule are parenthesized in the English translations. Consider:

31   An Overview of Surface Syntax

Mao (35)a. Kātahi rāua   ka haere; ka kite-a   mai, ka
           then they=du uns go   uns see-Pass here uns
           'So they set off, and when (they) were seen

           karanga.
           call
           approaching (the village), the call went out
           (lit. ...and when (they) were seen (by the vill-
           age), (people) called).' (Orbell 40)

Sam   b.   Ona asu ai lea i luga o   lana apu foe
           then dip Pro that to above Pred his paddle
           '(He) scooped up (water) with his paddle

           ona   punitia lea o   mata o aitu a   e
           then blocked that Pred eye of spirit and uns
           so the eyes of the spirits were blinded (with

           ta'u atu ai lona igoa.
           tell away Pro his name
           water), and then shouted his name.' (Stuebel
           228)

Kap   c.   Ka tinae,   e   there hua tono tinae,
           uns pregnant nonpast cut   just her stomach
           'When a pregnancy occurred, (they) just cut the

           e   hāhi, ka khape ti   tama.
           nonpast slit uns take the child
           stomach, slit (it) open and took the child (out
           of it).' (Elbert 90)

1.4.2. Clitic Placement

Tongan and several Samoic-Outlier languages have a rule of
Clitic Placement which moves a pronoun to second position in
the clause, immediately to the right of the tense-aspect-mood
particle. Cliticized pronouns have special clitic morphology
and are not marked for case; they form a single phonological
unit with the tense-aspect-mood particle, which itself may
undergo idiosyncratic changes.

   The Clitic Placement rules have varying restrictions, the
most interesting of which involves the class of pronouns that
they affect. We discuss the Tongan and Samoan rules, which

32   An Overview of Surface Syntax

are restricted to pronominal subjects and so argue for the existence of the category subject in these languages.

1.4.2.1. <u>Tongan</u>. Sentences (36) and (37) are related by Clitic Placement in Tongan, which is a copying rule:

 (36) Na'a ne taa'i 'e ia pē ia.
    past he hit   Erg he Emp him
    '<u>He</u> hit himself.'

 (37) Na'e taa'i pē ia 'e ia.
    past hit   Emp him Erg he
    'He hit himself.'

This rule creates a copy of a pronominal subject and places it in second position in the clause, immediately to the right of the tense-aspect-mood particle. The original subject surfaces as an independent pronoun if it is emphatic or contrastive; otherwise it is deleted by zero-pronominalization, as in:

 (38)a. Na'a ne taa'i pē ia.
     past he hit   Emp him
     'He hit himself.'

   b. Na'a ne puke.
     past she sick
     'She was sick.'

Clitic Placement must be stated to refer specifically to the tense-aspect-mood particle, since it can apply to any clause containing one, including tensed clauses (as above), clauses whose tense-aspect-mood particle serves as a complementizer, and clauses containing a predicate PP:

 (39)a. Pea na'e 'alu 'a e   tangatá 'o   ne folau
     and past go   Abs the person Comp he sail
     'Then the man went and he sailed

    mama'o.
    far
    away.'

b.   Na'a ku 'i Fisi.
     past I at Fiji
     'I was in Fiji.' (C.M. Churchward 1953: 21)

But it does not affect clauses without one, notably clauses formed from a predicate nominal preceded by the predicate particle <u>ko</u> (see 1.2.3). A rough statement of the rule is thus 'Make a copy of a pronominal subject and attach it to the right of the tense-aspect-mood particle of its clause'.[2]

Clitic Placement is optional for third singular pronouns but obligatory otherwise:

(40)a.   'Oku ou 'ahuina.
         prog I besmoked
         'I'm covered with smoke.'

   b.   Na'a nau 'ilo 'a e   tangata 'i he 'ana.
        past they know Abs the man   in the cave
        'They found a man in the cave.'

(41)a.   *'Oku 'ahuina au.
         prog besmoked I
         (I'm covered with smoke.)

   b.   *Na'e 'ilo 'e kinautolu 'a e   tangata 'i he
         past know Erg they   Abs the man   in the
         (They found a man in the

         'ana.
         cave
         cave.)

And, significantly, it is restricted to pronouns that are subjects. It applies to intransitive subjects:

(42)   Na'a ke hola mama'o.
        past you run far
        'You ran far away.'

As well as various types of transitive subjects (see 2.1.3):

(43)a. Na'a ku sio ki he fo'i manupuna.
        past I look to the one bird
        'I saw a bird.'

34   An Overview of Surface Syntax

      b.   Na'a ma   'ave 'e kimaua ho'o telefone.
          past we=du take Erg we=du   your telephone
          '<u>We</u> took away your telephone.'

But not to direct objects or oblique NPs. Compare (44) with (45), in which the rule has not applied:

  (44)a. *Na'a ne ui   'e he tangatá.
        past she call Erg the man
        (The man called her.)

     b. *Te u 'omi 'e Sione 'a e siaine.
        uns I bring Erg John Abs the banana
        (John will bring me some bananas.)

     c. *'Oku ou ngalo   e   pēpē.
        prog I forgotten the baby
        (The baby is forgotten because of me.)

  (45)a. Na'e ui   ia 'e he tangatá.
        past call her Erg the man
        'The man called her.'

     b. 'E 'omi 'e Sione 'a e siaine ki-ate au.
        uns bring Erg John Abs the banana to-pro me
        'John will bring me some bananas.'

     c. 'Oku ngalo   e   pēpē 'i-ate   au.
        prog forgotten the baby Caus-pro me
        'The baby is forgotten because of me.'

Sentences like these argue that the statement of Clitic Placement should refer specifically to subjects, and therefore subject should be recognized as a syntactic category of Tongan. (See Chapter 3 for discussion of how subject is to be defined.) The argument is important, because, as shown in Chapter 2, Tongan subjects do not form a unified morphological category with respect to case marking.

1.4.2.2. <u>Samoan</u>. Samoan Clitic Placement relates sentences like (46) and (47):

An Overview of Surface Syntax

(46) a. Sā mātou mānunu'a i le masini.
past we wounded=pl Caus the machine
'We were wounded by the machine.'

b. 'Olo'o 'e tautala lēmū.
prog you speak soft
'You're speaking softly.'

(47) a. Sā mānunu'a 'i mātou i le masini.
past wounded=pl pl we Caus the machine
'<u>We</u> were wounded by the machine.'

b. 'Olo'o tautala lēmū ia 'oe.
prog speak soft that you
'<u>You</u>'re speaking softly.'

This rule moves pronominal subjects which are neither emphatic nor contrastive to second position in the clause, immediately to the right of the tense-aspect-mood particle.

Clitic Placement appears to be a chopping rather than a copying rule, since clauses containing both an independent subject pronoun and a (coreferential) subject clitic are usually rejected by speakers (cf. though Milner 1962):

(48) 'Ou te tā-ina (*e a'u) le piano.
I uns play-Trans Erg I the piano
'I play the piano.'

Further, it must refer specifically to the tense-aspect-mood particle, for reasons the same as those given above for Tongan Clitic Placement. A rough statement of the rule is then 'Attach a nonemphatic, noncontrastive pronominal subject to the right of the tense-aspect-mood particle of its clause'.

Samoan Clitic Placement has several morphological quirks of note. First, if it applies to a clause introduced by the unspecified tense-aspect-mood <u>e</u>, this particle takes the form <u>te</u> and inverts with the clitic. Consider (48) and:

(49) a. Pe 'e te fefe i fōma'i?
Q you uns afraid at doctor
'Are you afraid of doctors?'

b. Pe-e fefe 'oe i fōma'i?
    Q-uns afraid you at doctor
    'Are you afraid of doctors?'

Second, the rule does not affect third singular intransitive subjects in the speech of most Samoans, a point discussed further in 4.2.3.1:

(50) a. *Na te sau 'i Hawai'i.
         he uns come to Hawaii
         (He'll come to Hawaii.)

   b. E   sau 'oia 'i Hawai'i.
       uns come he   to Hawaii
       'He'll come to Hawaii.'

Of more general interest is the fact that Clitic Placement will move only subjects. It applies to intransitive subjects (with the exception described immediately above):

(51) 'Ua 'ou mālūlū.
      prf I   cold
      'I'm cold.'

And to various types of transitive subjects (see 2.1.4):

(52) a. Sā   mātou leoleo i tickets o le lū'au.
         past we   guard at tickets of the luau
         'We were guarding the tickets at the luau.'

   b. Sā   'ou va'ai 'i-āte ia ma sā   ia va'ai mai
       past I   look to-pro him and past he look here
       'I looked at him and then he looked

       fo'i 'i-āte a'u.
       also to-pro me
       at me.'

   c. Sā   ia tulei a'u 'i lalo o le fa'asitepu.
       past he push me to below of the step
       'He pushed me down the stairs.'

   d. Sā   na 'aumai-a   se meaalofa o le Easter
       past he bring-Trans a gift   of the Easter
       'He brought an Easter present

37 An Overview of Surface Syntax

```
        'i-āte a'u.
        to-pro me
        to me.'
```

But it does not affect direct objects or oblique NPs:

(53) a. *Sā   lātou tausi e   le teine.
         past they care Erg the girl
         (The girl took care of them.)

   b.   *'Olo'o ia fasi e   leoleo e to'alua.
         prog   he hit Erg police uns two
         (Two policemen are beating him up.)

   c.   *'Ua 'ou galo   (ai) o lātou igoa 'uma.
         prf I   forgotten Pro pl=their name all
         (All of their names were forgotten by me.)

(54) a. Sā   tausi lātou e   le teine.
         past care them Erg the girl
         'The girl took care of them.'

   b.   'Olo'o fasi 'oia e   leoleo e to'alua.
         prog   hit him Erg police uns two
         'Two policemen are beating him up.'

   c.   'Ua galo   i-āte   a'u o lātou igoa 'uma.
         prf forgotten Caus-pro me pl=their name all
         'All of their names were forgotten by me.'

The fact that the rule is restricted to subjects argues that subject is a syntactic category of Samoan, despite the failure of subjects in this language to form a unified category with respect to case marking. Further arguments for the category subject are presented in Chapter 3.

1.4.3. Relativization

Throughout Polynesian, relative clauses are formed simply by deleting or pronominalizing the noun coreferential to the head (henceforth the <u>relative noun</u>). Because anaphors generally in these languages can be deleted by zero-pronominalization (see 1.4.1) or surface as pronouns, it might be supposed that relative nouns are no different from them; if so, there would be no need to posit a distinct Relativization rule (Clark 1976). This subsection argues against such a proposal, using facts from Tongan. The argument establishes not only that Tongan has a Relativization rule, but also that its zero-pronominalization rule must be global.

The Tongan relative clause follows its head and forms an NP with it. The fact that the relative clause forms part of a larger NP constituent is shown by the ability of its last element to bear the definitive accent, which is restricted to NPs (see 0.2):

(55) 'Oku 'i fē   'a e puha na'e toó?
      prog at where? Abs the box [past fall]
      'Where is the box that fell?' (C.M. Churchward 1953: 70)

The relative noun is either deleted or pronominalized:

(56) a. 'Oku mau lolotonga kumi   'a e   tamasi'i
        prog we Prog   search Abs the child
        'We're looking for the boy

        na'e hola.
        [past run]
        who ran away.'

     b. Meimei ko   e 'aho kotoa pē 'oku i ai ha
        almost Pred the day all Emp prog exist a
        'Almost every day there are some

        ni'ihi   'oku nau puke.
        some=pl [prog they sick]
        who are sick.' (C.M. Churchward 1953: 205)

The process deleting the relative noun in (56a) can be referred to as the <u>deletion strategy</u>, and that pronominalizing the relative noun in (56b) as the <u>pronominalization strategy</u>. We now consider whether the strategies can be distinguished from more general processes of anaphora.

Morphologically the output of the strategies resembles

that of other anaphoric processes, and consequently relative clauses do not look very different from other sentence types. Relative clauses that have undergone the deletion strategy resemble sentences whose pronouns have been deleted by zero-pronominalization. Compare (56a) and:

(57)   Na'e hola.
       past run
       '(He) ran away.'

Relative clauses that have undergone the pronominalization strategy resemble clauses containing ordinary pronouns. Compare (56b) and:

(58)   'Oku nau puke.
       prog they sick
       'They are sick.'

These parallels might lead one to think that there are no separate relativization strategies, and the deletion strategy is merely an instance of zero-pronominalization while the pronominalization strategy is an instance of ordinary pronominalization. However, other facts suggest that the strategies are distinct.

First, zero-pronominalization in Tongan is optional, so ordinary anaphors always have the option of being deleted or surfacing as pronouns. This is illustrated for subjects and direct objects in (59):

(59)a. Na'e fiema'u 'e he fine'eikí 'a e   tangatá
        past want   Erg the woman   Abs the man
        'The woman wanted of the man

        ke (ne) ha'u.
        sbj he   come
        that he come.'

   b.   Na'e 'alu 'a e   fefiné pea u'u (ia) 'e he
        past go   Abs the woman and bite her   Erg the
        'The woman went and the dog bit

kulī.
dog
her.'

But the deletion strategy is required for relative nouns in certain syntactic functions. For instance, relative nouns that are direct objects cannot surface as pronouns, but must be deleted (cf. C.M. Churchward 1953: 71):[3]

(60) a. Ko   e hā   'a e me'a na'e hoko ki he
       Pred the what? Abs the thing past happen to the
       'What (is the thing that) happened to the

       tamaikí   na'a ke tafulu'i (*kinautolu)?
       children [past you scold   them]
       children that you were scolding?'

   b. 'Oku 'ikai 'ilo 'e ha taha 'a e   tangata
      prog not know Erg a one Abs the person
      'Nobody knows the man

      na'e taa'i (?ia) 'e he fefine.
      [past hit   him Erg the woman]
      who the woman hit.'

The same is true for relative nouns that are third singular intransitive subjects:[4]

(61) a. Ko e hā   na'e hoko   ki he tamasi'i
       Pred the what? past happen to the child
       'What happened to the boy

       na'e (*ne) tō?
       [past he fall]
       who fell?'

   b. Na'a ke fe'iloaki mo   e tamasi'i na'e (*ne)
      past you meet   with the child   [past he
      'Did you meet with the boy who

      lele holo 'i tu'á?
      run around at outside]
      ran around outside?'

Compare (62), in which the relative nouns are intransitive subjects but not third singular, and the pronominalization strategy is allowed:

41   An Overview of Surface Syntax

(62) a. Ka-e   moui ai a-e   ongo siana naa
         but-uns alive Pro Abs-the   du   man   [past
         'But the two men that jumped into the

         na   hopo ki he fuu fa.
         they=du jump to the tree pandanus]
         tree were saved.' (Gifford 151)

     b. Ko   kimoutolu kuo mou   toki a'u   maí,
         Pred you=pl   [prf you=pl just arrive here]
         'You who have just arrived must

         kuo pau ke mou   ō   leva ki he 'ōfisí.
         prf must sbj you=pl go=pl now to the office
         go to the office at once.' (C.M. Churchward
         1953: 128)

If the deletion strategy were merely an instance of zero-pronominalization, it would be difficult to account for sentences like (60-61), in which the relative noun must disappear. Therefore, sentences of this type argue that the deletion strategy is distinct.

Second, zero-pronominalization deletes pronouns regardless of their syntactic function in the clause; in particular, it can delete pronouns in oblique cases:

(63) a. Na'a ku fakamanatu kinautolu, ka na'e ngalo
         past I remind   them   but past forgotten
         'I reminded them, but the picture was

         ('i-ate   kinautolu) 'a e   fakatātā.
         Caus-pro them   Abs the picture
         forgotten by them.'

     b. Na'e ha'u 'a e   polisí pea na'a ku 'oange (ki
         past come Abs the police and past I give   to
         'The policeman came and I gave

         ai) 'a e   fakamatala.
         Pro Abs the information
         him the information.'

But the deletion strategy does not affect relative nouns in oblique cases. Such nouns must undergo the pronominalization strategy instead:[5]

42   An Overview of Surface Syntax

(64) a.   Fakahā mai ki-ate au 'a e   tamasi'i 'oku
          show here to-pro me Abs the child   [prog
          'Show me the child by whom

          ngalo   *(ai) 'a e   lea faka-Tongá.
          forgotten Pro Abs the lg Tongan]
          the Tongan language was forgotten!'

    b.   Ko e Siale eni   na'a ku lau   ki aí.
          Pred the Charlie this [past I refer to Pro]
          'This is the Charlie to whom I referred.' (C.M.
          Churchward 1953: 91)

Examples like these might seem to suggest that zero-pronominalization could not penetrate into relative clauses, were it
not for sentences like the following, which show that the
rule regularly deletes pronouns in relative clauses as long
as they are not the relative noun:

(65)   ...oku ke iloi totonu a-e   mea   oku
             prog you know right Abs-the place [prog
          'Do you know the place where (she) is buried

          tanu ai?
          bury Pro]
          (lit. ...where (they) buried (her))?' (Gifford
          51)

Thus, in order to account for (64-65), the deletion strategy
must be separate from zero-pronominalization.

Finally, ordinary pronominalization allows anaphors of
NPs that would be marked with 'i 'at' or ki 'to' to assume one
of two morphological forms: they can surface as independent
pronouns preceded by these prepositions or as pronominal clitics, ai and ki ai, respectively:

(66) a.   Na'a ku 'oange ki-ate ia 'a e   tohí.
          past I give   to-pro her Abs the book
          'I gave her the book.'

    b.   Na'a ku 'oange ki ai 'a e   tohí.
          past I give   to Pro Abs the book
          'I gave her the book.'

But the pronominalization strategy does not allow this option. Instead, relative nouns in either of these cases must surface in their clitic forms:

(67) a. Ko   e   fefine ko   ia   'oku 'ofa ai 'a
         Pred the woman   Pred that [prog love Pro Abs
         'As for the woman who the man loves,

         e   tangatá, ko   'ene ha'u mei Australia.
         the man]   Pred her come from Australia
         she comes from Australia.'

     b. Ko   e   hā   'a e   me'a na'e hoko   ki he
         Pred the what? Abs the thing past happen to the
         'What (was the thing that) happened to the

         tamaikí   na'a ke 'ita ki ai?
         children [past you angry to Pro]
         children who you were angry at?'

Compare the effect of the pronominalization strategy on relative nouns preceded by mo 'with', which are allowed to surface as independent pronouns, since a clitic form is not independently available to them:

(68)   Ko   e   tangata tonu pē   ia   na'a ne fa'a
         Pred the man   indeed Emp that [past he often
         'That was the very man with whom he

         fakakaungāme'a mo   iá.
         associate   with him]
         habitually associated.' (C.M. Churchward 1953: 128)

The contrast between (66) and (67) argues that the pronominalization strategy must be separate from ordinary pronominalization, as well.

In summary, while the choice between zero-pronominalization and ordinary pronominalization is free, that between the two strategies for Relativization is not. The deletion strategy is required for direct objects and third singular intransitive subjects; the pronominalization strategy is required for oblique NPs. Further, while ordinary pronominalization allows certain oblique anaphors to occur in one of two morphological forms, the pronominalization strategy does not. The differences argue that the strategies cannot be collapsed with more general anaphoric processes. Thus Tongan has a distinct Relativization rule.

Arguments comparable to these can also be constructed for Relativization in Maori, Samoan, Pukapukan, and Kapingamarangi, though they are not presented here. (All of these languages have arguments of the type (67) and --with the possible exception of Kapingamarangi-- (64); Kapingamarangi apparently has arguments of the type (60), and Maori and Pukapukan have similar arguments dealing with subjects.) In subsequent chapters I simply assert that Relativization can be motivated in these languages.

Finally, it is worth pointing out that the existence of Relativization in Tongan does not suffice to account for ungrammatical sentences like the bad version of (64a), in which an oblique relative noun has been deleted. Sentences like this show that oblique relative nouns not only undergo the pronominalization strategy, but must also be prevented from undergoing zero-pronominalization after that. In order to achieve this, relative pronouns must somehow be 'flagged' as different from ordinary pronouns --a move which amounts to saying that Tongan zero-pronominalization is global. Further evidence for the global nature of this rule is presented in Chapter 3, n. 2.

NOTES

1. On the failure of preposed intransitive subjects or transitive direct objects to leave behind pronominal copies, see Chung and Seiter (1977).
2. Given this statement of the rule, sentences like:

(a) Mou   hopo.
     you=pl jump
     'Jump (pl)!' (C.M. Churchward 1953: 71)

appear to argue that imperative verbs are preceded by a tense-aspect-mood particle ∅, with no overt realization.

3. The bad versions of (60) are never volunteered by speakers and seem not to occur in narrative texts. Curiously, sentences of this type are less objectionable when the subject of the relative clause is an overt full noun, a fact for which I have no explanation.

4. This constraint holds for subjects at some derived level of structure. Thus, Tongan has a rule of Incorporation that strips a nonspecific direct object of its article and incorporates it into the verb, thereby detransitivizing the clause. (This rule may be the same as the Incorporation rule that affects certain oblique NPs of intransitive clauses, a possibility which is ignored here.) Subjects of clauses detransitivized by Incorporation are derived intransitive subjects, and if they are third singular, they must be relativized by the deletion strategy:

(a) Kuo ke sio ki he tangata na'a (*ne)
     prf you see to the man   [past he
     'Have you seen the man who was

     fakatau-kahoá?
     sell-necklace]
     selling necklaces?'

5. The notation *( ) means that the sentence is ungrammatical if the material inside the parentheses is omitted.

2. The Morphology of Case & Voice

The Polynesian languages exhibit great surface diversity in their morphology of case and voice. Although the same case and voice morphemes occur throughout the family, they are put to several different uses, and two major types of case systems result. This chapter first surveys the Polynesian scene as far as case and voice are concerned, and then describes the systems of five languages in depth. The discussion attempts to convey the diversity of case and voice in these languages; at the same time, it implicitly raises questions about the role of case marking in Polynesian syntax and its historical development, the investigation of which forms the major goal of this book.

2.1 presents the basic facts of case marking of subjects and direct objects. After an outline of accusative and ergative case marking, which are the two major types found in Polynesian, it describes the case systems of five representative languages: Maori, Tongan, Samoan, Kapingamarangi, and Pukapukan. 2.2 discusses the function of -Cia, a suffix found in many Polynesian languages which has been variously referred to as a passive suffix, a transitive suffix, or a marker of perfective aspect. It is argued that Maori -Cia indicates Passive, while Samoan -Cia has several functions, the most important of which is to indicate that a transitive subject has been extracted.

2.1. CASE MARKING

2.1.1. The Polynesian Situation

The two major types of case systems of Polynesian can be referred to as <u>accusative</u> and <u>ergative</u>, following a long tradition of the study of the morphology of case. In an accusative case system, transitive and intransitive subjects are treated as a unified morphological category as opposed to transitive direct objects, which are separate. In an ergative system, intransitive subjects and transitive direct objects are treated as a unified category as opposed to transitive subjects, which are separate.

To understand how these terms are applied within Polynesian it is necessary to have a rough picture of verb classification. Polynesian verbs (or, more properly, predicates) fall into two syntactic classes: intransitives, which are subcategorized for a subject but not a direct object; and transitives, which are subcategorized for both a subject and a direct object. Transitive verbs can further be classified as <u>canonical transitive</u> or <u>middle</u>, largely on the basis of their semantics. Canonical transitive verbs describe events which produce a direct, often physical effect on the direct object, while middle verbs describe events that do not affect the direct object immediately. Included among the middle verbs in most Polynesian languages are perception verbs ('see', 'listen to'), verbs of emotion and other psychological states ('love', 'want', 'understand'), verbs normally selecting animate direct objects, including some communication verbs ('meet with', 'help', 'call'), and verbs such as 'follow', 'wait for', and 'visit'.[1]

Transitive clauses containing a canonical transitive verb can be referred to as canonical transitive clauses; those containing a middle verb, as middle clauses.

Strictly speaking, the terms accusative and ergative refer only to the case marking of intransitive and canonical transitive clauses. Middle clauses exhibit a separate case pat-

48   The Morphology of Case and Voice

tern which resembles that used for intransitive clauses containing an oblique NP. With this caveat, we now proceed to the two major types of case systems, whose distribution correlates largely (but not entirely) with the linguistic subgrouping.

The accusative type of case system is found principally in East Polynesian languages. In this system, subjects of intransitive and canonical transitive clauses are unmarked; direct objects of canonical transitive clauses are preceded by the accusative marker i:

(1)   Accusative Case Marking:
         Verb   Subj   (intransitive)
         Verb   Subj   i DO   (transitive)

Subjects of middle clauses are also unmarked, while their direct objects are preceded by i or ki. Ki can be identified as the oblique preposition 'to', while i could be analyzed either as the accusative marker or as the oblique i 'at':

(2)   Middle Case Marking:
         Verb   Subj   i/ki DO

Both canonical transitive and middle clauses are eligible for Passive, which promotes the direct object to subject, turns the original subject into an oblique noun marked with the agent marker e, and attaches some form of the passive suffix -Cia to the verb:

(3)   Passive:
         Verb-Cia   e Agent   Subj
                     (=underlying   (=underlying
                     Subj)   DO)

The ergative type of case system is found in Tongic and in many Samoic-Outlier languages. In this system, subjects of intransitive clauses and direct objects of canonical transitive clauses are unmarked; subjects of canonical transitive clauses are preceded by the ergative marker e. NPs of the former type can be referred to as absolutives, and those of the latter type, as ergatives:

(4)   Ergative Case Marking:
       Verb   Subj   (intransitive)
       Verb e Subj   DO   (transitive)

In contrast, subjects of middle clauses are unmarked (like intransitive subjects), and their direct objects are preceded by one of the oblique prepositions i 'at' or ki 'to':

(5)   Middle Case Marking:
       Verb   Subj   i/ki DO

There is no syntactic Passive.

In addition to these two major systems, a number of composite types are found. Some languages (e.g. Maori) exhibit an accusative case system but make widespread use of Passive for canonical transitive clauses. Others (e.g. Samoan) have an ergative case system, but allow canonical transitive verbs to occur with a mysterious 'transitive' suffix, -Cia, cognate with the passive suffix of the accusative languages. Still others (e.g. Pukapukan) allow accusative or ergative case marking for transitive clauses, or have combined these patterns to produce a new case paradigm for all clause types (e.g. Kapingamarangi).

This diversity is surprising for such a closely related family of languages; it does not, however, interfere with two significant generalizations that hold for case marking throughout Polynesian. First, the case marking of canonical transitive clauses in the accusative languages resembles that of middle clauses in all Polynesian languages. Second, the case marking of passive clauses in the accusative languages resembles that of canonical transitive clauses in the ergative languages. These generalizations raise a number of synchronic and diachronic questions which are investigated in subsequent chapters.

The rest of this section describes the case systems of the five representative languages: Maori, an accusative language; Tongan and Samoan, two ergative languages; Kapingamarangi, a language whose accusative case system differs from (1-2); and Pukapukan, a language with a mixed accusative-ergative system.

2.1.2. Maori

Maori, an East Polynesian language, has the accusative case system of (1-3). Subjects of intransitive clauses are unmarked:

(6) a. Ka moe te tamaiti.
uns sleep the child
'The child is sleeping.'

b. Ka mate te iwi o Te Oripāroa.
uns die the people of Te Oriparoa
'The followers of Te Oriparoa were destroyed.'
(Orbell 98)

So are subjects of canonical transitive and middle clauses. Direct objects of canonical transitive clauses are marked with the accusative i:

(7) a. Ka whakareri a Rewi i ngā rama.
uns prepare prop Rewi Acc the=pl torch
'Rewi prepared the torches.' (Waititi 1969: 5)

b. Hura rawa ake te wahine rā i tana umu.
uncover Emp up the woman that Acc her oven
'The woman uncovered her oven.' (Orbell 90)

c. Hanga ana tētahi i tōna whare, hanga ana
build prog one Acc his house build prog
'Each of these two men was building himself a

           tētahi   i   tōna whare.
           one   Acc   his house
           house (lit. One was building his own house, the
           other was building his own house).' (Orbell 34)

    d.   Kātahi ia ka tīmata i   tōna haka, ka
           then   he uns begin Acc his haka uns
           'Then he started (to dance) his haka, chanting

           whakahua i   tōna ingoa.
           recite   Acc his name
           his name.' (Orbell 52)

Direct objects of middle clauses are marked with the oblique
ki 'to' or with i, which can be identified either as the oblique i 'at' or as the accusative marker. The choice between
i and ki is determined by considerations such as the degree
to which the direct object is affected by the event, and
whether or not it is fixed or known (Mark 1970):

  (8)a.   Ka hiahia au ki te pepehā tika.
          uns want   I to the proverb right
          'I want the right proverb.' (Mark 1970: 11)

    b.   Ka hiahia au i   te pepehā tika.
          uns want   I Acc the proverb right
          'I want the right proverb.' (Mark 1970: 11)

    c.   Hoatu kia kite i   te pai o tōu kāinga.
          move sbj see Acc the good of your house
          'Let (us) go and see this fine place of yours.'
          (Orbell 28)

    d.   Hoake kia kite koe ki te rangatira-tanga o
          move sbj see you to the chief-Nmlz   of
          'Come and (you will) see the greatness of my

          taku kāinga.
          my   house
          my home.' (Orbell 28)

   Both canonical transitive and middle clauses are eligible
for Passive, which promotes the direct object to subject,
turns the original subject into an oblique noun marked with
e, and attaches to the verb some alternant of the passive

52   The Morphology of Case and Voice

suffix -<u>Cia</u> (see Hale 1968):

(9) a.   Ka tuku-a   e   Paowa te waka.
         uns leave-Pass Agt Paowa the canoe
         'Paowa left the canoe.' (Orbell 74)

    b.   Ka tahu-na   te nanakia rā e   ngā   mano
         uns burn-Pass the monster that Agt the=pl men
         'The men set fire to the

         rā ki   te ahi.
         that with the fire
         monster.' (Orbell 40)

    c.   Kua moe-a   au e te nanakia.
         prf sleep-Pass I Agt the monster
         'A monster has taken me as his wife (lit. I
         have been slept with by a monster).' (Orbell 38)

    d.   I   kite-a   e   ia ki Te Pukemore.
         past see-Pass Agt him to Te Pukemore
         'He saw (them) on Mt. Pukemore.' (Orbell 30)

As is meant to be suggested by the English translations, the
Maori passive is the normal construction for canonical transitive clauses. The preference for Passive and the fact
that this rule alters grammatical relations are discussed
further in 2.2.1 (see also Chung 1977b).

2.1.3. <u>Tongan</u>

Tongan, one of the two Tongic languages, has an ergative case
system similar to (4-5).

Subjects of intransitive clauses occur in the absolutive
case, which is either unmarked or marked with <u>'a</u>. (The <u>'a</u>
is evidently descended from the pronominal-proper article in
Proto-Polynesian; see 1.3.2.)

(10) a. 'Oku fu'u hela'ia 'a 'Ālani 'i he ngāué.
         prog very tired   Abs Alan Caus the work
         'Alan is very tired because of work.'

b. 'Oku lolotonga puna ('a) e   vakapuna.
    prog Prog   fly   Abs the airplane
    'An airplane is flying.'

c. 'Oku lolotonga puna ha vakapuna.
    prog Prog   fly   a airplane
    'Some airplane or other is flying.'

Proper nouns in the absolutive are always preceded by 'a, and nonspecific nouns are always unmarked. Other types of nouns allow either form of the absolutive, with 'a occurring marginally before pronouns and demonstratives, sometimes before nouns preceded by a specific possessive pronoun, and preferably otherwise (C.M. Churchward 1953: 106). In this last case, use of 'a tends to be associated with slow or formal speech; lack of marking, with fast or informal speech.

Subjects of canonical transitive clauses occur in the ergative, marked with 'e, while direct objects are marked absolutive:

(11)a. 'Oku fa'u 'e hoku tokouá 'a e   tēpile.
        prog make Erg my   sibling Abs the table
        'My brother is making a table.'

b. Na'e tuli kinautolu 'e he sianá.
    past chase them   Erg the man
    'The man chased them.'

c. Na'e taa'i 'e Mele 'a Sione.
    past hit   Erg Mary Abs John
    'Mary hit John.'

d. Na'e 'ufi'ufi'i 'e Sione 'a e   tēpilé 'aki
    past cover   Erg John Abs the table with
    'John covered the table with

    ha ngatu.
    a tapa=cloth
    a tapa cloth.'

Subjects of middle clauses are marked absolutive and their direct objects are preceded by one of the oblique preposi-

54   The Morphology of Case and Voice

tions 'i 'at' or ki 'to'. The choice of 'i or ki is usually lexically governed, but sometimes determined by factors such as the animacy of the direct object or its distance from the subject:

    (12)a. Kuo pau ke talangofua kotoa ki he lao.
            prf must sbj obey   all to the law
            'Everyone must obey the law.'

       b. 'Oku manako ia 'i he ta'ahiné.
           prog like he at the girl
           'He likes the girl.'

       c. 'Oku ou muimui 'i he kā.
           prog I follow at the car
           'I'm following the car.' (I'm right behind it.)

       d. 'Oku ou muimui ki he kā.
           prog I follow to the car
           'I'm following the car.' (The car is on the
           horizon or is the head car in a parade.)

2.1.4. Samoan

Samoan, a Samoic-Outlier language, also has an ergative case system. Subjects of intransitive clauses are unmarked:

    (13)a. 'Ole'ā ōmai   lātou.
            fut   come=pl they
            'They will come.'

       b. Na   maliu 'oia i   le ma'i.
           past die   he Caus the sick
           'He died from sickness.'

       c. Ua tele le ofo   o le malaga ia te i
           prf great the surprised of the party at-pro pl
           'Great was the surprise of the party at

           laua.
           them=du
           them.' (Stuebel 230)

Subjects of canonical transitive clauses are marked with e, and their direct objects are unmarked:

(14) a. Sā   saisai e ia lona to'alua i   le maea.
         past tie   Erg he his spouse with the rope
         'He tied up his wife with a rope.'

   b.   Ona sasa ai lea o   Saleimoa e   Moso i
         then hit Pro that Pred Saleimoa Erg Moso with
         'Then Moso hit the Saleimoa people with

         le too.
         the pole
         the pole.' (Stuebel 229)

   c.   'Ana lē sola 'oia, semanū   e   maua 'oia
         if   not run he   probably uns catch him
         'If he hadn't run away, the police probably

         e   leoleo.
         Erg police
         would have caught him.'

   d.   E   iloa 'uma e   ia tali.
         uns know all Erg he answer
         'He knows all the answers.'

In addition, the verb of a canonical transitive clause is sometimes suffixed with an alternant of the 'transitive' suffix -Cia, usually -a or -ina. When this happens, the clause exhibits VOS word order at least as often as VSO, in violation of the more general word order tendencies (see 1.1.1):

(15) a. Ua fai-a   e   Savea Siuleo Pulotu.
         prf make-Trans Erg Savea Siuleo Pulotu
         'Savea Siuleo made Pulotu.' (Stuebel 234)

   b.   Sā   su'e-ina   a'u e   le fānau   a
         past search-Trans me Erg the children of
         'Fo'isia's children were looking

         Fo'isia.
         Fo'isia
         for me.'

   c.   Sā   'āmata-ina   e   lātou le pese.
         past begin-Trans Erg they the song
         'They began the song.'

The function of the transitive -Cia, so-called because it

occurs only in canonical transitive clauses, has heretofore been rather obscure. It is discussed at greater length in 2.2.2.

Subjects of middle clauses are unmarked, while their direct objects are preceded by one of the oblique prepositions i 'at' or 'i 'to' (<*ki by regular phonological change).[2] As the prepositions differ only by a glottal stop, NPs marked with them are more easily distinguished by their anaphors, ai and 'i ai, respectively. The choice between i and 'i is determined by factors such as the animacy of the direct object, its newness to the discourse, and the degree to which it is focused on (see Chung 1973b):

(16) a. 'Ua tago le teine 'i lona ulu.
        prf touch the girl to her head
        'The girl touched her head.'

    b. 'Ua 'alo tagata i-āte a'u.
        prf dodge person at-pro me
        'People ignored me.'

    c. 'Āfai e   leai se tupe, e   leai se mea   e
        if   uns not a   money uns not a   thing uns
        'If there's no money, there is nothing to

        popole ai.
        worry Pro
        worry about.' (pronominal copy of i)

    d. 'Ou te le'i māfaufau 'i ai muamua.
        I   uns not think   to Pro before
        'I wasn't thinking about it before.' (pronominal copy of 'i)

Finally, some middle verbs are eligible for a derivational process which attaches to them some alternant of the transitivizing suffix -Cia, thereby turning them into canonical transitive verbs. As such, they govern the ergative case pattern of (14), not the middle case pattern of (16):

The Morphology of Case and Voice

(17) a. 'Ua 'alo-fia   a'u e   tagata.
        prf dodge-Suff   me Erg person
        'People ignored me.'

   b. 'Ua alofa-gia 'i-tātou e   le nu'u.
       prf love-Suff pl-us   Erg the village
       'We are well-treated by the village.' (Milner 1966: 17)

Although the transitivizing -<u>Cia</u> is descended historically from the same source as the transitive -<u>Cia</u>, the two must now be considered distinct. Further discussion of the transitivizing suffix is postponed to 6.3.3. Arguments that neither -<u>Cia</u> is a passive suffix go back as far as Milner (1962); see also Cook (1978) and 2.2.2.1.

2.1.5. Kapingamarangi

Kapingamarangi, a Samoic-Outlier language, has an accusative case system that appears impressionistically to be a composite of the Maori and Samoan types. This subsection discusses the marking of postverbal subjects and direct objects only, since the analysis of unmarked NPs preceding the verb has already been dealt with in 1.1.2.

In Kapingamarangi, subjects of intransitive clauses appear either unmarked or marked with the nominative markers <u>e</u> or <u>ko</u>. From the available textual material (Elbert 1948) it is difficult to tell what determines the distribution of these markers:

(18) a. E, heke mai te ika.
        oh slide here the fish
        'Oh, a fish slides in.' (Elbert 70)

   b. Ka rere mai ei mē i ono   nua o ti ariki.
       uns fly here Pro it at pl=his top of the priest
       'It flew over the priest.' (Elbert 73)

   c. Tē mataku e   au i   toku aroh(o) i ti koe.
       not afraid Nom I   Caus my   love   at pro you
       'I am not afraid because of my love for you.'
       (Elbert 147)

58   Te Morphology of Case and Voice

      d.   Ne   hōhō rā   ko Ia ki rara.
          past near that Nom he to below
          'When he was almost down...' (Elbert 93)

Subjects of canonical transitive clauses also appear unmarked or in the nominative:

  (19)a. Roua ka keri aka ti kau   'rā.
        Roua uns dig up the people that
        'The people dug up Roua.' (Elbert 118)

     b. E   khumi e   au.
        nonpast grab Nom I
        'I'll grab (it).' (Elbert 80)

     c. Ka khumi ko ti miharī.
        uns grab Nom the receiver
        '...picked up by the radio receiver.' (Elbert 146)

     d. Tana u   rā ku kaiā ko thangata.
        his crab that prf steal Nom the=person
        'Someone had stolen his crab.' (Elbert 98)

So do subjects of middle clauses:

  (20)a. Ka kitē Ia niā   'hina tokorua ka noho i
        uns see he the=pl woman two   uns sit at
        'He saw two women sitting

        tono pāhi.
        his side
        beside him.' (Elbert 82)

     b. Au ku kitē e   au a   mē.
        I prf see Nom I pro him
        'I saw him.' (Elbert 33)

     c. Mā tērā ku kitā ko ti thama tērā.
        and that prf see Nom the boy that
        'The boy saw her.' (Elbert 110)

Although there is a statistical tendency for subjects of middles to be unmarked and subjects of canonical transitives to be marked overtly with e or ko, this is not absolute, and it is clear that each type of subject allows either the nominative or lack of marking.

Direct objects of canonical transitive clauses appear either unmarked or marked with the accusative i:

 (21)a. Uku rima e   khumi e au ti niu.
    pl=my hand nonpast grab Nom I the tree
    'I'm holding the tree with my hands.' (Elbert 65)

  b. Keiokō Aparē ka hakamhūni tūmā ti ahi a mā.
    then Apare uns hide extra the fire of her
    'Apare hid the extra (taros) in the woman's fire.' (Elbert 63)

  c. Thāne rā e   kae i tana u.
    the=man that nonpast take Acc his trap
    'The man took his fish trap.' (Elbert 78)

Direct objects of middle clauses are either unmarked, marked with i, or with ki. Ki can be identified as the oblique ki 'to', while i and lack of marking can be analyzed either as the locative (i) 'at' or as the accusative:

 (22)a. Ti kau 'rā ku mhata ki ti manu.
    the people that prf look to the bird
    'The people looked at the bird.' (Elbert 72)

  b. Keiokō ti ahina ku hakarongo nherekhai
    then the woman prf hear   the=pl=word
    'The woman listened to the instructions of the

    ti kē.
    the turtle
    turtle.' (Elbert 71)

  c. Koe rā ka noho, ka hakarongo i ti koe.
    you that uns sit uns hear   Acc pro you
    'You stay here, see how (you) feel.' (Elbert 91)

  d. Nia tama tiki hakarongo ki ti herekhai
    the=pl child not hear to the word
    'The boys did not obey their mother's

    tinau tinana.
    their=du mother
    instructions.' (Elbert 86)

While there is a tendency for direct objects of middles to be marked with i or ki rather than unmarked, this is --again-- not absolute; cf. (20).

Finally, canonical transitive verbs and middle verbs can be suffixed with the transitive suffix -Cia, which occurs principally in future or unrealized clauses. When this happens, the form of the nominative case is frequently e and never ko; otherwise the case pattern remains unaffected:[3]

(23) a. Koe ti ika e uta-ina koe a Hina?
you the fish nonpast carry-Trans you prop Hina
'Are you the fish who will carry Hina?' (Elbert 70)

b. Koe e tē ranga-hia e koe ou
you nonpast not tell-Trans Nom you pl=your
'You didn't remember your

hihimata.
antenna
antennae.' (Elbert 124)

c. Iri-hia mai i au.
fan-Trans here Acc me
'Fan me.' (Elbert 175)

d. Kōtou e rongo-no e kōtou i ti
you=pl nonpast hear-Trans Nom you=pl Acc the
'You hear what she's said (lit. You hear her

mā mē tērā noko hai.
thing her that past say
thing that (she) said).' (Elbert 92)

Ignoring the failure of ko to cooccur with the transitive suffix, the following picture emerges: subjects are marked with e or ko, direct objects of canonical transitives are marked with i, and in addition any subject or direct object may exhibit no marker. The choice of these options is influenced by verb classification and the presence or absence of -Cia, in a fashion reminiscent of Samoan. However, it should not obscure the fact that when these NPs are overtly marked,

one set of markers is used for transitive and intransitive
subjects and a distinct marker is used for transitive direct
objects. Thus the basic organization of the case system is
accusative.

2.1.6. Pukapukan

Pukapukan, a Samoic-Outlier language and the last of the languages to be described here, has a mixed accusative-ergative
case system. This system differs from that of other Polynesian languages and therefore is worth examining in some detail.

Intransitive clauses in Pukapukan take their subjects in
the nominative, which is generally unmarked:

(24) a. Na   we-lele te kau.
         past pl-run the people
         'The people ran.'

   b.   Na   lilo   te kete   i   te tāne.
        past gotten the basket Caus the man
        'The basket belongs to the man.'

Exceptionally, the nominative marker for proper nouns and the
third singular pronoun is i, followed by the pronominal-proper article a (see 1.3.2):

(25) a. Na   wano i   a-na   lā   Victoria Park.
         past go   Nom pro-he across Victoria Park
         'He went across Victoria Park.'

   b.   Yapu   loa i a   Leiakunavai.
        pregnant Emp Nom prop Leiakunavai
        'Leiakunavai became pregnant.' (Beaglehole and
        Beaglehole 1067)

Underlyingly transitive clauses, whether canonical transitive or middle, allow three surface case patterns. For the
moment I refrain from discussing the syntax associated with
these patterns and refer to them simply as 'accusative',

'passive', and 'ergative', following the morphology.

In the 'accusative' pattern, the underlying subject is nominative and the underlying direct object is marked with the accusative marker i, as in the canonical transitive clauses of (26) and the middle clause of (27):

(26) a. Ka aumai te wawine i te puka.
fut bring the woman Acc the book
'The woman is going to bring the book.'

b. Kakati loa i te yiku o te tawola.
bite Emp Acc the tail of the whale
'(He) bit the tail of the whale.' (Beaglehole and Beaglehole 1041)

c. Ko velevele i a Palaoa i ona
prog clear Nom prop Palaoa Acc pl=his
'Palaoa was clearing his large channel

mataava i tona alai.
channel in his coral
in his coral barrier.' (Beaglehole and Beaglehole 1133)

(27) Ko mina i a-na i te ika.
prog want Nom pro-he Acc the fish
'He wants the fish.'

In the 'passive' pattern, the underlying subject is marked with the agentive/ergative marker e, the underlying direct object is nominative, and some alternant of the 'passive' suffix -Cia, usually -a, -ina, or -ngia, is attached to the verb. In violation of the more general word order tendencies, the clause exhibits VOS word order as often as VSO (see 1.1.1). Consider the canonical transitive clauses of (28) and the middle clauses of (29):

(28) a. Na teretere-ina nā wāwā e Turi.
past peel-Pass the=pl taro Agt Turi
'Turi peeled the taro.'

b. Na vayi-ngia e te wawine te yakari.
past split-Pass Agt the woman the coconut
'The woman split the coconut.'

(29) a. Ko   mina-ngia te yua e-ku.
        prog want-Pass the water Agt-me
        'I want the water.'

    b. Kite-a   mai te toe   ika e   te akula.
       see-Pass here the other fish Agt the swordfish
       'The swordfish saw another fish.' (Beaglehole
       and Beaglehole 1042)

In the 'ergative' pattern, finally, the underlying subject is marked with e, the underlying direct object is nominative, and the -Cia suffix does not appear. This pattern is illustrated for canonical transitive clauses by (30) and for middle clauses by (31):

(30) a. Na   aumai e-ku te pānga.
        past bring Erg-I the mat
        'I brought the mat.'

    b. Lomilomi ai e   tana wawine ma na   tama
       massage Pro Erg his woman and the=pl boy
       'His two knees were massaged by his wife and

       lua tulivae ia.
       two knee   that
       the children.' (Beaglehole and Beaglehole 1089)

(31) a. ?Ko mina e-ku te yua.
        prog want Erg-I the water
        'I want the water.'

    b. eia koa kite ai e   Te Pou...
       then prf see Pro Erg Te Pou
       'Then when Te Pou saw (them)...'

Morphologically it appears that the only difference between the 'passive' and 'ergative' patterns is the presence or absence of -Cia. It will be shown in Chapter 7, however, that the clause types exhibiting these patterns differ syntactically in several respects, and so the choice of different labels is justified. For the moment I simply assert that the 'passive' and 'ergative' patterns are distinct. This explicitly does not involve the claim that clauses in the 'passive' pattern are invariably derived by a Passive rule, a point which is developed further in Chapter 7.

In general, the three patterns are governed by the large majority of transitive verbs, although the 'ergative' pattern is less acceptable than the 'accusative' or 'passive' for certain middle verbs. Variation among the patterns is determined principally by what other syntactic rules have applied. In clauses to which no other rules have applied (zero-pronominalization excepted), the three patterns appear to vary freely and are associated with few discernable shades of meaning. Speakers of Pukapukan sometimes suggest that the 'ergative' pattern indicates emphatic action; this is difficult to confirm on the basis of textual examples. Speakers also suggest that the 'passive' pattern is used for unrealized events. Although there is some tendency for the 'passive' pattern to occur in imperatives or clauses introduced by the subjunctive particle ke, it is not restricted to these contexts; compare:

(32) Yuki-a   ma   na   ngakau ke yeye
     pierce-Pass with the=pl mind sbj unconscious
     'Pierce their minds so that (they) are uncon-

     wua, ke wakavavale-ina.
     just sbj weaken=pl-Pass
     scious, so that (they) are stupified.' (Beaglehole and Beaglehole 1155)

(33) Yolo-wia mai e   tona mana.
     push-Pass here Agt his power
     '(The person) was pushed in by his power.'
     (Beaglehole and Beaglehole 1109)

The main differences among the patterns appear rather to occur in the areas of register and stylistics. As far as register is concerned, the 'accusative' is identified as formal, polite, and proper; the 'ergative' as informal, casual, and slightly improper; and the 'passive' as neutral. Stylistically, the three patterns are sometimes used to organize different sections of narrative texts, although their precise functions remain somewhat unclear. For instance, a narrative can begin in the 'accusative' pattern and shift to 'ergative' subsequently (Beaglehole and Beaglehole 1938b: 1086-89), or begin in the 'ergative' pattern and shift to 'accusative' subsequently (Beaglehole and Beaglehole 1938b: 1009-11). The same device is also used for short sequences of events. As an alternative, the patterns are sometimes assigned so that the topic of the narrative is consistently nominative (Beaglehole and Beaglehole 1938b: 993-95).

Even when these considerations are taken into account, there remain many instances in which the choice of case pattern cannot be attributed to any clear factors. In such situations I assume that the patterns are in free variation, although the real situation is doubtless more complex.

Significantly, the three patterns do not vary as freely in clauses whose subject or direct object has been removed by certain rules --a phenomenon discussed further in Chapter 7. For the moment, all that concerns us is that Pukapukan has a mixed case system unique in Polynesian: it allows 'accusative' case marking, 'ergative' case marking, and a third type --'passive' case marking-- as well.[4]

2.2. THE -Cia SUFFIX: PASSIVE, TRANSITIVE, OR PERFECTIVE?

Many Polynesian languages have a -Cia suffix which is attached to verbs in one particular case pattern, and in this sense intimately connected to the morphology of case. The suffix has aroused (and doubtless will continue to arouse) much controversy in the literature. For Samoan, for instance,

66   The Morphology of Case and Voice

it has been proposed that -Cia is a passive suffix, a transitive suffix, and a marker of perfective aspect. Curiously, the same sorts of proposals have been made for Maori, despite the fact that Maori -Cia and Samoan -Cia have rather different distributional properties.

This section examines the functions of Maori -Cia and Samoan -Cia and argues that both have to do with voice, where this term is understood very loosely to mean the way in which the underlying subject of a clause appears on the surface. In particular, Maori -Cia indicates Passive; Samoan -Cia serves primarily to indicate that a transitive subject has been extracted. Finally, the hypothesis is examined that -Cia in these languages might serve partly or wholly as a marker of perfective aspect.

2.2.1. The Maori Passive

In 2.1.2, the Maori -Cia suffix was described as a marker of Passive. Consider the passive (34), which is related to the active (35) on this analysis:

(34)   Ka whana-a   a   Hōne e   te hōiho.
        uns kick-Pass   prop John Agt the horse
        'John was kicked by the horse.'

(35)   Ka whana te hōiho i   a   Hōne.
        uns kick   the horse Acc prop John
        'The horse kicked John.'

(Active is used here to refer to the clause type in which a single NP is both underlying subject and surface subject.)

One striking characteristic of the passive is that it occurs more frequently than the active, unlike passives in other languages (e.g. English). This fact, noted as early as Williams and Williams (1950[1862]), has been supported in recent discussions by observations like the following:

(a) The passive is more frequent than the active in narratives, particularly for canonical transitive clauses. Clark (1973b), for instance, gives statistics for some fifty pages of texts that show the passive occurring 244 times and the active only 188 times. According to Patrick Hohepa and Kenneth Hale, the passive is used 75-85% more often than the active.

(b) The passive is required for certain clause types typically thought of as 'active'; in particular, for nonreflexive imperatives formed from canonical transitive clauses. Compare the passive imperatives of (36) with their active counterparts:

(36) a. Tua-ina   te rākau.
        fell-Pass the tree
        'Fell the tree!'

     b. Pūhi-a.
        shoot-Pass
        'Shoot (it)!'

(37) a. *Tua i   te rākau.
        fell Acc the tree
        (Fell the tree!)

     b. *Patu i   te poaka.
        kill Acc the pig
        (Kill the pig!)

(c) The passive occurs in contexts that would seem strange or unnatural for an English passive. In (38), for instance, the passives within the adverbial clause correspond to English actives:

(38)   Ka hiahia-tia e   te tāne kia moe-a,
        uns want-Pass   Agt the man sbj sleep-Pass
        'Whenever a man wanted to sleep (with her),

        kāore e   pai   te iwi.
        not   nonpast agree the people
        the people did not agree.' (Biggs, Hohepa, and Mead 46)

Observations of this sort have led Sinclair (1976) to claim that clauses like (34) are superficially transitive, and Clark (1973b) to suggest that they serve in large part to indicate the perfective. Here, on the contrary, it is argued that these clauses have undergone a Passive rule which alters grammatical relations in the expected way (see Williams and Williams (1950[1862]) for an early statement of this view). 2.2.1.1 scrutinizes the frequency of Passive more closely; 2.2.1.2 and 2.2.1.3 give two arguments that it alters grammatical relations. 2.2.1.5 raises the issue of perfectivity and suggests that, in the most general account, passive clauses serve only indirectly to signal perfective aspect, if at all.

2.2.1.1. <u>Frequency</u>. The proposals that the Maori passive is not really a passive are primarily motivated by its high frequency. Because passive clauses occur far more often than active clauses, the argument goes, they should not be viewed as syntactically derived from the active. However, it can be shown that the frequency of the passive is a late or superficial phenomenon, in that it is systematically overriden by the requirements of other rules. This weakens the case for assuming that frequency gives clues to underlying structure.

Thus, the passive never occurs in clauses whose underlying subjects have been deleted by the three types of Equi in Maori: <u>ki te</u> Equi, <u>hei</u> Equi, and Participle Formation (see 3.2.1). These rules apply only to embedded clauses that are active:

(39)a. E   haere mai ana tērā...ki te patu i   a
        uns go   here prog that   Comp kill Acc prop
        'She came up to kill Uta as

69   The Morphology of Case and Voice

>   Uta hei kai   māhana.
>   Uta for food for=her
>   food for herself.' (Orbell 70; <u>ki te</u> Equi)
>
> b. Ka haere a   Pētera rāua   ko   Paki ki te
>   uns go   prop Peter   they=du Pred Paki to the
>   'Peter and Paki went to the burial ground
>
>   urupā   ki te kari i   te rua.
>   cemetery Comp dig Acc the hole
>   to dig a hole.' (Waititi 1969: 30; <u>ki te</u> Equi)
>
> c. Ka tuku-a   mai ko   tētahi parirau hei
>   uns put-Pass here Pred one   wing   Comp
>   '(It) stretches out a wing to scoop
>
>   hao   i   te tangata.
>   scoop Acc the person
>   up the man.' (Orbell 102; <u>hei</u> Equi)

Further, the passive never occurs in clauses whose underlying subjects have been extracted by Relativization or Clefting, although it tends to be found in clauses whose underlying direct objects have undergone these rules. In these cases the choice of active vs. passive seems determined by a preference for the rules to apply to NPs in the unmarked case (Clark 1973b):

> (40)a. te tāne... i   whakarere nei i   a   ia
>   the man   [past   abandon   this Acc pro her]
>   'the man...who had abandoned her' (Orbell 94;
>   Relativization)
>
> b.   te kōtimana e   pūhi-a   ana e   te hau
>   the thistle [uns blow-Pass prog Agt the wind]
>   'the thistle that is blown by the wind' (Biggs,
>   Hohepa, and Mead 76; Relativization)
>
> c.   Ko   Houmea tonu e   horo   nei i
>   Pred Houmea still nonpast swallow this Acc
>   'It's Houmea who is swallowing the fish
>
>   ngā   ika o tō waka.
>   the=pl fish of your canoe
>   in your canoe!' (Orbell 64; Clefting)

Apparently, the only clause types for which Passive is strongly preferred are imperative clauses, clauses which have undergone zero-pronominalization:

(41) a. Ka rere mai te tuakana, tapa-hia ana te
uns run here the sibling cut-Pass prog the
'The elder brother ran up and (he) cut

rāhiri.
rope
the rope.' (Orbell 20)

b. Ka kawe-a ki rō whare kia kai-nga e
uns take-Pass to inside house sbj eat-Pass Agt
'(She) took (them) into the house so that her

tāna tāne.
her husband
husband could eat (them).' (Orbell 60)

Or have not undergone any other rules:

(42) a. Ka mau-ria mai e ia ngā manu.
uns carry-Pass here Agt him the=pl bird
'He brought back the birds.' (Orbell 50)

b. Kātahi ka whakakā-ngia e Tamahae te raiti.
then uns light-Pass Agt Tamahae the light
'Then Tamahae turned on the light.' (Waititi 1969: 42)

The fact that the high frequency of Passive occurs principally in clauses of these last types is borne out by nineteenth century texts. In some fifty pages of Orbell (1968), for instance, the passive is used for all 28 transitive imperatives, and for 259 out of 346 canonical transitive clauses of types (41-42). However, it is used for none of the 26 transitive clauses whose subjects have been deleted by Equi; in the 10 relative clauses in which a transitive subject or direct object is relativized, the choice of active or passive is determined by which construction will allow the relative noun to occur in the unmarked case.

As will be discussed in 3.1.3, the Maori Equi rules can be identified as 'deeper' rules, Relativization and Clefting as superficial rules, and zero-pronominalization as perhaps the last rule of all. This makes it tempting to correlate the increasing frequency of the passive with the increasing superficiality of *other* rules affecting the clause. Even without going this far, however, the facts described above argue that the preference for Passive is late: it takes effect only after conditions on other rules (i.e. Equi, Relativization, and Clefting) have been satisfied. In this sense, its high frequency compared to the active is superficial. The point does not, of course, refute proposals that the Maori passive is really superficially transitive or perfective; but it does undermine their original motivation.

2.2.1.2. *Relativization*. An argument that passive clauses have different grammatical relations from their active counterparts is provided by the Maori Relativization rule. This rule, like its Tongan counterpart (see 1.4.3), consists of a deletion strategy and a pronominalization strategy (see Williams and Williams 1950[1862]). The deletion strategy is used to relativize intransitive and transitive subjects:

(43) a. Ka puta mai te wairua o te tamaiti i
uns come here the spirit of the child [past
'The spirit of the child who had died

mate.
die]
came.' (Orbell 8)

b. Ka hari hoki ki tana kai e whakatangi
uns happy also to his food [nonpast sound
'(He) was greatly delighted with his food which

mai rā i te pūtātara.
here that Acc the horn]
was sounding the trumpet.' (Orbell 14)

72   The Morphology of Case and Voice

The pronominalization strategy is used for transitive direct objects and for certain oblique NPs:

(44)a. E   mōhio ana au ki te tangata i   patu
        uns know prog I to the man   [past hit
        'I know the man who John

        ai   a   Hōne.
        Pro prop John]
        hit.'

   b.   ...te take   i   whakarēre-a ai a
           the reason [past abandon-Pass Pro prop
        '...the reason why Te Oriparoa abandoned

        Hinepoupou e   Te Oripāroa, he umu korora.
        Hinepoupou Agt Te Oriparoa] a   oven pigeon
        Hinepoupou was because of a meal of pigeons.'
        (Orbell 90)

   c.   Ko   te whare i   noho ai ia, i   wera
        Pred the house [past sit Pro he] past burn
        'The house that he stayed in was burned

        i   te ahi.
        Caus the fire
        by the fire.'

Now when Relativization attempts to affect the NPs of a passive clause, the underlying direct object is relativized via the deletion strategy:

(45)a. Ka   puta ki waho   ngā   tamariki i
        uns come to outside   the=pl   children [past
        'Then out came the sons she

        horo-mia   nei.
        swallow-Pass   this]
        had swallowed.' (Orbell 68)

   b.   Ka   haere atu te wahine rā   ki te wāhi
        uns go   away the woman that to the place
        'The woman went to the place that had been

        i   tohu-ngia mai.
        [past   show-Pass here]
        pointed out (to her) (by the whale).' (Orbell 24)

The underlying subject cannot be relativized at all, as pointed out by Tamati Reedy:

(46) *Ko   te wahine ka patu-a   ai   te tangata
       Pred the woman   [uns hit-Pass Pro the man
       (The woman by whom the man was hit

       rā,   he hoa   nō-ku.
       that] a   friend of-me
       is a friend of mine.)

Assuming Keenan and Comrie's (1977) Accessibility Hierarchy, the ability of the underlying direct objects of (45) to undergo the deletion strategy argues that they are subjects when Relativization applies. Further, the inability of the underlying subject of (46) to undergo either strategy argues that it is neither subject nor direct object, but rather some (unrelativizable) type of oblique NP. Both conclusions point to the fact that passive clauses have different grammatical relations from active clauses. Significantly, they differ in the way that we would expect if passive clauses are derived from their active counterparts by a Passive rule.

2.2.1.3. he. A second argument that the passive has different grammatical relations from the active is provided by the nonspecific article he. As noted by Kenneth Hale and Patrick Hohepa (class lectures, 1969), this article qualifies nouns only when they are the subjects of intransitive clauses (see also Chung and Timberlake 1974; Chung 1977b; Reedy 1977). Consider the intransitive subjects of:

(47)a. Ka puta he whakaaro mō te wahine rā.
        uns come a thought for the woman that
        'A thought came to the woman.' (Orbell 42)

     b. Kua riro   he tamaiti i   a   Hēmi.
        prf taken a child   Caus prop Jim
        'A child has been taken away by Jim.'

74   The Morphology of Case and Voice

> c. Ka   mau   tonu he pakanga a Tangaroa ki
>   uns continue still a war   of Tangaroa to
>   'Tangaroa's war against Tane continues
>
>   a   Tane.
>   prop Tane
>   everlastingly.' (Grey 3)

<u>He</u> does not qualify nouns that are subjects of middle clauses, subjects of canonical transitive clauses, direct objects, or oblique NPs:

> (48)a. *Ka patu he tangata i   te wheke.
>   uns kill a man   Acc the octopus
>   (A man killed the octopus.)
>
>   b. *I   kite te tamaiti i   he ngārara.
>   past see the child   Acc a monster
>   (The child saw a monster.)
>
>   c. *Ka tua-ina   te rākau ki   he toki.
>   uns fell-Pass the tree with a axe
>   (The tree was felled with some axe or other.)

Now in a passive clause, <u>he</u> cannot qualify the underlying subject, as might be more or less expected:

> (49)   *I   patu-a   e   he tangata a   Hōne.
>   past hit-Pass Agt a man   prop John
>   (Some man hit John.)

But it can qualify the underlying direct object:

> (50)a. Ka hopu-kia   e   ia he poaka.
>   uns catch-Pass Agt him a pig
>   'He caught a pig.' (Orbell 8)
>
>   b. Ka panga-ina atu e   Paowa he pōwhatu ki
>   uns throw-Pass away Agt Paowa a stone   to
>   'Paowa threw a stone on the
>
>   taua ahi.
>   that fire
>   fire.' (Orbell 74)
>
>   c. Kua hiahia rātou kia hau-a   he waka mō
>   prf want   they sbj hew-Pass a canoe for
>   'They wanted a canoe to be hewn

>   rātou.
>   them
>   for them.' (Biggs, Hohepa, and Mead 83)

Its ability to do so argues that the underlying direct object of the passive is the subject of an intransitive clause. Thus the passive differs from its active counterpart both in grammatical relations and in transitivity. As before, it differs in a way that we would expect if it is derived from the active by a Passive rule.

2.2.1.4. <u>Passive</u>. To summarize the arguments of the preceding two paragraphs, the underlying direct object of the passive acts as a subject while its underlying subject acts like an oblique NP; in this respect, it contrasts with the active, whose underlying subject and direct object act as subject and direct object, respectively. Given what we know about linguistic typology (see Perlmutter and Postal 1977, for instance), a straightforward conclusion to be drawn from this is that the passive is related to the active by a Passive rule that alters grammatical relations in the expected way; i.e. it promotes the direct object to subject and removes the original subject to an oblique grammatical relation. Certainly the burden of proof falls on those who would want to account for the shift in grammatical relations by some other means.

Contrary to Sinclair (1976) and Clark (1973b), therefore, the Maori passive <u>is</u> related to the active by a Passive rule. See Chung and Timberlake (1974) and Chung (1977b) for further discussion.

2.2.1.5. <u>On Passive and the Perfective</u>. Having argued for the existence of Passive, we can raise the question of wheth-

76   The Morphology of Case and Voice

er it might be favored or required in perfective clauses, and in this sense a marker of perfective aspect (Clark 1973b). In other words, does Maori grammar include a condition like:

(51)   Apply Passive to clauses with a perfective interpretation.

(Observe that, for reasons given in 2.2.1.1, such a condition could not take effect until after rules such as Equi, Relativization, and Clefting had applied.) A condition like (51) would be plausible given the existence of other languages of the world in which passive and perfective are correlated (e.g. Western Austronesian languages; see Gonda 1952); however, it is not fully supported in Maori. This paragraph first examines the facts bearing on (51) and then advances a different condition to account for the frequency of Passive.

On the one hand, Passive applies overwhelmingly to canonical transitive clauses which are perfective, i.e. which view the event as a complete or undifferentiated whole (Clark 1973b). This tendency, which is particularly noticeable in narratives, would appear to support a condition like (51):

(52)a.   Ka   tango-hia   te   whaea   e   te   patupaiarehe.
          uns seize-Pass the mother Agt the fairy
          'The fairy seized the woman.' (Orbell 8)

    b.   Ka   purupuru-a e   Te Heiraura ngā   puta o
         uns plug-Pass   Agt Te Heiraura the=pl hole of
         'Te Heiraura plugged up the holes of their

         tō rāua   whare.
         their=du house
         house.' (Biggs, Hohepa, and Mead 45)

Clauses like (52) which have not undergone Passive are correspondingly rare in texts (but see Orbell 1968: 14, 24).

On the other hand, Passive also applies to clauses which have an imperfective interpretation, i.e. which view the

77   The Morphology of Case and Voice

event as internally differentiated. Consider the narrative
examples:

    (53)a.   Ka   whati-ia   tonu-tia   mai.
              uns break-Pass still-Pass here
              '(He) kept on breaking (it).' (Biggs, Hohepa,
              and Mead 31)

        b.   Kei ngā   pō   mārama,...e   kite-a   atu
              at the=pl night clear   uns see-Pass away
              'On clear nights,...Rona can be seen with

              ana   a   Rona me   tana tahā.
              prog prop Rona with her   calabash
              her calabash.' (Biggs, Hohepa, and Mead 20)

        c.   E   mōhio-tia ana e   ngā   pūkōrero o
              uns know-Pass prog Agt the=pl orator   of
              'The orators of today know that this was

              naianei, ko   te pā   tēnei...
              today   Pred the fort this
              the fortress...' (Biggs, Hohepa, and Mead 88)

(53a) describes a repetitive event; (53b), a habitual event;
and (53c), a present state. (See Comrie (1976) and Chung and
Timberlake (1978) on the identification of such events as
imperfective.) While Passive is not as overwhelming in imperfective clauses as in clauses like (52), it applies as
often as not. Compare the active:

    (54)a.   Hanga ana tētahi i   tōna whare, hanga ana
              build prog one   Acc his house build prog
              'Each of these two men was building himself

              tētahi i   tōna whare.
              one   Acc his house
              a house.' (Orbell 34)

        b.   Whakapē noa i   te whare; a, kāore hoki
              crush   vain Acc the house and not   also
              '(It) tried to push over the house, but in

              i   hinga.
              past fall
              vain; (the house) would not fall.' (Orbell 104)

Further, Passive need not apply to perfective clauses containing a middle verb, i.e. a verb whose direct object is not immediately or physically affected by the action. While the rule sometimes affects middle clauses:

(55) a. Ka kite-a   atu e rāua   e   rere haere
         uns see-Pass away Agt them=du uns fly go
         'They saw the bird flying toward them

         mai ana taua manu.
         here prog that bird
         (lit. They saw that the bird was flying...).'
         (Orbell 86)

     b. Ka rango-na   e   ia te haruru o ngā   mano
         uns hear-Pass Agt him the sound of the=pl men
         'He heard the sound of all the

         rā.
         that
         men.' (Orbell 40)

More frequently it does not:

(56) a. Ka kite rāua   i waho   i te oneone e
         uns see they=du at outside on the sand uns
         'They saw footprints on the ground (lit. They

         takoto ana ngā   tapuwae.
         lie   prog the=pl footprint
         saw on the sand that there were footprints).'
         (Orbell 80)

     b. Ka rapu a   Tu i   tetahi whakaaro ma-na.
         uns seek prop Tu Acc one   thought for-him
         'Tu sought some advice for himself.' (Grey 4)

Finally, the rule appears not to apply at all in narrative to clauses containing a reflexive (Clark 1973b) or a cognate direct object. Consider the reflexive sentences of (57) and the cognate-object sentences of (58), which could well be interpreted as perfective:

(57) a. Ka whakakino a   Paowa i   a   ia.
         uns make=ugly prop Paowa Acc pro him
         'Paowa made himself ugly.' (Orbell 76)

b. Ka tārona   i   a   ia.
    uns strangle Acc pro her
    '(She) strangled herself.' (Orbell 4)

(58)a. Ka tangi taua wahine i   ōna   tangi mō
        uns cry that woman Acc pl=her cry   for
        'The woman cried her cries for her

        āna   tamariki.
        pl=her children
        children.' (Biggs, Hohepa, and Mead 91)

b. Ka karanga atu anō i   taua karanga āna.
    uns call   away Emp Acc that call   of=her
    'Again she repeated her question.' (Orbell 24)

In short, Passive applies almost always in narrative to perfective, canonical transitive clauses; sometimes to imperfective or middle clauses; and never to clauses containing a reflexive or cognate direct object. Although perfective aspect figures in this distribution, it accounts for only a portion of the facts.

While (51) could perhaps be viewed as one of several disjunctive conditions on Passive, we would prefer to replace it with a unified description of the facts. We can begin to construct one by observing that the direct objects of the clause types listed above differ in the degree to which they are affected by the event. (a) Reflexive and cognate direct objects are not affected at all, given that they are not referentially independent. Cognate objects do not refer; the reference of reflexives is determined by their antecedents. (b) Direct objects of middle verbs, by definition, are not immediately or physically affected, though they may be affected indirectly. (c) Similarly, direct objects of imperfective clauses are affected only in part, in that the event being described is not viewed as complete (see Comrie 1976; Chung and Timberlake 1978). (d) Only direct objects of perfective, canonical transitive clauses qualify as completely affected, both by virtue of the inherent meaning of the verb and the aspectual value assigned to the clause.

The frequency of Passive in these different clause types correlates roughly, but revealingly, with this classification: the more the direct object is affected by the event, the more likely Passive is to apply. This suggests that Maori grammar may include a condition like:

(59)   Apply Passive to clauses containing an affected direct object.

Condition (59) will describe the virtually obligatory character of Passive in perfective, canonical transitive clauses, as well as its failure to apply in clauses with reflexive or cognate direct objects. Liberally interpreted, it may also account for the intermediate frequency of the rule in imperfective clauses and its relatively low frequency in middle clauses.

It may be, however, that a liberal interpretation of (59) is not required. Observe that in the imperfective (53-54), Passive has applied if the clause describes a repetitive or habitual event, but not if it describes a progressive or unsuccessful one. Clauses of these types differ precisely in whether their direct objects can be said to have been affected <u>at</u> <u>least</u> <u>once</u>. In repetitive/habitual clauses, an incomplete series of events is described; while the direct object has not been affected by the entire series, it may well have been affected by some member of it. In progressive/unsuccessful clauses, though, typically only a single event is described, and the direct object has not been completely affected by it. Therefore, in its application to imperfective clauses, Passive may be obeying (59) in a strict sense.

Assuming that these observations generalize to all imperfective clauses in narrative and can perhaps be extended to middle clauses, (59) will provide a general account of the high frequency of Passive. The question can then be raised of what motivates this condition. Although there appears to be no evidence bearing specifically on this issue, I would like to suggest that (59) results from a further condition in Maori, of the form:

(60)   Other things being equal, affected NPs (or themes in the sense of Gruber 1970) appear as surface subjects.

The guess that (60) is part of Maori grammar will be useful in Chapter 6.

2.2.2.   The Samoan Transitive Suffix

In 2.1.4, Samoan -Cia was described as a 'transitive' suffix optionally attached to canonical transitive verbs:

(61)   Sā   su'e-ina   a'u e   le fānau   a
       past search-Trans me   Erg the children of
       'Fo'isia's children were looking

       Fo'isia.
       Fo'isia
       for me.'

(62)   Sā   su'e   a'u e   le fānau   a Fo'isia.
       past search me   Erg the children of Fo'isia
       'Fo'isia's children were looking for me.'

As the description suggests, -Cia can in principle appear on any canonical transitive verb --a characteristic which has made its function both a mystery and a point of controversy in the literature on Samoan. Pratt (1960[1911]: 25), for instance, identifies -Cia as a passive suffix, noting at the same time that "passive verbs with an active meaning...are of very frequent use". S. Churchward (1951: 72) suggests that -Cia might serve in part as an anaphor for direct objects, while Milner (1962, 1973) has proposed that it is a marker of perfective aspect.

Here, on the contrary, it is argued that -<u>Cia</u> indicates that a canonical transitive subject has been extracted. The distribution of this suffix therefore depends in large part on what <u>other</u> rules have applied. 2.2.2.1 argues that -<u>Cia</u> does not change grammatical relations; 2.2.2.2 discusses its basic distribution. Finally, 2.2.2.3 describes some remaining cases and argues that, in these, -<u>Cia</u> serves more as a marker of mood than of aspect.

2.2.2.1. <u>Arguments Against a Relation-Changing Rule</u>. Milner (1962) and Cook (1978) give several arguments that -<u>Cia</u> is not a passive suffix, which are briefly repeated here. These show that the underlying subject of a transitive clause acts as a subject even when -<u>Cia</u> is attached to the verb.

Thus, the underlying subject is eligible for Clitic Placement, which affects only subjects (see 1.4.2.2). Compare (63), in which -<u>Cia</u> occurs, with (64), in which it does not:

    (63)   Sā   'ou faitau-ina le tusi.
               past I   read-Trans the book
               'I read the book.'

    (64)   Sā   'ou faitau le tusi.
               past I   read   the book
               'I read the book.'

The underlying subject can also undergo Equi, which deletes only subjects (see 3.2.3):

    (65)   Na   mātou mānana'o e   fa'agalo-ina le mea
               past we   want=pl uns forget-Trans the thing
               'We wanted to forget what

               'ua tupu.
               prf happen
               had happened.'

    (66)   Na   mātou mānana'o e   fa'agalo le mea
               past we   want=pl uns forget   the thing
               'We wanted to forget what

'ua tupu.
prf happen
had happened.'

And Raising, which raises only subjects (see 3.3.3):

(67) Sā fa'apea e ia 'ona fai-a le fale.
      past thus Erg he Comp do-Trans the house
      'He built the house like this.'

(68) E fa'apea e Ioane 'ona fai le fale.
      uns thus Erg John Comp do the house
      'John will build the house like this.'

In addition, it can be shown that the underlying direct object acts as a direct object rather than an oblique NP, even if -Cia appears on the verb. Thus, the underlying direct object can undergo Quantifier Float regardless of animacy or linear position, a property which is restricted to subjects and direct objects (see 3.4.4.4):

(69) Sā 'ou 'ai-a 'uma-ina fa'i.
      past I Eat-Trans all-Trans banana
      'I ate up all the bananas.'

(70) O le a latou ai uma le nono a lo'u atalii.
      fut   they eat all the nonu of my son
      'They will eat all of my son's nonu fruit.'
      (Stuebel 165)

(The -Cia appearing on the quantifier in (69) is the result of an optional Agreement rule.)

Arguments like these establish that -Cia does not alter grammatical relations, and both (61) and (62) are superficially transitive clauses. To this extent the label 'transitive suffix' seems justified.

2.2.2.2. Missing Subjects. Although -Cia can in principle appear on any canonical transitive verb, its distribution in conversation and narratives is rather different. This paragraph argues that -Cia serves primarily as a flag for transitive subjects that have been removed by certain superficial rules.

To begin with, -Cia occurs infrequently in practice in clauses to which no syntactic rules have applied (but see 2.2.2.3). Consider:

(71) a. 'Ana lē sola 'oia, semanū   e   maua 'oia
         if not run he   probably uns catch him
         'If he hadn't run away, probably the police

         e   leoleo.
         Erg police
         would have caught him.'

    b.   Ona sasa ai lea o   Saleimoa e   Moso i
         then hit Pro that Pred Saleimoa Erg Moso with
         'Then Moso hit the Saleimoa people with

         le too.
         the pole
         the pole.' (Stuebel 229)

It is also infrequent in clauses whose subject or direct object has been removed by zero-pronominalization:

(72) a. Sā   fai mai Fo'isia 'ole'ā 'ave se   tupe   e
         past say here Fo'isia fut   take a   money   uns
         'Fo'isia said that (I) should take some money

         fa'atau ai   se 'ogāumu uila.
         buy   Pro a oven   electric
         with which (I) should buy an electric oven.'

    b.   Ona pue   ai lea e   le auao ma ave i
         then catch Pro that Erg the auao and take to
         'The auao seized (him) and took (him) to

         Pulotu.
         Pulotu
         Pulotu.' (Stuebel 228)

Further, -Cia occurs rarely in embedded clauses whose subject or direct object has been removed by major rules such as Raising or Equi. In (73), the embedded subject has been deleted by Equi:

(73)a. Fiafia tele Fo'isia e   'ai le ota.
        happy very Fo'isia uns eat the raw=fish
        'Fo'isia likes very much to eat raw fish.'

   b.   La   te   o   ifo e   aami le puga.
        they=du uns go=pl down uns fetch the coral
        'They should both go down to get the rock.'
        (Stuebel 161)

In (74), it has undergone Raising:

(74)   E   mafai e   Ioane 'ona kuka le mea'ai.
       uns can   Erg John Comp cook the food
       'John can cook the food.'

And in (75), the direct object has undergone a different raising rule that affects any NP (see 3.5.2):

(75)   Sa   faapea le fasiga   o i latou ona fai.
       past thus   the beating of pl them Comp do
       'The mistreatment of them took place in the following way.' (Stuebel 163)

Where -Cia appears is rather in clauses whose subjects have been moved or deleted by superficial rules, or whose subjects are not overt because they are generic. For instance, the suffix is strongly preferred in clauses whose (canonical transitive) subjects have undergone Clitic Placement:

(76)a. Sā   'ou su'e-ina   le lā'au-pese.
        past I   search-Trans   the machine-song
        'I was looking for the taperecorder.'

   b.   E   alu i-a   Leosia na te faasino ina
        uns go to-prop   Leosia he uns show-Trans
        '(She) should go to Leosia so that he could

        ane   lana tane.
        along   her man
        show (her) her husband.' (Stuebel 233)

It is also strongly preferred in clauses whose subjects have been extracted by Relativization:

86   The Morphology of Case and Voice

(77) a. 'O   fea   le tamāloa na   maitau-ina
         Pred where? the man   [past count-Trans
         'Where is the man who counted the

         tupe?
         money]
         money?'

    b.   O   ni   isi   nuu   e   vaafaatau uma
         Pred some=pl other village uns messenger all
         'In other villages all the chiefs who made

         alii   e   fai-a   le taua.
         chief [uns do-Trans   the war]
         war were messengers (to the spirits).' (Stuebel
         173)

Or Clefting:

(78) a. 'O   le 'afā   sā   fa'aleaga-ina fale.
         Pred the storm past destroy-Trans house
         'It was the storm that destroyed the houses.'

    b.   O   Leaga ua faaigoa-ina ana   fanau   o
         Pred Leaga prf name-Trans pl=his   children Pred
         'Leaga named his children

         Leaga.
         Leaga
         Leaga.' (Stuebel 174)

Finally, it usually appears when a canonical transitive subject is the generic agent and thus not overt:

(79) a. Sā   'ou asiasi 'i-āte 'i lātou 'a'o fa'amanatu-
         past I   visit to-pro pl them when celebrate-
         'I visited them while Independence Day

         ina   le aso tū   to'atasi.
         Trans the day stand alone
         was being celebrated.'

    b.   E   ta'u-a   i latou o   le auao.
         uns tell-Trans pl them Pred the auao
         'They were called auao.' (Stuebel 227)

The relatively high frequency of -Cia in clauses of these types is borne out by statistics from nineteenth century texts. In some twenty pages of Stuebel (1896), for instance, -Cia is found in 36 out of 58 canonical transitive clauses whose subjects have undergone Clitic Placement; all 5 clauses whose subjects have been extracted by Relativization or Clefting; and all 45 clauses having the generic agent as subject. But it occurs in only 65 out of 448 canonical transitive clauses falling into the other categories described above. (A further breakdown of this last group of clauses is given in 2.2.2.3.)

Crucially, nonsubjects which have been extracted by superficial rules do not condition the suffix in the same way. For instance, if the direct object rather than the subject has been removed by Relativization or Clefting, -Cia tends not to be attached to the verb in contemporary Samoan:

(80) a. Na   mātou 'ai-a-ina   le pua'a na
       past we   eat-Trans-Trans   the pig   [past
       'We ate the pig that

       fasi e   le tama.
       kill Erg the boy]
       the boy killed.' (Relativization)

    b. 'O   a'u sā   su'e   e   le fānau   a
       Pred I   past search Erg the children of
       'It is me that Fo'isia's children were

       Fo'isia.
       Fo'isia
       looking for.' (Clefting)

Similarly, if an oblique NP has been extracted, -Cia occurs only rarely:

(81)   'O   le ā   le mea   na   tā ai   e   le
        Pred the what?   the thing [past hit Pro Erg the
        'What was the thing that the boy hit

        tama le maile?
        boy   the dog]
        the dog with?' (Relativization)

Taken together, these facts argue that -_Cia_ sometimes serves as a flag for missing canonical transitive subjects, either ones that have been moved or extracted by superficial rules or ones that for morphological reasons cannot be overt (i.e. generic agents). Observe that the suffix is not an anaphor for transitive subjects; rather, it serves to signal that the subject has been removed by a <u>particular type</u> of rule. Its distribution therefore is determined largely by what other rules have applied. Oddly, the relevant rules include not only Clitic Placement and extractions, which count as superficial for the purposes of the rule typology of Chapter 3, but also the lexical rule which assigns no morphology to generic agents. Why this last rule should pattern with the others is difficult to motivate synchronically (but see 6.3.3 for a possible historical explanation).

Assuming that a single rule of -_Cia_ Insertion is responsible for the suffix in (76-79), this rule will have the form:

(82)   Attach -_Cia_ to a canonical transitive verb if the subject of the clause (a) is the generic agent, or (b) has been moved or extracted by a superficial rule.

Observe that part (b) of the rule is global.

The generalization that -_Cia_ signals a missing transitive subject is based on relative frequency, and so must be qualified in two ways. First, since the suffix is in principle optional, it occasionally does not occur in sentences of the types (76-79). See Cook (1978) for discussion of the discourse conditions under which -_Cia_ is omitted in these sentence types. Second, since -_Cia_ can in principle appear on any canonical transitive verb, there is a portion of its distribution which (82) does not account for. Some of these remaining cases are discussed immediately below.

2.2.2.3. On the Transitive Suffix and the Perfective.

As suggested above, -Cia occasionally appears in clauses from which nothing has been extracted. Consider:

(83) a. Sā   su'e-ina   a'u e   le fānau   a
         past search-Trans me Erg the children of
         'Fo'isia's children were looking

         Fo'isia.
         Fo'isia
         for me.'

   b. ...seia tuu-ina   mai lava e   i latou
           until place-Trans here Emp   Erg pl they
       '...until they had given (him)

         o   se mea.
         Pred a thing
         something.' (Stuebel 172)

Although sentences of this type are relatively infrequent, they are nonetheless grammatical, and so some account must be given of them.

One possible account, originally proposed by Milner (1962, 1973), holds that -Cia might mark perfective aspect in clauses of this type. Under such a hypothesis, Samoan grammar would include not only (82) but also a separate rule like:

(84)   Attach -Cia to a canonical transitive verb if
        the clause is perfective.

Such a hypothesis would seem supported by speakers' comments that -Cia can make the event 'fuller' or locate it in the more distant past --effects similar to those of perfective aspect, which treats events as single, undifferentiated wholes. Nonetheless, it is not borne out by the full range of facts.

To begin with, speakers' reactions to -Cia in clauses like (83) are not limited to those above. In addition, speakers observe that -Cia can make the event progressive or stress

90   The Morphology of Case and Voice

that several participants are involved, as pointed out by Kenneth Cook. Effects like these are typically associated with the imperfective, which treats events as internally differentiated. This raises the possibility that the suffix may not be consistently associated with one aspect over the other.

Further, there are imperfective and perfective contexts in which -Cia seems to occur indifferently. Consider sentences of the form 'X was V-ing when Y V-ed', which have been much discussed in the literature on aspect. In these, the first clause describes a progressive event and the second, a single event framed by it; the former is identified as imperfective and the latter, as perfective. -Cia can occur within either:

(85) a. 'Ina 'ua tāpuni-(ina) e   Ioane le tusi,
         Comp prf close-Trans Erg John the book
         'When John closed the book, they

         'olo'o vala'au 'i lātou.
         prog   shout   pl they
         were shouting.'

    b.   Sā   mātou fo'i   mai, 'olo'o kuka-(ina) e
         past we   return here prog   cook-Trans Erg
         'When we returned, the children were

         tamaiti le keke.
         children the cake
         baking a cake.'

If anything, there is a slight preference for -Cia in the imperfective clause --a preference which appears to contradict (84) directly.

Finally, -Cia is preferred or required in various types of negative sentences, which describe incomplete events and thus are often imperfective. The suffix tends to occur in negative sentences describing single incomplete events:

(86) a. Sā   le'i meli-a   e   le falemeli le
         past not mail-Trans Erg the postoffice the
         'The postoffice didn't deliver the

```
                    tusi.
                    letter
                    letter.'

        b.   Ua vavalu tasi talo, a   e   le  valu-a
             prf scrape one  taro and uns not scrape-Trans
             'Then (she) scraped one taro, but left another

                    tasi talo.
                    one  taro
                    taro unscraped.' (Sierich 1902: 175)
```

It is required in negative imperatives, which specifically direct the hearer that an event should remain incomplete:

```
(87)    'Aua lē  lafo-*(ina) 'i ai  se tusi.
        impv not send-Trans  to Pro a  letter
        'Don't send them a letter!'
```

Compare the affirmative:

```
(88)    Lafo-(*ina) 'i ai  se tusi.
        send-Trans  to Pro a  letter
        'Send them a letter!'
```

And it is required in negative generic statements, which describe events that never become complete:

```
(89)    E  lē  loka-*(ina) e   leoleo tagata gaoi.
        uns not lock-Trans Erg police person steal
        'Policemen do not arrest burglars.'
```

Compare:

```
(90)    E   loka e   leoleo tagata gaoi.
        uns lock Erg police person steal
        'Policemen arrest burglars.'
```

The imperfective nature of these sentence types argues that -Cia does not mark perfective aspect in any systematic sense. Therefore, (84) should be rejected for some other account of the presence of the suffix in sentences like (83).

It may seem a short step from this conclusion to the claim that -Cia marks the imperfective rather than the perfective.

92   The Morphology of Case and Voice

However, its failure to occur with particular frequency in imperfective contexts other than (86), (87), and (89) would make such a claim unappealing. The only systematic distributional facts that I have been able to find suggest instead that -Cia may tend to occur in unrealized clauses: future clauses, purposive clauses, and the antecedent and consequent clauses of conditions:

(91)   Ona alu ai lea o   Tiitii...ina ia
       then go Pro that Pred Tiitii Comp sbj
       'Then Tiitii went...so that (he) could

       utu-fia   o   le la'i   i se pupu.
       fill-Trans Pred the west=wind in a case
       put the west wind in a box.' (Stuebel 166)

Given that negative sentences also describe unrealized events, the possibility arises that -Cia may serve secondarily as a marker of unrealized mood --a hypothesis which is supported to some extent by statistics from texts. For instance, in the twenty pages of Stuebel (1896) mentioned in 2.2.2.2, -Cia occurs in all 10 negative sentences and in 25 out of 158 (i.e. 16%) other instances of unrealized clauses. Compare its appearance in 30 out of 280 (i.e. 11%) realized clauses like (83a).

It can be tentatively suggested, then, that -Cia may be a marker of unrealized mood, and Samoan may include not only (82) but also a rule like:

(92)   Attach -Cia to a canonical transitive verb in
       an unrealized clause.

This second -Cia Insertion rule calls forth two remarks. First, such a rule still does not account for sentences like (83a), with which this discussion began, because such sentences describe realized events. Some consolation for this may perhaps be found in the fact that -Cia is not, after all,

very frequent in sentences of this type. Second, it should
be stressed that (92) is not on a par with (82) in contemporary Samoan, but instead determines the distribution of -Cia
in only a small proportion of cases. This strengthens the
conclusion that -Cia serves primarily to indicate a missing
transitive subject.

2.2.3. Summary

This section has examined the functions of Maori -Cia and Samoan -Cia, two verb suffixes which have aroused much controversy in the literature. It was argued that Maori -Cia indicates Passive; the high frequency of Passive reflects a
condition that, other things being equal, affected NPs (or
themes) will appear as surface subjects. In contrast, Samoan
-Cia serves primarily to indicate that a canonical transitive
subject has been removed by certain superficial rules. Some
limited distributional evidence suggests that the suffix may
serve secondarily as a marker of unrealized mood.

NOTES

1. A few verbs in individual languages, e.g. Samoan iloa
   'know' and (for some speakers) lagona 'feel, perceive',
   are lexically marked as canonical transitives.
2. Pratt (1960[1911]: 9), who otherwise records glottal
   stop, observes that "no break [=glottal stop/SC] is now
   observed in the pronunciation" of 'i. I agree, and have
   previously treated i 'at' and 'i 'to' as disambiguated
   only by their pronominal copies. However, several linguists have informed me that they consistently perceive
   the initial glottal stop of 'i. This is the reason for
   its appearance in the text.
3. In the texts, no clauses are found in which the verb is

suffixed with -*cia*, the subject is unmarked, and the direct object is marked with the accusative *i*. It is difficult to tell whether this gap is accidental or reflects some genuine restriction.

4. It is sometimes suggested that influence from Cook Islands Maori or some other East Polynesian language might have had a hand in shaping Pukapukan's mixed case system. However, arguments for such a suggestion are not compelling, and there are facets of the case system that would be difficult to motivate in terms of it (see Chapter 7). The issue of influence is examined at greater length in Chung (1976a).

3. Case Marking & Grammatical Relations

The diversity of case marking in Polynesian leads to two questions, which form the topic of this chapter. First, does case marking reveal anything about syntactic structure? And second, what are the categories around which the syntax of these languages is organized? Both questions raise the larger issue of the degree to which morphology and syntax are interrelated. They have received two types of answers in the general linguistic literature, which can be referred to as the <u>integrated</u> position and the <u>independent</u> position.

According to the integrated position, the categories picked out by the case marking of a language are the same categories that its syntactic rules refer to. Such a position claims that the syntax of every language should parallel its morphology in an important sense. It predicts that the Polynesian languages should exhibit great diversity in their syntax, parallel to the diversity of case systems described in Chapter 2.

According to the independent position, formulated by Anderson (1976) and Perlmutter and Postal (1974), among others, the categories picked out by the case marking of a language need not be the same as those that its syntactic rules refer to. Therefore, a language's syntax and its morphology are not necessarily organized along the same lines. This position allows for the possibility that those categories central to syntactic organization may be relatively constant across languages --and, in particular, that grammatical relations such as <u>subject</u> and <u>direct object</u> may be universal elements of clause structure. On this view, the Polynesian languages should manifest a deeper syntactic similarity, in that many of their processes refer to the categories subject or direct object.

This chapter presents facts from Polynesian arguing against the integrated position and in favor of the independent position. It is argued that Polynesian languages have a class of syntactic rules, including e.g. Raising, which can be identified as major or 'central' in terms of current rule typologies; these refer to subject or direct object if they mention any subtypes of NPs. Given that these categories are not picked out by ergative case marking, the fact that rules refer to them even in the ergative languages refutes the integrated position. Further, their presence throughout Polynesian suggests that they might well be universal. The evidence is therefore consistent with a theory of grammar, such as relational grammar (Perlmutter and Postal 1974, 1977), which takes grammatical relations as basic terms of syntactic description.

3.1 presents the integrated and the independent positions in greater detail and lays out the strategy for this chapter. 3.2 through 3.5 describe the major rules of three Polynesian languages: Maori, Tongan, and Samoan. It is shown that Equi and Raising in these languages refer to subject if they mention any subtypes of NPs; a number of other rules refer to direct object. 3.6 surveys the Polynesian scene more generally and draws conclusions.

3.1. TWO POSITIONS ON CASE MARKING AND SYNTAX
This section states the two positions on case marking and syntax and constructs a strategy for arguing against one and for the other. 3.1.1 describes the integrated position and the

independent position; 3.1.2 points out that both can be separated from the issue of how syntactic categories are formally defined. 3.1.3 observes that a strong case can be made for subject and direct object if they can be shown to figure in the major or 'central' rules of Polynesian syntax. The question is then raised of how major rules can be independently identified, and a rough rule typology is developed.

3.1.1. The Integrated Position and the Independent Position

The two positions discussed here differ in their claims about whether morphology and syntax are organized in parallel fashion.

The integrated position claims that the categories organizing the syntax of a language will be the same as those picked out by its case morphology. Assuming that the case marking of subjects and direct objects is assigned by rule(s), it can be stated as follows:

> (1) The Integrated Position:
> In any given language, the NP categories picked out by the case marking rule(s) are exactly those to which other syntactic rules can refer.

In particular, (1) claims that languages with an accusative type of case marking should also have an 'accusative' syntax: their syntactic rules should pick out subjects or direct objects if they refer to any categories of NPs. But languages with an ergative type of case marking should have an 'ergative' syntax: their rules should refer to absolutives (i.e. intransitive subjects and transitive direct objects) or ergatives (i.e. transitive subjects) if they mention any categories of NPs. The claim extends in the obvious way to languages with a mixed accusative-ergative case marking or with a special case pattern for middle clauses. Observe that it is not claimed that all rules of a language refer to case marking. Rather, all rules, including the case marking rules, refer to some more abstract NP categories which are claimed to be reflected precisely by the case morphology.

(1) appears implicitly in a good deal of traditional literature on case marking and syntax, although it is rarely, if ever, stated in explicit form. It seems to lie behind the longstanding confusion of 'subject' and 'NP in the nominative case', which can be found occasionally even in the writings of a linguist as astute as Jespersen (1924). It figures in traditional discussions of ergativity, particularly those concerned with the 'passive' character of languages with ergative case marking (e.g. Schuchardt 1895; Uhlenbeck 1916, as described in Sapir 1917). For Polynesian, such a position is advocated most explicitly by Biggs (1974: 407), who observes for the ergative Polynesian languages:

> It is disturbing (to me) to find such a basic function as subject being marked on the one hand by two different cases, and, on the other hand, homonymously with the object. I can't help wondering whether what is being called the "object of an intransitive verb" [Read probably "object of a transitive verb"/SC] would not be better regarded as the subject (and goal), with the nominal in the ergative case being regarded as an agent (but not as subject), and comparable to agents of passive verbs in English. My doubts spring from my continuing belief that grammars of languages should be based on linguistic analyses which rely heavily on a correlation between grammatical categories and observable features (surface features) of the language concerned.

Biggs goes on to argue that absolutive in ergative Polynesian languages functions like subject in accusative Polynesian languages for the purposes of NP indispensability.

Ignoring for the moment the complications presented by middle clauses and mixed accusative-ergative case systems, we can restate the integrated position specifically for Polynesian languages as:

(2)   The Integrated Position Applied to Polynesian:
In languages with accusative case marking, syntactic rules will refer to __subject__ or __direct object__ if they mention any categories of NPs. In languages with ergative case marking, syntactic rules will refer to __absolutive__ or __ergative__ if they mention any categories of NPs.

In contrast, the position to be argued for here --the independent position-- claims that morphology and syntax need not be organized along the same lines. On this view, the categories picked out by the case morphology of a language may differ from the categories central to syntax, which may be relatively constant across languages.

Supporters of the independent position have advanced the additional, strong claim that grammatical relations --i.e. categories like subject-- are central to the syntax of all languages. Anderson (1976), for instance, argues that the large majority of ergative languages have syntactic rules that refer to subjects. Perlmutter and Postal (1974, 1977) have proposed that relations such as subject, direct object, and indirect object are universals of clause structure, referred to crucially by a wide variety of syntactic rules.

Adopting a version of this claim, we can state the independent position as:

(3)   The Independent Position:
The NP categories picked out by the case marking rule(s) of a language may differ from the categories to which other syntactic rules refer. However, all languages have rules refer-

ring to subject and direct object, which are
central to syntactic organization.

The application of (3) to Polynesian seems clear: all Polynesian languages, regardless of case system, should have syntactic rules referring to subject and/or direct object.

3.1.2. On Defining Categories

Some brief remarks should be made about what is meant by subject and direct object in (3).

The strategy adopted here assumes only an informal and pretheoretical characterization of subject and direct object. As such, it does not rely on any of the more formal definitions of these categories that have appeared in the literature. Some of these, and their application to Polynesian languages, include:

Subject and direct object are implicitly defined in terms of linear order in several generative semantics works (e.g. McCawley 1970). For Polynesian, assuming an underlying VSO word order, this would mean that the subject would be the first NP following the verb and the direct object, the second NP.

Subject and direct object are defined in terms of dominance by Chomsky (1965). For Polynesian, assuming the existence of a verb phrase in underlying structure, this would mean that the subject is the NP immediately dominated by S, and the direct object is the NP immediately dominated by VP.

Finally, subject, direct object, and other grammatical relations are treated as unanalyzable primitives by Perlmutter and Postal (1974, 1977), who assert that they are not defined in terms of structural configurations.

The arguments to be given below neither assume these definitions nor argue for any particular one of them over the

101 Case Marking and Grammatical Relations

others. Rather, they establish the correctness of the independent position for Polynesian languages regardless of whether subject and direct object are defined in terms of dominance or taken as primitives. Separate arguments that these categories should not be defined in terms of linear order are given by Anderson and Chung (1977) and Chung (1976a).

Throughout, subject and direct object are referred to indifferently as syntactic categories or grammatical relations.

3.1.3. A Rule Typology
Finally, a strategy must be constructed for arguing against the integrated position and for the independent position.

It is fairly easy to conceive of types of arguments against the integrated position. For instance, the integrated position will be contradicted if any ergative Polynesian language exhibits rules referring to subjects, regardless of what these rules are. Thus the existence of Tongan Clitic Placement and Samoan Clitic Placement, which are restricted to subjects (see 1.4.2), provides the beginnings of a refutation of (1).

The independent position presents a slightly more complex case. It claims not only that rules can be found in every language referring to subject and direct object, but also that these categories are central to the organization of syntax. Therefore, in order to evaluate it, some notion is required of which rules of Polynesian syntax are 'central' and which are not.

The strategy adopted here is to extend to Polynesian languages the typology of cyclic vs. postcyclic rules which has been developed in the transformational literature (e.g. Lakoff 1965; Postal 1972; Perlmutter 1973; Hankamer 1974; Kayne 1975; and others). This typology recognizes two groups

of rules, cyclic and postcyclic, which are distinguished by
method and order of application. Cyclic rules obey the principle of the strict cycle (Chomsky 1973); postcyclic rules do
not. Further, while cyclic rules may not be ordered among
themselves, and postcyclic rules may not be either, all cyclic rules crucially precede all postcyclic ones. The ordering criterion suggests that cyclic rules are deeper or syntactically more central than postcyclic rules, in the sense
that they apply first.

English rules classified as cyclic within this typology include Passive, Subject-to-Subject Raising, Subject-to-Object
Raising, Equi, Quantifier Float, Dative Movement, and others;
rules classified as postcyclic include Clitic Placement (in
French; see Kayne 1975), Wh-Movement (i.e. the rule involved
in forming relative clauses and questions, among other constructions), Topicalization, Clefting, and others.

Interestingly, there seems to be rough agreement in the
literature that the extension of this typology has something
right about it, although the methods by which the two groupings are reached vary widely. For instance, Chomsky (1975,
1977) proposes a different rule typology which recognizes
only two transformations in the core grammar of English:
'Move NP' and 'Move wh-phrase into Comp'. When constrained,
'Move NP' produces the same output as Passive and Subject-to-Subject Raising, while 'Move wh-phrase' has the same output
as Wh-Movement, Topicalization, Clefting, and other rules.
The division between the two transformations is similar to
that between (some) cyclic and (some) postcyclic rules. Further, Perlmutter and Postal (1974) adopt a typology which
distinguishes very broadly between term-creating rules --i.e.
rules that create subjects, direct objects, or indirect objects-- and all other rules. The term-creating rules include

Passive, Subject-to-Subject Raising, Subject-to-Object Raising, Dative Movement, and so forth; the other rules include Relativization, Topicalization, Clefting, and so forth. Again, the division approximates that between cyclic and postcyclic rules (although some cyclic rules, e.g. Equi, are not term-creating in Perlmutter and Postal's sense).

In each of these alternative typologies, there are reasons for thinking that the rules corresponding to the cyclic grouping are deeper or more central. Essentially, they have outputs which could be generated independently as underlying or initial structures. Thus, Chomsky's 'Move NP' is structure-preserving; Perlmutter and Postal's term-creating rules assign (new) grammatical relations to NPs, where grammatical relations are the only relations besides clause membership borne by NPs in initial structures.

We can therefore be fairly confident in identifying some or all cyclic rules as deeper or syntactically central. According to the independent position, these are the rules that should refer to subject or direct object if they mention any categories of NPs.

A problem that arises in extending the cyclic vs. post-cyclic typology to Polynesian languages is that these languages offer very little evidence about rule ordering. Consequently, it is difficult to classify rules as cyclic or not according to their ordering properties. Several approaches could be taken to this. On the one hand, it could be assumed that the rule types possible in language are restricted tightly enough that, if a rule can be shown to be cyclic in one language, its analogues in other languages will be cyclic as well. See Bach (1971) and Andrews (1973) for proposals similar to this. On the other hand, one could try to classify rules as cyclic or not by means of subsidiary properties.

Such properties are likely to include bounding and lexical exceptions (or government; see Green 1974), which have often been observed to be typical of cyclic rules, but not of postcyclic ones.

The strategy of this chapter combines both of these approaches. It recognizes two main groups of syntactic rules, **major** and **superficial**, which are distinguished by crosslinguistic and language-internal properties. Major rules correspond to rules that can be shown to be cyclic in some other language; they have lexical exceptions or are governed; their domain of application is limited to one or, at most, two clauses (i.e. they are bounded). Superficial rules correspond to postcyclic rules in other languages; they do not have lexical exceptions; and their domain of application need not be restricted to any number of clauses (i.e. they are unbounded).

One result which will emerge from this chapter is that most major rules create or destroy grammatical relations; superficial rules do not. Although this is not a defining feature of the typology, it should be mentioned at the outset.

Finally, in the interests of making the typology more accurate, two further groups of rules are defined: **morphology** rules and **anaphora** rules. As the name suggests, morphology rules serve exclusively to insert morphology. They are recognized as a distinct group because they are classified ambivalently by the major vs. superficial typology, being governed and bounded on the one hand but analogous to postcyclic, global rules on the other (see Andrews 1971 and Timberlake 1979). Anaphora rules consist of zero-pronominalization (see 1.4.1) plus the interpretive rules for ordinary pronominal anaphors. They are recognized as distinct because they are pragmatically controlled (in the sense of Hankamer and Sag

1976), and because clauses to which they have applied often act like clauses that have undergone no rules at all (see 2.2). Both characteristics suggest that they are perhaps the last rules to apply.

The major vs. superficial typology is outlined below, along with the elaborations just mentioned. The rules listed in the classification are discussed either in this chapter or in other chapters (see the index for precise references).

<u>Major</u> <u>Rules</u>
Equi
Raising
Passive (Maori)
Promotion (Maori)
Object Incorporation
Quantifier Float

<u>Superficial</u> <u>Rules</u>
Relativization
Clefting
Topicalization
Question Movement
Subject Preposing
    (Pukapukan)
Clitic Placement

<u>Morphology</u> <u>Rules</u>
Case Marking
-<u>Cia</u> Insertion (Samoan)
Distribution of <u>he</u> (Maori)

<u>Anaphora</u> <u>Rules</u>
Zero-Pronominalization
  (Pronoun Interpretation)

At this point no assumptions are made about relative ordering; see though 4.4.

We are now ready to survey the major rules of Polynesian languages to see if they argue against the integrated position and bear out the predictions of the independent position. 3.2 through 3.5 examine the major rules of three of the representative languages --Maori, Tongan, and Samoan-- and argue that they refer to subject or direct object if they mention any categories of NPs.

3.2. SUBJECT-REFERRING RULES: EQUI

Most if not all Polynesian languages have an Equi rule which deletes an NP of an embedded clause (the target) under coreference with some NP of the next higher clause (the controller). It is argued here that the Equi rules of Maori, Tongan, and Samoan require their targets to be subjects, and so refer to the category subject. As such, they support the independent position. At the same time, the presence of rules of this type in Tongan and Samoan, both ergative languages, argues that the integrated position is not correct.

3.2.1 deals with Maori Equi; 3.2.2, with Tongan Equi; and 3.2.3, with Samoan Equi. A putative Equi rule in Tongan which allows its target to be any NP is discussed later, in 3.5.1.

3.2.1. Maori

Maori has three Equi rules, ki te Equi, hei Equi, and Participle Formation, which are consistent with either the independent position or the integrated position. Because the rules have identical restrictions on the target, only ki te Equi is discussed in any detail. The situation as regards the other rules is outlined briefly at the end of this subsection.

3.2.1.1. Basic Description.
Ki te Equi relates sentences (4) and (5):

(4)   Ka hiahia au ki te haere.
      uns want I Comp go
      'I want to go.'

(5)   Ka hiahia au kia haere au.
      uns want I sbj go   I
      'I want that I should go.'

This rule applies in certain two-clause structures in which one clause contains a verb of volition, effort, motion, sending, or command, and the other clause is embedded directly under it. Embedded clauses of this type are usually introduced by the subjunctive tense-aspect-mood particle kia:

(6) a. Ka whakaaro au kia haere ia.
        uns think   I sbj go   he
        'I decided that he would go.'

    b. Kua hiahia rātou kia hau-a   he waka mō
        prf want they sbj hew-Pass a canoe for
        'They wanted a canoe to be hewn for

        rātou.
        them
        them.' (Biggs, Hohepa, and Mead 83)

If a target in the embedded clause is coreferential with a controller in the higher clause, it is generally deleted by ki te Equi, subject to conditions to be described below. When this happens, kia is replaced by the complementizer ki te (Hale 1968):

(7) a. Ka whakaaro au ki te haere.
        uns think   I Comp go
        'I decided to go.'

    b. Kua hiahia a   Rewi ki te moe.
        prf want prop Rewi Comp sleep
        'Rewi wanted to sleep.'

    c. Ka haere ia ki te toitoi-tuna.
        uns go   he Comp fish-eel
        'He went to fish for eels.' (Waititi 1969: 6)

Like the infinitival morphology of other languages (e.g. English), ki te bears certain resemblances to nominal morphology: ki is homophonous with the preposition 'to' and te is homophonous with the specific singular article. Nonetheless, it can be shown that embedded clauses introduced by ki te are reduced clauses and not derived nouns or nominalizations.

To begin with, these clauses do not allow their verbs to

be replaced by nominalizations formed with the nominalizing suffix -Canga (see 6.5.1):

(8) a. ?*I   hiahia au ki te patu-nga i   te poaka.
       past want I Comp kill-Nmlz Acc the pig
       (I wanted to kill the pig.)

    b. I   hiahia au ki te patu i   te poaka.
       past want I Comp kill Acc the pig
       'I wanted to kill the pig.'

Derived nouns regularly allow this sort of replacement, however:

(9) a. no te kaha-kore-tanga
       for the able-not-Nmlz
       'for the inability' (Grey 4)

    b. mō   tana kaha
       for his able
       'for his ability' (Biggs, Hohepa, and Mead 86)

Further, clauses introduced by ki te do not allow their transitive direct objects to occur in the possessive:

(10) a. *I   hiahia au ki te patu o te   poaka.
        past want I Comp kill of the pig
        (I wanted to kill the pig.)

     b. *Ka   haere ia ki te toitoi o ngā   tuna.
        uns go   he Comp fish   of the=pl eel
        (He went to fish for the eels.)

But derived nouns and nominalizations regularly allow this:

(11) a. He tata rawa te   whakaeke o te   poti o Paerau
        a near Emp the converge of the boat of Paerau
        'Close was (its) converging on the boat of
        mā.
        associates
        Paerau and his men.' (Waititi 1969: 134)

     b. te patu-nga o te ngārara-hua-rau
        the kill-Nmlz of the Ngarara-hua-rau
        'the killing of Ngarara-hua-rau' (Biggs, Hohepa,
        and Mead 36)

109   Case Marking and Grammatical Relations

The contrast between (8) and (10), on the one hand, and (9) and (11), on the other, argues that embedded clauses introduced by ki te are verbal in character.

Ki te Equi can be distinguished from other deletion rules by its insertion of the ki te complementizer. If the rule has applied, the complementizer must be inserted; consider the following examples, due to Tamati Reedy:

 (12)a. E āhei ia ki te haere.
    nonpast able he Comp go
    'He is able to go.'

  b. *E āhei ia kia haere.
    nonpast able he sbj go
    (He is able to go.)

And if the rule has not applied, the complementizer cannot be inserted, as shown by:

 (13)a. Ka whakaaro au ki te haere.
    uns think I Comp go
    'I decided to go.'

  b. *Ka whakaaro au ki te haere au/ia.
    uns think I Comp go I/he
    (I decided for me/him to go.)

These properties distinguish ki te Equi from other deletions, in particular zero-pronominalization, which deletes an NP coreferential with some NP in previous discourse and does not result in any special morphology. A rough statement of the rule is then: 'Delete the target in an embedded clause under coreference with a controller in the next higher clause, and insert ki te, subject to further conditions (described below)'.

3.2.1.2. *Ki te Equi as a Major Rule*. The fact that ki te Equi is a major rule is established by the following.

To begin with, the rule is the counterpart of Equi in

English, which is widely recognized to be cyclic (see Perlmutter and Soames, forthcoming).

Further, it is restricted to two-clause structures and therefore bounded. <u>Ki te</u> Equi will not operate into an embedded clause across an intervening negative verb, for instance. Consider:

(14) a. Kei te hiahia a   Hōne ki te poro i   te
         at the want prop John Comp chop Acc the
         'John wants to chop down the

         rākau.
         tree
         tree.'

   b. *Kei te hiahia a   Hōne ki te kaua e
       at the want prop John Comp don't nonpast
       (John wants not to chop down

       poro i   te rākau.
       chop Acc the tree
       the tree.)

In (14b), both the negative <u>kaua</u> 'don't' and the embedded verb <u>poro</u> 'cut down' are preceded by their own tense-aspect-mood particles, a fact which establishes that they are in separate clauses. Compare (15), in which Equi has not applied:

(15)   Kei te hiahia a   Hōne kia kaua e
        at the want prop John sbj don't nonpast
        'John wants that the tree should not

        poro-a   te rākau.
        chop-Pass the tree
        be chopped down (by him/them).'

Finally, <u>ki te</u> Equi is governed and exhibits a number of lexical exceptions, first pointed out by Tamati Reedy. The rule is optional for <u>hiahia</u> 'want' (cf. (4-5)), but obligatory for most other governing verbs if its structural description is met:

(16) a. Ka   whakaaro au ki te haere.
         uns think   I Comp go
         'I decided to go.'

     b. *Ka   whakaaro au kia haere au.
         uns think   I sbj go   I
         (I decided that I should go.)

The rule must apply, and its structural description must be met, for āhei 'be able':

(17) a. E   āhei ia ki te haere.
         nonpast   able he Comp go
         'He is able to go.'

     b. *E   āhei ia kia haere ia/a   Hōne.
         nonpast   able he sbj go   he/prop John
         (He is able that he/John should go.)

It can be concluded from this that ki te Equi is indeed a major rule.

3.2.1.3. <u>Restriction to Subjects</u>. Having established this, we can now raise the question of whether ki te Equi refers to any categories of NPs. The answer is that it is restricted to targets that are both subjects and semantic agents/experiencers.

Thus, the rule deletes intransitive subjects (see (7)):

(18) a. Kāore a   Pare i   pai   ki te puta mai.
         not   prop Pare past agree Comp come here
         'Pare did not agree to go outside.' (Orbell 4)

     b. E   kore rā te wairua e   haere mai
         nonpast not that the spirit nonpast go   here
         'Spirits don't come back

         ki te whawhai.
         Comp fight
         to fight.' (Orbell 34)

As well as transitive subjects, whether subjects of canonical transitives or middles:

112 Case Marking and Grammatical Relations

    (19)a.   E   hiahia ana a   Hōne ki te patu i   ngā
           uns want   prog prop John Comp kill Acc the=pl
           'John wants to kill the

           manu.
           bird
           birds.'

       b.   Ka whakareri te   tira   ki te whakahoki i
          uns prepare   the company Comp   return   Acc
          'The people prepared to return him

          a ia ki tōna kāinga tupu.
          pro him to his home   ancestral
          to his ancestral home.' (Waititi 1969: 28)

       c.   Ka tono au i   aku   mōkai ki te tahitahi i
          uns send I Acc pl=my slave Comp   sweep   Acc
          'I ordered my servants to sweep

          te whare.
          the house
          the house.'

       d.   Ka āhua mai   ki te mātakitaki i   a   Te
          uns crowd here Comp   look   Acc prop Te
          '(The fairies) crowded round to gaze at Te

          Kanawa.
          Kanawa
          Kanawa.' (Orbell 30)

But it does not delete transitive direct objects:

    (20)   *E hiahia ana a   Hōne ki te patu (ai) te
           uns want   prog prop John Comp hit   Pro the
           (John wants the girl to hit

          kōtiro.
          girl
          (him).)

Or oblique NPs:

    (21)a. *Ka haere ia ki te hōmai (ai) e   Rewi te
           uns go   he Comp   give   Pro Agt Rewi the
           (He went for Rewi to give the book (to

          pukapuka.
          book
          him).)

113 Case Marking and Grammatical Relations

    b. *Kua hiahia rātou ki te hau-a   e   ia te
         prf want   they Comp hew-Pass Agt him the
         (They wanted him to hew the

         waka (mō rātou).
         canoe for them
         canoe (for them).)

(The *ai* in these examples reflects the fact that nonsubjects are often copied by extraction rules.)

Further, *ki te* Equi only deletes subjects if they are also semantic agents, as in (19), or experiencers, as in (7b). It does not delete subjects that are semantic patients, regardless of whether they are attached to underlying stative verbs:[1]

  (22)a. *I   hiahia koe ki te riro i   te   wahine.
          past want you Comp taken Caus the woman
          (You wanted to be taken away by the woman.)

      b. I   hiahia koe kia riro koe i   te   wahine.
          past want you sbj taken you Caus the woman
          'You wanted that you should be taken away by
          the woman.'

Or are the derived subjects of passive clauses:

  (23)a. *I   hiahia au ki te patu-a   e   Rewi.
          past want I Comp hit-Pass Agt Rewi
          (I wanted to be hit by Rewi.)

      b. I   hiahia au kia patu-a   (au)   Rewi.
          past want I sbj hit-Pass I   Agt Rewi
          'I wanted that I should be hit by Rewi.'

      c. Ka kawe-a   ki rō   whare kia kai-nga e
          uns take-Pass to inside house sbj eat-Pass Agt
          '(She) took (them) into the house for her

          tāna tāne.
          her man
          husband to eat (lit. ...so that (they) could
          be eaten by her husband).' (Orbell 60)

Finally, the rule does not delete semantic agents or exper-

iencers unless they are also subjects when it applies. <u>Ki te</u>
Equi does not affect agents of passive clauses, which are no
longer subjects, although they have the semantics of agents/
experiencers:

(24)a. *I   hiahia au ki te patu-a   te poaka.
         past want I Comp hit-Pass the pig
         (I wanted to kill the pig.)

   b.   *Ka whakaaro a   Hōne ki te inu-mia   te
         uns think   prop John Comp drink-Pass the
         (John decided to drink the

         wai.
         water
         water.)

(25)a.   I   hiahia au kia patu-a   (e   au) te poaka.
         past want I sbj hit-Pass Agt me the pig
         'I wanted that I should kill the pig.'

   b.   Ka whakaaro a   Hone kia inu-mia   (e   ia)
         uns think   prop John sbj drink-Pass Agt him
         'John decided that he would drink

         te wai.
         the water
         the water.' (Clark 1973b: 4)

In (25), the passive agent of the embedded clause can optionally disappear through zero-pronominalization.

Taken together, these facts argue that the target of <u>ki te</u>
Equi must be both a subject and a semantic agent/experiencer.
The latter restriction is common for Equi rules in other languages (see also 3.2.3); the former argues that <u>ki te</u> Equi
refers to the category subject. Because Maori is an accusative language and its case marking rules treat subjects as a
unified category, <u>ki te</u> Equi is consistent with the integrated position. Observe, however, that it is consistent with
the independent position as well.

3.2.1.4. **Hei Equi and Participle Formation**. Roughly the same conclusion can be reached for the two other Equi rules of Maori, hei Equi and Participle Formation. Hei Equi operates in certain two-clause structures containing an embedded adverbial clause of purpose. It deletes a target which is coreferential to a controller in the higher clause, and inserts the complementizer hei:

    (26) a. Ka tuku-a   mai ko   tētahi parirau hei hao
            uns put-Pass here Pred one   wing   for scoop
            '(It) stretches out a wing to scoop

            i   te tangata.
            Acc the person
            him up.' (Orbell 102)

       b. Ko   koe ki waho,   hei pakipaki i   tā tāua
            Pred you to outside, for collect Acc our=du
            'You outside, to keep our troops

            ope.
            company
            together.' (Biggs, Hohepa, and Mead 79)

Participle Formation operates in certain other two-clause structures containing an adverbial clause of purpose. It deletes a target under coreference with a controller in the higher clause, and removes the tense-aspect-mood particle of the embedded clause as well:

    (27) a. Hoki   ana te wahine rā   ki te whare tangi
            return prog the woman   that to the house cry
            'The woman returned to the house to weep

            ai.
            Pro
            for him.' (Orbell 22)

       b. Ka tae   mai te taraka mau i   ngā
            uns arrive here the truck take Acc the=pl
            'The truck arrived to take the men to the

            tāngata ki te   ngahere.
            men   to the forest
            forest.' (Waititi 1969: 42)

These rules, like <u>ki te</u> Equi, are restricted to targets which are both subjects and semantic agents (or, perhaps, subjects and semantic agents/experiencers). They therefore refer to the category subject, and are consistent with either the integrated or the independent position.

3.2.2. <u>Tongan</u>

Tongan, an ergative language, has an Equi rule which argues against the integrated position and in favor of the independent one.

3.2.2.1. <u>Basic Description</u>.

Tongan Equi relates sentences like (28) and (29):

(28) Pea na'e 'alu 'a e   tangatá 'o   folau mama'o.
      and past go Abs the man   Comp sail far
      'Then the man went and sailed away.'

(29) Pea na'e 'alu 'a e   tangatá 'o   ne folau
      and past go Abs the man   Comp he sail
      'Then the man went and he sailed

      mama'o.
      far
      away.'

This rule operates in certain two-clause structures in which one clause contains a verb of motion or directed action, and the other clause is an embedded clause introduced by the complementizer <u>'o</u>:

(30)a. Pea hanga a   Muni o   ne huai   hake a-e
       and turn Abs Muni Comp he throw up   Abs-the
       'And Muni turned and lifted up the

       fangu.
       calabash
       calabash.' (Gifford 134)

  b.   Na'e ha'u ai pē 'a Kinikinilau ia 'o
       past come Pro Emp Abs Kinikinilau that Comp
       'Kinikinilau came and they

```
                    na       nonofo ai pē.
                    they=du  stay=pl Pro Emp
                    lived there together.' (Fanua 21)
```

If a target in the 'o clause is coreferential with a controller in the higher clause, it is optionally deleted by Equi:

```
(31)a.   Ne    hanga hifo 'a  e   la'á 'o   'ofa 'i
         past  turn  down Abs the sun  Comp love at
         'The sun looked down and...took pity on

         si'ono foha.
         his    son
         Sisimataela'a.' (Fanua 33)

   b.    Mou     haua kimoutolu o    alu.
         you=pl  come you=pl    Comp go
         'You come out and go!' (Gifford 94)
```

The 'o complementizer of structures which can be affected by Equi has several characteristics of note. It is restricted to clauses embedded under verbs of motion or directed action:

```
(32)a.   Na'a ne tu'u hake 'o   'alu.
         past he stand up  Comp go
         'He stood up and went.'

   b.   *Na'a ku feinga 'o   u mavahe 'aneafi.
         past I  try    Comp I leave  yesterday
         (I tried and left yesterday.)
```

In this respect it differs from the subjunctive tense-aspect-mood particle ke, which is more of an all-purpose marker for embedded clauses:

```
(33)a.   Na'a ne tu'u hake ke  'alu.
         past he stand up  sbj go
         'He stood up to go.'

   b.    Na'a ku feinga ke  u mavahe 'aneafi.
         past I  try    sbj I leave  yesterday
         'I tried to leave yesterday.'
```

'O is also glossed 'and', a gloss suggesting that it serves

as a coordinating conjunction. However, it can be argued that it is not so much a conjunction as a complementizer of result.

To begin with, 'o occurs only when the event described by the embedded clause is the specific result of that described by the higher clause. In (34), the events are not construed as related in this direct fashion, and the conjunction pea 'and' appears instead:

(34) a. *Na'a nau 'oange ki ai 'a e tohí 'o 'alu
      past they give to Pro Abs the book Comp go
      (They gave him the book and he

      ia.
      he
      left.)

b. Na'a nau 'oange ki ai 'a e tohí pea 'alu
   past they give to Pro Abs the book and go
   'They gave him the book and he

   ia.
   he
   left.'

In (35), which is a true coordinate structure, no result interpretation is possible, and pea must appear:

(35) a. *Ko e tufunga ia 'o ko e tangata
      Pred the carpenter he Comp Pred the person
      (He is a carpenter and I am a

      faifakatau au.
      seller   I
      salesman.)

b. Ko e tufunga ia pea ko e tangata
   Pred the carpenter he and Pred the person
   'He is a carpenter and I am a

   faifakatau au.
   seller   I
   salesman.'

Further, clauses introduced by 'o act like ordinary subordinate clauses, in that they allow NPs to be freely extracted from them. Consider:

(36) a. Na'a nau ha'u 'o 'omai 'a e pīsí ma'a-ku.
past they come Comp bring Abs the peach for-me
'They came and brought the peaches to me.'

b. Ko e pīsí na'a nau ha'u 'o 'omai
Pred the peach past they come Comp bring
'It is the peaches that they came and brought

ma'a-ku.
for-me
to me.'

c. Ko au na'a nau ha'u 'o 'omai ki ai 'a
Pred me past they come Comp bring to Pro Abs
'It is me that they came and brought the

e pīsí.
the peach
peaches to.'

But true coordinate clauses obey the Coordinate Structure Constraint (Ross 1967); they do not allow this sort of extraction:

(37) a. 'Oku ou sai'ia au 'i he tamasi'í, pea 'oku ke
prog I like I at the boy and prog you
'I like the boy and you

sai'ia koe 'i he ta'ahiné.
like you at the girl
like the girl.'

b. *Ko e ta'ahiné 'oku ou sai'ia au 'i he
Pred the girl prog I like I at the
(It is the girl that I like the boy

tamasi'í, pea 'oku ke sai'ia koe ai.
boy and prog you like you Pro
and you like.)

These facts argue that the 'o of (30-31) is not a coordinating conjunction but an adverbial complementizer, rather like the infinitival *and* of English He went *and* bought some whiskey. For arguments that the *and* in sentences of this type is not a coordinating conjunction either, see Ross (1967: 93-94).

Because Equi simply deletes the target in an 'o clause without resulting in any other change in morphology, it might be wondered whether this rule is distinct from zero-pronominalization, an ungoverned, unbounded deletion rule (see 1.4.1). The properties to be outlined below show that Equi can be distinguished from zero-pronominalization and other deletion rules. In anticipation of them, it is simply asserted here that Equi exists. The rule has roughly the form: 'Delete a target in an 'o clause under coreference with a controller in the next higher clause, subject to further conditions (described below)'.

3.2.2.2. <u>Equi as a Major Rule</u>. As might be expected, Tongan Equi qualifies as a major rule.

It is the counterpart of English Equi, which is cyclic, as already noted above.

It is also bounded. Equi cannot reach across an intervening clause to find a target; instead, it must locate target and controller in adjacent clauses connected by the complementizer 'o:

(38) a. Na'a ne tu'u hake 'o 'alu.
past he stand up Comp go
'He stood up and went.'

b. *Na'a ne tu'u ki 'olunga 'o pau ke 'alu.
past he stand to above Comp must sbj go
(He stood up and had to go.)

Compare:

(39) Kuo pau ke ne 'alu.
prf must sbj he go
'It was necessary that he go.'

Because the 'o complementizer requires a connection of direct result between the next higher clause and the clause to which 'o is attached, sentences like (38b) are not fully acceptable even if Equi has not applied. This suggests that the fact that the rule is bounded may follow ultimately from the semantic requirements imposed by the complementizer.

Finally, Equi is governed by verbs of motion or directed action. It also exhibits lexical exceptions: the rule is optional for most governing verbs, including 'alu 'go', ha'u 'come', hanga 'turn', and taa'i 'hit', but obligatory for hanga 'do', a transitive verb with rather unusual properties (see 6.3.1.3). Consider:

(40) a. Na'a mau hanga 'o fakaafe'i ia ki he party.
past we do Comp invite him to the party
'We invited him to the party.'

b. Na'a ne hanga 'o muimui'i homau tunga'ane.
past he do Comp follow our brother
'He followed our brother.'

(41) a. *Na'a mau hanga 'o mau fakaafe'i ia ki he
past we do Comp we invite him to the
(We invited him to the

party.
party.
party.)

b. *Na'a ne hanga 'o ne muimui'i homau tunga'ane.
past he do Comp he follow our brother
(He followed our brother.)

3.2.2.3. <u>Restriction to Subjects</u>. Having shown that Equi is a major rule, we now turn to its restriction on the target: it is restricted to targets that are subjects. The rule deletes intransitive subjects:

(42) a. 'E ha'u 'a Kuku Tangata 'o 'ita he
uns come Abs Kuku Tangata Comp angry because
'Father will come and be very angry when he

kuo mate 'a e fu'u siaine.
prf die Abs the tree banana
finds this banana tree toppled over!' (Fanua 44)

122 Case Marking and Grammatical Relations

  b. Na'a ne 'alu 'o tūkia he va'akaú.
    past he go Comp trip the stick
    'He went and tripped on the stick.'

  c. Na'a ku taa'i ia 'o mate.
    past I hit him Comp die
    'I hit him and he died.'

Subjects of canonical transitive clauses:

  (43)a. Na'e 'alu 'a e tangatá 'o taa'i 'a e
     past go Abs the man Comp hit Abs the
     'The man went and hit the

    kulī.
    dog
    dog.'

  b. Na'e tō mai ha matangi 'o haveki 'a e
    past fall here a wind Comp break Abs the
    'Some wind came and blew down the

    falé.
    house
    house.'

And subjects of middle clauses:

  (44)a. Na'e 'alu 'a e ta'ahiné 'o ala ki he
     past go Abs the girl Comp touch to the
     'The girl went and touched the

    pēpē.
    baby
    baby.'

  b. Ne hanga hifo 'a e la'á 'o 'ofa 'i
    past turn down Abs the sun Comp love at
    'The sun looked down and...took pity on

    si'ono foha.
    his son
    Sisimataela'a.' (Fanua 33)

But it does not delete absolutive direct objects:

  (45)a. *Na'a ku puna atu 'o ne ma'u.
     past I jump away Comp he catch
     (I jumped up and he grabbed (me).)

123   Case Marking and Grammatical Relations

      b. *Na'e hanga mai 'a e   tamasi'i 'o mau
          past turn here Abs the child   Comp we
          (The boy turned and then we

          fakatokanga'i ai.
          recognize   Pro
          recognized (him).)

(46)a. Na'a ku puna atu 'o ne ma'u au.
          past I jump away Comp he catch me
          'I jumped up and he grabbed me.'

      b. Na'e hanga mai 'a e   tamasi'i 'o mau
          past turn here Abs the child   Comp we
          'The boy turned and then we

          fakatokanga'i ai ia.
          recognize   Pro him
          recognized him.'

Direct objects of middle clauses:

(47)a. *Na'a nau omi   'o mau fakamālō.
          past they come=pl Comp we thank
          (They came and we thanked (them).)

      b. Na'a nau omi   'o mau fakamālō ki ai.
          past they come=pl Comp we thank   to Pro
          'They came and we thanked them.'

Or genuine oblique NPs:

(48)a. *Na'e ha'u 'a Simione 'o mau 'ave 'a e
          past come Abs Simione Comp we take Abs the
          (Simione came and we took the

          lolé.
          candy
          candy away (from him).)

      b. ?Na'e ha'u 'a Simione 'o mau 'ave 'a e
          past come Abs Simione Comp we take Abs the
          'Simione came and we took the

          lolé mei 'i-ate ia.
          candy from at-pro him
          candy away from him.'

The requirement that targets of Equi be subjects is not

124   Case Marking and Grammatical Relations

combined with particularly narrow semantic restrictions: targets may either cause the event of the embedded clause or else be physically or psychologically affected by it. Thus in (43), the target is a semantic agent; in (42a), a semantic experiencer; and in (42b) and (42c), a semantic patient. However, if a target is a nonagent, it must be affected by the event in some way, as is the case in (42).

It can be concluded that Equi is restricted to targets that are subjects, and so refers to the category subject.

Given that Tongan is an ergative language, its case marking rules pick out intransitive subjects and transitive direct objects (i.e. absolutives) as a unified category as opposed to transitive subjects (i.e. ergatives). The integrated position predicts that other rules in such a language should pick out these same categories if they mention any subtypes of NPs. Therefore, the presence of the Equi rule just described, which refers to subjects regardless of their case marking, provides a counterexample to the integrated position. It simultaneously supports the independent position, which claims that subject and direct object figure prominently in the syntax of all Polynesian languages.[2]

3.2.3. Samoan

Equi in Samoan, another ergative language, also argues that the independent position is to be preferred to the integrated position.

3.2.3.1. Basic Description. Samoan Equi relates sentences like (49) and (50):

  (49) 'Ua mānana'o 'i mātou e mālō i le pālota.
      prf want=pl pl we uns win in the election
      'We want to win in the election.'

(50)   'Ua mānana'o 'i mātou mātou te mālō i le
       prf want=pl   pl we   we   uns win in the
       'We want that we should win in the

       pālota.
       election
       election.'

This rule applies in certain two-clause structures in which one clause contains a verb of motion, volition, effort, force, or persuasion, and the other clause is embedded directly under it. Such embedded clauses are introduced by the unspecified tense-aspect-mood particle e (te if Clitic Placement has applied), which is used generally for unrealized clauses:

(51)a. Po 'ua 'e taumafai 'e te fia alu 'ese?
       Q prf you try   you uns want go away
       'Did you try that you should run away?'

   b. Sā lātou fa'amālosi 'i-āte a'u 'ou te nofo
       past they encourage to-pro me I uns stay
       'They encouraged me that I should stay

       i le fale.
       at the house
       at home.'

If the target in the embedded clause is coreferential with a controller in the higher clause, it is optionally deleted by Equi, subject to conditions to be described below:

(52)a. Po 'ua 'e taumafai e fia alu 'ese?
       Q prf you try   uns want go away
       'Did you try to run away?'

   b. Sā 'ou fa'amālosi 'i-āte ia e alu 'i le
       past I   encourage to-pro him uns go to the
       'I encouraged him to go to

       ā'oga.
       school
       school.'

Since Equi deletes the target without having any other effect on the embedded clause, it appears similar to zero-pronominalization; however, the facts about to be discussed argue that it exists as a distinct rule. Its form is roughly: 'Delete a target in an embedded clause under coreference with a controller in the next higher clause, subject to further conditions (described below)'.

3.2.3.2. <u>Equi</u> <u>as</u> <u>a</u> <u>Major</u> <u>Rule</u>. Equi meets all of the criteria for a major rule.

It is the counterpart of English Equi, a cyclic rule.

It is also bounded: it cannot delete a target which is separated from its controller by an intervening embedded clause. Compare (53), in which Equi has applied, with (54), in which it has not:

(53)   *'Ou te mana'o e fai mai 'oia sā va'ai
       I   uns want uns say here he past see
      (I want that he should say that (I)

      'i-āte ia.
      to-pro him
      saw him.)

(54)   'Ou te mana'o e fai mai 'oia sā 'ou
      I   uns want uns say here he past I
      'I want that he should say that I

      va'ai 'i-āte ia.
      see   to-pro him
      saw him.'

It also appears to have lexical exceptions. In general, Equi is optional for a large class of governing verbs, including <u>manatu</u> 'think', <u>taumafai</u> 'try', <u>fa'amālosi</u> 'encourage', <u>fiu</u> 'tired (of)', and so forth. But in the grammars of many speakers, the verbs <u>alu</u> (plural <u>ō</u>) 'go' and <u>mana'o</u> 'want' exhibit an additional, rather unusual restriction: they do not allow Equi to be controlled by a first or second singular clitic pronoun if the target occurs in an intransitive clause. In (55), all of these conditions are met and

Equi cannot apply:

    (55)a. *'Ua 'ou mana'o e   alu e   moe.
             prf I want   uns go uns sleep
             (I want to go to sleep.)

       b. *Pe 'e te mana'o e   alu atu 'i lo'u fale?
            Q you uns want   uns go away to my   house
            (Do you want to go to my house?)

    (56)a. 'Ua 'ou mana'o 'ou te alu 'ou te moe.
             prf I want   I   uns go I   uns sleep
             'I want to go to sleep.'

       b. Pe 'e te mana'o 'e te alu atu 'i lo'u fale?
            Q you uns want   you uns go away to my   house
            'Do you want to go to my house?'

       c. 'Ou te alu 'ou te tafao i Hollywood.
            I   uns go I   uns loaf in Hollywood
            'I'm going to loaf in Hollywood.'

In contrast, in (57), the controller is a first or second singular independent pronoun, and Equi can apply:

    (57)a. 'Ua 'ou mana'o e   alu a'u e   moe.
             prf I want   uns go I   uns sleep
             'I want that I should go to sleep.'

       b. 'O 'oe e   mana'o e   sau taeao.
            Pred you uns want   uns come tomorrow
            'It is you that wants to come tomorrow.'

In (58), the controller is a clitic, but not first or second singular:

    (58)a. Na   mātou mānana'o e   'a'ai, 'a e   peita'i
             past we   want=pl uns eat=pl and uns but
             'We wanted to eat, but the food

             'ua 'ave 'ese mea'ai.
             prf take away food
             had been taken away.'

       b. Sā   lātou mānana'o e   ō   'i le 'āiga.
            past they want=pl uns go=pl to the house
            'They wanted to go home.'

Further, in (59), the target is in a middle or canonical transitive clause, and Equi is allowed:

(59) a. Sā 'ou alu atu e fesili po 'o le ā
past I go away uns ask Q Pred the what?
'I went outside to ask what

le mea 'ua tupu.
the thing prf happen
had happened.'

b. 'E te mana'o e faitau le tusi?
you uns want uns read the book
'Do you want to read the book?'

Finally, in (60), the governing verb is not <u>alu</u> or <u>mana'o</u>:

(60) a. 'Ua 'ou fiu e alu 'i Los Angeles.
prf I tired uns go to Los Angeles
'I'm tired of going to Los Angeles.'

b. 'Ou te lē fiafia e tā'ele i le sami.
I uns not happy uns swim in the ocean
'I don't like to go swimming in the ocean.'

Recalling that clitic subjects in Samoan are nonemphatic (see 1.4.2.2), we can state the restriction as follows: for <u>alu</u> and <u>mana'o</u>, Equi cannot be controlled by a nonemphatic first or second singular subject if the target occurs in an intransitive clause. The motivation for such a restriction is not at all clear. What is important is that it appears to hold only for <u>alu</u> and <u>mana'o</u> (and, for occasional speakers, <u>manatu</u> 'think'), and thus can be regarded as a particularly unusual type of lexical exception.

It follows from all of the above considerations that Equi is a major rule. Interestingly, the properties that establish this also serve to differentiate it from zero-pronominalization, an extremely free deletion rule.

3.2.3.3. <u>Restriction to Subjects</u>. As expected by now, Equi exhibits a restriction on the target: it affects only tar-

gets that are both subjects and semantic agents/experiencers.
Thus, the rule deletes intransitive subjects:

(61) a. Lua   te ō   e   momoe?
        you=du uns go=pl uns sleep=pl
        'Are you two going to sleep?'

    b. 'Ua māfaufau Ioane e   alu.
        prf think   John uns go
        'John decided to go.'

Subjects of canonical transitive clauses:

(62) a. Fiafia tele Fo'isia e   'ai le ota.
        happy very Fo'isia uns eat the raw=fish
        'Fo'isia likes very much to eat raw fish.'

    b. Na   mātou taumafai e   fa'a'uma le galuega.
        past we   try   uns finish   the work
        'We tried to finish the work.'

    c. Ona oo   atu ai lea o   le alii mai
        then arrive away Pro that Pred the chief from
        'Then the chief arrived from Upolu

        Upolu e   tuli-loa le lupe.
        Upolu uns chase-Emp the pigeon
        to catch the pigeon.' (Stuebel 232)

And subjects of middle clauses:

(63)   'Ua māfaufau Ioane e   asiasi 'i lona tuafafine.
        prf think   John uns visit to his sister
        'John decided to visit his sister.'

But it does not delete absolutive direct objects:

(64) a. *Mātou te le'i mānana'o e   maua e   leoleo.
        we   uns not want=pl uns catch Erg police
        (We didn't want to be caught by the police.)

    b. *Sā   mana'o le fafine e   fa'agalo 'uma e
        past want   the woman uns forget   all Erg
        (The woman wanted everyone to forget

        tagata.
        person
        (her).)

130 Case Marking and Grammatical Relations

(65) a. Mātou te le'i mānana'o e maua e leoleo
we uns not want=pl uns catch Erg police
'We didn't want that we should be caught by

mātou.
us
the police.'

b. Sā mana'o le fafine e fa'agalo 'uma e
past want the woman uns forget all Erg
'The woman wanted that everyone should forget

tagata naia.
person her
her.'

Direct objects of middle clauses:

(66) a. *Sā lātou lē mānana'o e fesoasoani a lātou
past they not want=pl uns help pl=their
(They didn't want their friends to help

uō.
friend
(them).)

b. Sā lātou lē mānana'o e fesoasoani a lātou
past they not want=pl uns help pl=their
'They didn't want their friends to

uō 'i-āte 'i lātou.
friend to-pro pl them
help them.'

Or oblique NPs:

(67) *Na mātou taumafai e 'uma le galuega.
past we try uns done the work
(We tried that the work should get done (because of us).)

Further, Equi requires its target to be a semantic agent, as in (62), or an experiencer, as in (61a), as well as a subject. It does not delete subjects that are semantic patients, as shown by:

(68) a. *Sā mātou mānana'o 'ia pa'u'ū.
past we want=pl sbj fall=pl
(We wanted to fall.)

Case Marking and Grammatical Relations

   b. *E   le'i mana'o 'oia e   lavea i-ā   'i
        uns not   want   she uns hurt Caus-pro pl
        (She didn't want to be hurt by

        lātou.
        them
        them.)

   c. Sā   mātou mānana'o 'ia pa'u'ū mātou.
       past we   want=pl sbj fall=pl we
       'We wanted that we should fall.'

Finally, the rule will not delete semantic agents or experiencers unless they are also subjects. This is shown, for instance, by its failure to affect the stative agent of the embedded clause in (69), which is semantically an agent but syntactically oblique (see 1.3.5):[3]

(69)a. *Na   mātou mānana'o e   galo   le mea
         past we   want=pl   uns forgotten the thing
         (We wanted what had happened to be forgotten

         'ua tupu.
         prf happen
         (by us).)

   b. Na   mātou mānana'o e   galo   i-āte   'i
       past we   want=pl   uns forgotten Caus-pro pl
       'We wanted what had happened to be

       mātou le mea   'ua tupu.
       us   the thing prf happen
       forgotten by us.'

Equi is, therefore, restricted to targets that are both subjects and semantic agents/experiencers.

Recall that Samoan is an ergative language and its case marking rules pick out ergatives as opposed to absolutives. The fact that its Equi rule picks out (certain) subjects, whether they are marked absolutive or ergative, provides an argument against the integrated position. At the same time, it supports the independent position, which claims that subject is one of the categories central to the syntax of all Polynesian languages.[4]

132   Case Marking and Grammatical Relations

3.2.4. Summary

To sum up, the Equi rules discussed above for Maori, Tongan, and Samoan all refer to the category subject. Tongan Equi appears not to mention any other categories, while the Maori and Samoan rules refer to the semantic roles agent and experiencer in addition. The fact that all of the rules pick out subjects regardless of their case marking argues that the independent position is to be preferred to the integrated one --an argument that will be strengthened in the sections below.

3.3. SUBJECT-REFERRING RULES: RAISING

Many Polynesian languages have a Raising rule which raises an NP from an embedded clause to become the subject of a modal, aspectual, or negative verb. This section examines the Raising rules of Maori, Tongan, and Samoan, and argues that they are restricted to subjects. They therefore refer to the category subject and support the independent position. At the same time, the presence of rules with this restriction in Tongan and Samoan, both ergative languages, strengthens the case against the integrated position.

3.3.1 describes Maori Raising; 3.3.2, Tongan Raising; and 3.3.3, Samoan Raising. A distinct Raising rule in Samoan that affects NPs of any syntactic type is discussed later, in 3.5.2.

3.3.1. Maori

Raising in Maori, an accusative language, is consistent with both the integrated and the independent positions.

3.3.1.1. Background: Negative Sentences. Maori Raising operates in negative sentences containing the negative verbs

133 Case Marking and Grammatical Relations

kore 'not', kāhore 'not', kīhai 'not (past)', ēhara 'not (for
certain predicate nominals or predicate PPs)', or kaua 'not
(imperative)'. Such sentences are biclausal, the negative
acting as the verb of the higher clause and the negated
clause, as its sentential subject:

(70)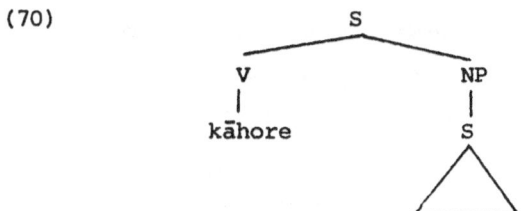

Several arguments are given in Chung (1970) for the biclausal
structure (70). Here I briefly summarize the characteristics
that indicate that negatives in Maori are higher verbs.

To begin with, kore 'not' is generally preceded by its own
tense-aspect-mood particle (Hohepa 1969b), while the other
negatives can be segmented into combinations of tense-aspect-
mood particle plus negative stem (e.g. kā+hore). Given that
tense-aspect-mood particles in Maori are associated with all
and only verbs (see 1.2.1 and 1.2.3), this argues that negatives have verbal status.

Further, negatives attract certain verbal modifiers, such
as the pronominal copy ai, which otherwise occur only with
verbs (see 1.2.2 and 1.2.3). Consider:

(71)a. Ko   tēnā te take e   kore ai a   Hōne
        Pred that the reason nonpast not Pro prop John
        'That is the reason why John won't

        e   mate āpōpō.
        nonpast die   tomorrow
        die tomorrow.'

    b. Ko   tēnā te take kāhore ai i   hiahia
        Pred that the reason not   Pro past want
        'That is the reason why the man didn't

134   Case Marking and Grammatical Relations

>te tangata ki te hopu-ika.
>the man   Comp catch-fish
>want to go fishing.'

Finally, the negated clause is introduced by the tense-aspect-mood particles for embedded, rather than matrix, clauses (see 1.2.1). These are distinguished by the fact that they indicate nonpast tense (embedded clause e) rather than unspecified tense-aspect (matrix ka), and do not indicate perfect aspect (matrix kua):

>(72)   Kāore e   kata   a   Mere.
>   not   nonpast laugh prop Mary
>   'Mary won't laugh.'

Negated clauses with perfect aspect are preceded by the subjunctive particle kia:

>(73)   Kāore anō kia whiti te rā.
>   not   yet sbj shine the sun
>   'The sun hasn't risen yet.'

Facts like these provide the beginnings of a demonstration that negative sentences are biclausal, the negative acts as the verb of its own clause, and the negated clause is embedded under it. See Chung (1970) for further details.

3.3.1.2. <u>Basic Description</u>. We now turn to Maori Raising, which relates sentences like (74) and (75):

>(74)a. Kīhai a   Tamahae i   haere.
>   not prop Tamahae past go
>   'Tamahae didn't go.'
>
>   b. Kāore anō te rā kia whiti.
>   not   yet the sun sbj shine
>   'The sun hasn't risen yet.'
>
>(75)a. Kīhai i   haere a   Tamahae.
>   not   past go   prop Tamahae
>   'Tamahae didn't go.'

b. Kāore anō kia whiti te rā.
    not yet sbj shine the sun
    'The sun hasn't risen yet.'

This rule takes an NP from the negated clause and raises it to the next higher clause, where it becomes the derived subject of the negative verb. It is obligatory for pronouns, as pointed out by Tamati Reedy:

(76)a. Kaua tātou e   haere.
        don't we   nonpast go
        'Let's not go!' (Biggs 1969: 64)

b. *Kaua e   haere tātou.
    don't nonpast go   we
    (Let's not go!)

And, though optional for full nouns, it applies so frequently that it is sometimes treated as if it were required for them as well (Williams and Williams 1950[1862]; Biggs 1969).

In order to show that Raising has the effect just described, it is necessary to argue that the raised NP is the (surface) subject of the higher clause, but originated in the embedded clause. The arguments that establish this include the following.

(a) To begin with, the raised NP originates in the lower clause. This can be shown by the usual subcategorization arguments involving a missing NP.

(b) The raised NP is also the (surface) subject of the higher clause. It appears in the unmarked case, which is the normal case for subjects, and has the word order of a subject, occurring to the immediate right of the negative verb. In addition, it can be qualified by the nonspecific article he.

As described in 2.2.1.3, the nonspecific article he can qualify intransitive subjects but no other types of nouns. Consider the intransitive subjects of:

(77)a. Ka hinga he rākau.
        uns fall a tree
        'Some tree or other fell.'

   b.   Ka whanatu he tāngata kia titiro ki a   Paowa
        uns run=up a people sbj look   to prop Paowa
        'Everyone ran up to watch Paowa

        e   haere mai ana.
        uns go   here prog
        coming.' (Orbell 78)

Subjects qualified by he are eligible for an optional rule which moves them to the beginning of the clause, immediately to the left of the tense-aspect-mood particle, subject to discourse conditions of a weak sort:

(78)   He tangata ka haere ki te moana.
        a person uns go   to the ocean
        'A man went to the ocean.'

In contrast, transitive subjects cannot be qualified by he. This is true whether they follow the verb in surface structure:

(79)a. *Ka patu he tangata i   te wheke.
         uns kill a person Acc the octopus
         (A man killed the octopus.)

   b.   *I   kite he wahine i   te nanakia.
         past see a woman Acc the monster
         (A woman saw the monster.)

Or have been moved to the left by the preposing rule:[5]

(80)   *He kurī i   ngau i   a   Pipo.
         a dog past bite Acc prop Pipo
         (A dog bit Pipo.)

And even when they are shielded from sentence-initial position by a preposed time adverb:

(81)   *Āpōpō   he wahine ka patu i   te tuna.
         tomorrow a woman uns kill Acc the eel
         (Tomorrow a woman will kill the eel.)

Case Marking and Grammatical Relations

Now when Raising has applied to a negative sentence, the raised NP can be qualified by <u>he</u> even if it originally served as transitive subject in the negated clause. Consider:

(82) a. Kāhore he tangata e   hanga i   te whare.
         not   a person nonpast build Acc the house
         'No one will build the house.'
         'It is not the case that anyone will build the house.'

    b.   Kāhore anō he wahine kia patu i   te tuna.
         not   yet a woman sbj kill Acc the eel
         'Women haven't yet killed eels.'

Sentences like (82) argue that the raised NP is no longer the subject of the negated clause. It must now be serving as the subject of an intransitive clause, since only intransitive subjects can be qualified by <u>he</u>. Given that negative verbs can be shown independently to be stative intransitives (see Hohepa 1969b; Chung 1970), the evidence is fairly compelling that the raised NPs of (82) are the surface subjects of the negative verb.

(It follows from this that the distribution of <u>he</u> is not determined at underlying structure, but only after Raising has had a chance to apply. This is consistent with the fact that its distribution is not determined until Passive has had a chance to apply; see 2.2.1.3.)

(c) Finally, it is necessary to argue that the rule responsible for (74) is not a kind of Equi; that is, the raised NP does not originate in the higher clause and then trigger deletion of a coreferential target in the embedded clause. This can be established by considering the properties of controlled deletion rules in Maori and contrasting them with the properties of Raising.

Thus, the raised NP clearly does not control zero-pronominalization in the negated clause. This is because zero-pronominalization deletes its targets optionally (see 1.4.1), while Raising always leaves a hole in the negated clause:

(83) a. Kāore a Mere e kata.
  not prop Mary nonpast laugh
  'Mary won't laugh.'

 b. *Kāore a Mere e kata ia.
  not prop Mary nonpast laugh she
  (Mary won't laugh.)

Further, the raised NP does not control any of the three Equi rules in Maori: <u>ki te</u> Equi, <u>hei</u> Equi, or Participle Formation. This point is established by the following.

First, Raising cannot produce the changes in complementizer morphology associated with <u>ki te</u> Equi, <u>hei</u> Equi, or Participle Formation. For instance, it cannot replace the subjunctive particle of a negated clause with the complementizer <u>ki te</u>, as shown in:

(84) a. *Kāhore anō a Tamahae ki te haere.
  not yet prop Tamahae Comp go
  (Tamahae hasn't gone yet.)

 b. Kāhore anō a Tamahae kia haere.
  not yet prop Tamahae sbj go
  'Tamahae hasn't gone yet.'

Compare the following, in which <u>ki te</u> Equi has applied:

(85) a. E āhei ia ki te haere.
  nonpast able he Comp go
  'He is able to go.'

 b. *E āhei ia kia haere.
  nonpast able he sbj go
  (He is able to go.)

Second, Raising applies freely to semantic patients, while the Equi rules are restricted to semantic agents or experiencers. Compare the Raising sentences of (86) with the <u>ki te</u> Equi sentences of (87):

(86) a. E   kore   a   Hōne e   mate āpōpō.
         nonpast not   prop John nonpast die   tomorrow
         'John won't die tomorrow.'

     b. Kaua   ahau e   whakarēre-a.
         don't I   nonpast abandon-Pass
         'Let me not be cast aside!' (Biggs 1969: 64)

(87) a. *Ka   hiahia au ki te mate āpōpō.
         uns want   I Comp die tomorrow
         (I want to die tomorrow.)

     b. *I   hiahia au ki te patu-a   e   Rewi.
         past want   I Comp hit-Pass Agt Rewi
         (I wanted to be hit by Rewi.)

Third, structures that have undergone Raising have different extraction properties from structures that have undergone the Equi rules. In particular, in Equi structures, the direct object of the embedded clause can be freely extracted by Clefting, a rule which moves a focused subject or direct object to the left and marks it with the predicate particle ko (Hohepa 1969b; Chung 1977b):

(88) Ko   te poaka i   hiahia ai   a   Hōne ki te
      Pred the pig   past want   Pro prop John Comp
      'It is the pig that John wanted to

      patu.
      kill
      kill.'

But in a Raising structure, the direct object of the negated clause cannot be extracted by this rule:[6]

(89) a. *Ko   te kūmara   kāhore ai   a   Hōne i
         Pred the sweet=potato not   Pro prop John past
         (It is the sweet potato that John didn't

         waru.
         peel
         peel.)

     b. *Ko   wai   kīhai ai   mātou i   patu?
         Pred who? not   Pro we   past kill
         (Who didn't we kill?)

140   Case Marking and Grammatical Relations

The contrast between (89) and (88) argues that Clefting must be able to distinguish Raising structures from Equi structures. Therefore, structures of the former type should not be derived via an Equi rule.

The constraint on extraction illustrated in (89) has several further properties of note. First, it does not extend to all extraction rules: it does not prevent Relativization from extracting the direct object of a negated clause, for instance:

(90) a. Ko   wai   te mea   kīhai ai mātou i
         Pred who? the person [not   Pro we   past
         'Who is the person who we didn't

         patu?
         kill]
         kill?'

     b. Ko   te poaka te mea   kīhai ai i   patu
         Pred the pig the thing [not   Pro past kill
         'The pig is the thing that Sara didn't

         a   Hera.
         prop Sara]
         kill.'

Second, and interestingly, it prevents Clefting from extracting the direct object of a negated clause even if Raising has not applied. This is shown in:

(91) a. *Ko   te wahine kīhai ai i   tuku   te
         Pred the woman not   Pro past release the
         (It is the woman that the man didn't

         tangata.
         man
         release.)

     b. *Ko   te poaka kāhore ai i   patu a   Hera.
         Pred the pig   not   Pro past kill prop Sara
         (It is the pig that Sara didn't kill.)

Sentences like (91) suggest that, in order for the constraint to be stated most generally, negative sentences that have undergone Raising should be treated as similar to negative sentences that have not. Such a suggestion confirms that sentences like (74) and (75) are indeed related by Raising.

On the basis of arguments like these, it can be concluded that (74) and (75) are related by a Raising rule. The rule is stated roughly: 'Raise an NP from the negated clause to become the subject of the negative verb, subject to further conditions (described below)'.

3.3.1.3. **Raising as a Major Rule**. Raising in Maori qualifies as a major rule.

To begin with, it is the counterpart of Subject-to-Subject Raising in English, which has been shown to be cyclic (see Perlmutter and Soames, forthcoming).

It is also bounded: it will raise NPs only from the clause immediately below the negative verb.

Finally, Raising is governed by the negatives listed at the beginning of 3.3.1.1. It is not available for other higher verbs, such as _tika_ 'be right':

(92)a. *Ka tika tātou kia kite i te kāwana.
       uns right we   sbj see Acc the governor
       (It is right that we should see the governor.)

   b. Ka tika kia kite tātou i te kāwana.
      uns right sbj see we   Acc the governor
      'It is right that we should see the governor.'

3.3.1.4. **Restriction to Subjects**. Having shown that Raising is a major rule, we can ask whether it is restricted to any categories of NPs. The answer is that it is available for all and only NPs that are subjects in the negated clause.

Thus, Raising affects intransitive subjects:

(93)a. Kīhai a   Tamahae i   haere.
       not prop Tamahae past go
       'Tamahae didn't go.'

b. E   kore rā te wairua e   haere mai
    nonpast not that the spirit nonpast go   here
    'Spirits don't come back

    ki te whawhai.
    Comp fight
    to fight.' (Orbell 34)

Subjects of canonical transitive clauses:

(94) a. Kāhore a   Hōne i   patu i   te poaka.
         not   prop John past kill Acc the pig
         'John didn't kill the pig.'

     b. Kore rawa te kaiārahi e   whakamārama i
         not Emp the guide   nonpast explain   Acc
         'The guide will never explain that

         taua pakiwaitara.
         that story
         story.' (Waititi 1969: 105)

     c. He mea   tika e   kore ai a   Hemi
         a thing right nonpast not Pro prop Jim
         'It is true that Jim will not

         e   tuku   i   ngā   pirihimana.
         nonpast release Acc the=pl policeman
         release the policemen.'

And subjects of middle clauses:

(95) Kāore anō te nuinga o ngā   tamariki nei
      not   yet the majority of the=pl children this
      'Most of these children hadn't yet

      kia kite i   tētahi tereina.
      sbj see Acc one   train
      seen a train.' (Waititi 1969: 98)

It also affects derived subjects (=underlying direct objects) of passive clauses:

(96) a. Kāhore rāua   kia kite-a   mai e   ngā
         not   they=du sbj see-Pass here Agt the=pl
         'The people inside the house did not

         tāngata o te whare.
         people of the house
         see them.' (Orbell 86)

b. Kaua au e   whakaatu-ria.
    don't I   nonpast point-Pass
    'Do not say that I am here (lit. Don't point me
    out)!' (Orbell 94)

c. E   kore mātou e   tuku-na.
    nonpast not we   nonpast release-Pass
    'We will not be released.'

However, it does not affect transitive direct objects:

(97) a. *Kāhore (i) te poaka i   patu ai a   Hōne.
         not   Acc the pig   past kill Pro prop John
         (John didn't kill the pig.)

     b. *Kīhai (i) a   Pipo i   ngau (ai) te kurī.
         not   Acc prop Pipo past bite Pro the dog
         (The dog didn't bite Pipo.)

Or oblique NPs:

(98) a. *Kāhore (ki) te tāone i   haere (ai) a   Hōne.
         not   to the town past go   Pro prop John
         (John didn't go to town.)

     b. *Kīhai te māhita i   riro (ai) a   Hōne.
         not   the master past taken Pro prop John
         (John wasn't taken away by the master.)

Including agents (=underlying subjects) of passive clauses:

(99)   *Kāhore (e) ngā   tāngata kia kite-a (ai)
         not   Agt the=pl people sbj see-Pass Pro
         (The people didn't see

         rāua.
         they=du
         them.)

The idea that Raising is restricted to subjects receives confirmation from a curious Maori construction involving two unmarked NPs, one of which is the subject of the clause and the other of which is not. This construction is an elaboration of the clause type illustrated in (100), which has a stative verb as predicate (see 1.3.5):

(100)   Ka pau   te parāoa i   te kiore.
        uns exhausted the bread Caus the rat
        'The bread was consumed because of the rat.'

In (100), te parāoa 'the bread' is the surface subject of pau 'be exhausted', as shown, for instance, by its ability to relativize via the deletion strategy (see 2.2.1.2).

Optionally, stative clauses of this type may include a derived nominal which describes the action resulting in the state described by the verb. Consider:

(101)a. Ka pau   te parāoa i   te kiore te kai.
        uns exhausted the bread Caus the rat the eat
        'The bread was eaten up by the rat (lit. The bread was consumed by the rat through eating).'

    b. Ka mutu te tangata rā   rāua   ko te
        uns done the man   that they=du Pred the
        'When the man and the woman had finished

        wahine te   tangi.
        woman the weep
        weeping...' (Orbell 24)

The derivation of these constructions raises some interesting questions, which do not concern us here. (For instance, it is conceivable that the surface subjects of (101) originate as possessors of the derived nominal, as in 'the eating of the bread' or 'the weeping of the man and the woman', and then acquire subjecthood via a Raising rule. See Perlmutter (forthcoming).) What is of immediate interest is that the derived nominals of (101), though in the unmarked case, are not surface subjects. And, consistent with the restriction formulated above, Raising cannot affect them:

(102)a. *Kāhore te kai i   pau   te parāoa i
        not   the eat past exhausted the bread Caus
        (The bread was not eaten up by

        te kiore.
        the rat
        the rat.)

b. *Kāhore te kai i pau i te kiore
   not the eat past exhausted Caus the rat
   (The bread was not eaten up by

   te parāoa.
   the bread
   the rat.)

Compare (103), in which Raising has applied to the surface subject:

(103)   Kāhore te parāoa i pau i te kiore
        not the bread past exhausted Caus the rat
        'The bread was not eaten up by

        te kai.
        the eat
        the rat.'

The contrast of (102) and (103) argues that Raising does not extend to all unmarked NPs; it is evidently restricted instead to just those unmarked NPs that are subjects when it applies. Raising therefore refers to the category subject. Of course, since Maori is an accusative language and its case marking rules pick out subjects, this fact is consistent either with the integrated or with the independent position.

3.3.2. Tongan

Raising in Tongan, an ergative language, argues against the integrated position and in favor of the independent position.

3.3.2.1. Basic Description.

Raising in Tongan relates sentences like (104) and (105):

(104)   'E lava 'a e pēpē 'o lea.
        uns can Abs the baby Comp talk
        'The baby can talk.'

(105)   'E lava ke lea 'a e pēpē.
        uns can sbj talk Abs the baby
        'The baby can talk.'

146   Case Marking and Grammatical Relations

This rule operates in two-clause structures involving the higher verb lava 'be possible, be able, manage', a modal with root and epistemic meanings. Clauses embedded under lava are sentential subjects introduced by the subjunctive tense-aspect-mood particle ke:

(106)a. 'E lava ke tonu eni?
       uns can sbj right this
       'Can this be right?'

   b. Na'e puke lahi 'a e ki'i tamasi'í, ka na'e
      past sick very Abs the small child   but past
      'The child was very sick, but

      lava pē ke ne 'alu.
      can Emp sbj he go
      he could walk.'

Raising takes an NP from the embedded clause and raises it to become the derived subject of lava, subject to conditions to be spelled out below. When this happens, the subjunctive particle is replaced by the complementizer 'o:

(107)a. Tahá 'e lava ia 'o kaka.
       not uns can he Comp climb
       'It isn't as if he could climb.' (C.M. Churchward 1953: 289)

   b. Na'e puke lahi 'a e ki'i tamasi'í, ka na'a
      past sick very Abs the small child   but past
      'The child was very sick, but

      ne lava pē 'o 'alu.
      he can Emp Comp go
      he could walk.'

Despite some variation in usage, it appears that ke must be replaced by 'o once Raising has applied:[7]

(108)a. 'Oku lava 'e he tangata ko 'ená 'o langa
       prog can Erg the man   Pred that Comp build
       'That man can build

       'a e fale lelei.
       Abs the house good
       good houses.'

147 Case Marking and Grammatical Relations

    b. *'Oku lava 'e he tangata ko 'ená ke langa
        prog can Erg the man Pred that sbj build
       (That man can build

       'a   e   fale lelei.
       Abs the house good
       good houses.)

And it is not replaced by 'o otherwise:

    (109)a. ?'E lava 'o   u 'alu?
           uns can Comp I go
           'Can I go?'

       b. 'E lava ke u 'alu?
          uns can sbj I go
          'Can I go?'

The 'o complementizer can thus be regarded as a morphological consequence of Raising, rather like the infinitival morphology resulting from Raising in more familiar languages (e.g. English). Recall that the complementizer also appears in structures eligible for Equi (see 3.2.2.1).

In order to establish that Raising operates as just described, we must show that the raised NP originated in the embedded clause but now acts as the surface subject of the clause containing lava. The arguments supporting this include the following.

(a) The raised NP originates in the embedded clause, since it triggers Verb Agreement there.

Tongan has a Verb Agreement rule, governed by a small class of intransitive verbs, that optionally marks them as agreeing in number with their subjects. The agreement is morphologically suppletive: for instance, 'alu 'go' has the dual/plural form ō, and ha'u 'come', the dual/plural form omi:

    (110)a. Te mau ō   atu 'apō 'i he hongofulu.
          uns we go=pl away tonight at the ten
          'We are coming tonight at ten.'

b. Te mau 'alu atu 'apō 'i he hongofulu.
   uns we go away tonight at the ten
   'We are coming tonight at ten.'

Agreement is triggered only by subjects which are clausemates of the verb in question. Compare (110) with (111), in which the potential trigger is a nonsubject:

(111) a. *'E omi ia ki-ate kimautolu 'apongipongi.
       uns come=pl he to-pro us tomorrow
       (He is coming to us tomorrow.)

   b. 'E ha'u ia ki-ate kimautolu 'apongipongi.
      uns come he to-pro us tomorrow
      'He is coming to us tomorrow.'

And with (112), in which the potential trigger is a subject but not in the same clause as the agreeing verb:

(112) a. *'Oku mau loto ke omi (ia) 'apongipongi.
       prog we want sbj come=pl he tomorrow
       (We want him to come tomorrow.)

   b. 'Oku mau loto ke ha'u (ia) 'apongipongi.
      prog we want sbj come he tomorrow
      'We want him to come tomorrow.'

Now in Raising sentences, the raised NP can trigger Agreement in the embedded clause, even though it occurs in the higher clause on the surface:

(113) a. Te nau lava 'o omi 'apongipongi?
       uns they can Comp come=pl tomorrow
       'Can they come tomorrow?'

   b. Te nau lava 'o ha'u 'apongipongi?
      uns they can Comp come tomorrow
      'Can they come tomorrow?'

Its ability to serve as trigger argues that it is the subject of the embedded clause at some previous level of derivation. For our purposes, this amounts to saying that it originates in the embedded clause.

(b) The raised NP acts as the subject of the clause containing <u>lava</u>, since it can undergo several clause-bounded rules there which are restricted to subjects (or subjects and direct objects).

For instance, Quantifier Float, described below in 3.4.4, is a clause-bounded rule triggered only by subjects and direct objects. This rule can be triggered by the raised NP in the higher clause:

(114)   'Oku lava kotoa 'e hoku ngaahi kaume'a 'o
        prog can all   Erg my   pl   friend Comp
        'My friends all can cook

        haka 'a e   me'akai faka-Siaina.
        cook Abs the food   Chinese
        Chinese food.'

Clitic Placement is a clause-bounded rule that is required for most pronominal subjects and not allowed otherwise (see 1.4.2.1). This rule regularly affects the raised NP in the higher clause if it is pronominal:

(115)a. Te ke lava pē koe 'o   hola mama'o.
        uns you can Emp you Comp run far
        'You can run away by yourself.'

     b. Te mou   lava 'o   kaukau momoko?
        uns you=pl can Comp bathe cold
        'Will you be able to take cold baths?' (Shumway
        1971: 309)

Finally, Possessor Marking is a rule that assigns the <u>'a</u> form of the possessive to subjects of nominalized verbs but to no other associated NPs. This rule regularly affects the raised NP if the higher verb (i.e. <u>lava</u>) has been nominalized:

(116)   Na'a nau fiefia 'i   ho'o lava 'o   fakahā
        past they happy Caus your can Comp show
        'They appreciated your being able to tell them

        vave ange ki-ate kinautolu.
        fast away to-pro them
        so quickly.' (<u>ho'o</u> is an <u>'a</u> possessive pronoun)

The ability of the raised NP to undergo all of these rules confirms that it is indeed the subject of the higher clause.

(c) Finally, the raised NP does not originate in the higher clause and later trigger deletion of a coreferential target in the embedded clause; rather, it originates in the embedded clause and is then raised. This point is made most forcefully by case marking.

As described in 2.1.3, Tongan has a case system which assigns different case marking to subjects depending on transitivity. Intransitive subjects appear in the absolutive; canonical transitive subjects, in the ergative:

(117) a. Na'e 'alu 'a Mele.
past go Abs Mary
'Mary went.'

b. Na'e taa'i 'e Mele 'a Sione.
past hit Erg Mary Abs John
'Mary hit John.'

Assignment of these cases is determined by the transitivity of the clause to which the subject is attached. Thus in complex structures like (118), which have undergone Equi, the case marking of the higher subject (i.e. the controller) is determined by the transitivity of the higher clause, not by the clause containing the deleted target:

(118) a. Pea na'e 'alu 'a e tangatá 'o folau mama'o.
and past go Abs the man Comp sail far
'Then the man went and sailed away.'

b. Na'e 'alu 'a e kau sōtia 'o maumau'i
past go Abs the pl soldier Comp destroy
'The soldiers went and destroyed

'a e vaka.
Abs the ship
the ship.'

However, in Raising sentences, the case marking of the

151 Case Marking and Grammatical Relations

raised NP is determined by the transitivity of the <u>embedded</u> clause rather than the clause in which it actually surfaces. If the embedded clause is intransitive, the raised NP is absolutive:

(119) a. Te   ke toe   lava koe 'o   ki'i kai?
          uns   you again can   you Comp small eat
          'Can <u>you</u> eat just a little more?'

     b. *Te   ke toe   lava 'e   koe 'o   ki'i kai?
          uns you again can   Erg you Comp small eat
          (Can <u>you</u> eat just a little more?)

If the embedded clause is canonical transitive, the raised NP is ergative:

(120) a. Te   ke lava 'e   koe 'o   lau   'eku mata'itohi?
          uns you can   Erg you Comp read my   handwriting
          'Can <u>you</u> read my handwriting?'

     b. 'Oku lava 'e he tangata ko   'ená 'o   langa
          prog can Erg the man   Pred that Comp build
          'That man can build

          'a   e   fale lelei.
          Abs the house good
          good houses.'

(121) a. *Te   ke lava koe 'o   lau   'eku mata'itohi?
          uns you can you Comp read my   handwriting
          (Can <u>you</u> read my handwriting?)

     b. *'Oku lava 'a   e   tangata ko   'ená 'o   langa
          prog can Abs the man   Pred that Comp build
          (That man can build

          'a   e   fale lelei.
          Abs the house good
          good houses.)

Further confirmation that the case marking of the raised NP is governed by the embedded clause comes from sentence types in which transitivity has been altered. For instance, Tongan has an Incorporation rule that strips a nonspecific direct object of its article and incorporates it into the verb, thereby detransitivizing the clause. Subjects of clauses detransitivized by Incorporation occur in the absolutive:

(122) a. Na'e haka-ika 'a e sianá.
past cook-fish Abs the man
'The man cooked fish.'

b. *Na'e haka-ika 'e he sianá.
past cook-fish Erg the man
(The man cooked fish.)

Compare (123), in which Incorporation has not applied and the subject is ergative:

(123) Na'e haka 'e he sianá 'a e ika.
past cook Erg the man Abs the fish
'The man cooked a fish.'

Now when Incorporation has applied in the embedded clause of a Raising structure, the raised NP occurs in the absolutive, as well. Consider:

(124) a. Te ke lava koe 'o haka-ika?
uns you can you Comp cook-fish
'Can <u>you</u> cook fish?'

b. ??Te ke lava 'e koe 'o haka-ika?
uns you can Erg you Comp cook-fish
(Can <u>you</u> cook fish?)

These facts suggest that case marking is sensitive to derived transitivity, and also to the clause membership of a subject at some point before surface structure. At the same time, they argue that the raised NP does not originate in the higher clause. Recall that in Equi structures, the case marking of the controller is not determined by the transitivity of the embedded clause. Since the case marking of the raised NP <u>is</u> determined by the embedded clause, it follows that Raising structures are not derived by coreferential deletion.

The raised NP instead originates in the embedded clause, and is only later turned into the subject of the higher clause by Raising.

Arguments of these sorts establish that sentences like (104) and (105) are related by a Raising rule, of the form: 'Raise an NP from the embedded clause to become the subject of lava, and insert 'o, subject to further conditions (to be described below)'.

3.3.2.2. <u>Raising</u> as a <u>Major Rule</u>. As might be expected, Raising meets all of the conditions for a major rule.

It is the counterpart of Subject-to-Subject Raising in English, a cyclic rule.

It is also bounded: it cannot raise an NP from an embedded clause to the clause containing <u>lava</u> if another embedded clause intervenes:

    (125)   *Na'a ne lava pē 'o hā kuo ongosia.
               past he can Emp Comp appear prf tired
               (He managed to appear tired.)

Compare:

    (126)   Na'e hā mai kuo ne ongosia.
               past appear here prf he tired
               'It appeared that he was tired.'

Finally, Raising is governed by a single verb, <u>lava</u>, and is not triggered by other modal, negative, or aspectual verbs:

    (127)a. *Pea kamata 'a e kakai 'o kaikaila.
               and begin Abs the people Comp shout
               (Then the people began to shout.)

        b. Pea kamata ke kaikaila 'a e kakai.
           and begin sbj shout Abs the people
           'Then the people began to shout.'

It should be noted that <u>lava</u> governs Raising in both its

154 Case Marking and Grammatical Relations

epistemic ('be possible') and root ('be able, manage') senses, with the root sense triggering the rule more frequently. Lava thus poses a problem for the generative semantics position that claims that epistemic modals govern Raising, but root modals govern Equi (Ross 1969). See Pullum and Wilson (1977) for observations suggesting that the syntax of English modals is inadequately handled by such a position, as well.

3.3.2.3. <u>Restriction to Subjects</u>. Given that Raising is a major rule, it is significant that it affects only certain subtypes of NPs: it restricted to NPs that are subjects of the embedded clause.

Raising promotes the subjects of intransitive clauses:

(128)a. Tahá 'e lava ia 'o   kaka.
         not uns can he Comp climb
         'It isn't as if he could climb.' (C.M. Churchward 1953: 289)

     b. Ko   e   'uhinga kehe   ne   'ikai lava ai
         Pred the reason different past not   can Pro
         'However, sleep eluded him for different

         ia 'o   mohe.
         he Comp sleep
         reasons (lit. There were different reasons why
         he couldn't sleep).' (Fanua 88)

It also promotes the subjects of canonical transitive clauses:

(129)a. 'Oku ou lava 'o   ongo'i 'a e   tāme'a mei
         prog I can Comp hear   Abs the music from
         'I can hear the music (coming) from

         he fale ko   ē.
         the house Pred that
         that house.'

     b. 'E lava 'e he māhiná 'o   tamate'i 'a e
         uns can Erg the moon   Comp shut   Abs the
         'Is it possible for the moon to block out

155 Case Marking and Grammatical Relations

      la'á?
      sun
      the sun?'

  c. Te nau lava 'o fakatau 'a e falé, kapau
    uns they can Comp sell Abs the house if
    'They could sell the house, if

    te nau fiema'u.
    uns they want
    they want to.'

And the subjects of middle clauses:

 (130) 'Oku ke lava 'o sio ki ha me'a?
    prog you can Comp see to a thing
    'Can you see anything?'

But it does not apply to absolutive direct objects:[8]

 (131)a. *Na'e lava 'a e fefiné 'o taa'i 'e Sione.
     past can Abs the woman Comp hit Erg John
     (The woman could be hit by John.)

   b. *'E lava 'a e falé 'o nau fakatau, kapau
     uns can Abs the house Comp they sell if
     (They could sell the house, if

    te nau fiema'u.
    uns they want
    they want to.)

Direct objects of middle clauses:

 (132) *Te ke lava 'o nau 'eva mai he Sāpate?
    uns you can Comp they visit here the Sunday
    (Can they visit you on Sunday?)

Or oblique NPs:

 (133)a. *Na'a ne lava 'o mahino 'a e fekau
     past he can Comp clear Abs the message
     (He could understand the secret message

    fakapulipuli.
    secret
    (lit. The secret message could be clear to
    him).)

b. *Te   mau lava pē 'o   ngalo   ia.
   uns we can Emp Comp forgotten it
   (It could be forgotten by us/because of us.)

Since Raising is restricted to subjects, regardless of their case marking, its structural description must mention the category subject. The point is made particularly clearly by the contrast in case marking of the raised NPs of (128) and (129b). Raising thus strengthens the case against the integrated position, according to which rules in ergative languages could pick out absolutives or ergatives but should not mention categories like subject at all. At the same time, of course, it lends support to the independent position, which claims that subject and direct object are central to the syntax of all Polynesian languages.

3.3.3. Samoan

The last Raising rule to be discussed in this section is a Raising rule in Samoan, which also supports the independent position over the integrated position.

3.3.3.1. Basic Description. Samoan Raising is a copying rule which relates sentences like (134) and (135):

(134)   'Ou te mafai 'ona 'ou alu taeao.
        I   uns can   Comp I   go tomorrow
        'I can go tomorrow.'

(135)   E   mafai 'ona 'ou alu taeao.
        uns can   Comp I   go tomorrow
        'I can go tomorrow.'

This rule applies in certain two-clause structures containing the higher modal verbs mafai 'be able' or tatau 'be necessary', the higher aspectual verb 'āmata 'begin', or the higher manner verb fa'apea 'be (done) thus'. Clauses embedded under these verbs are sentential subjects introduced by the complementizer 'ona:

(136) a. E   mafai 'ona tātou nonofo.
          uns can   Comp we   stay=pl
          'We can stay.'

     b. Sā   tatau 'ona alu 'oia.
         past must Comp go he
         'He had to go.'

Essentially, Raising takes an NP from the embedded clause and turns it into the derived subject of the higher clause, at the same time leaving a pronominal copy of it in its original clause. If the raised NP is emphatic, the copy will surface either as a clitic in the embedded clause:

(137)   Pe 'e te mafai 'ona 'e tautala i   le gagana
         Q you uns can   Comp you speak   in the lg
         'Can you speak (in)

         Sāmoa?
         Samoan
         Samoan?'

Or as a full pronoun, in which case it has the sense of an emphatic reflexive:

(138)   E   mafai e   Ioane 'ona fai e   ia le kuka.
         uns can   Erg John Comp do Erg he the cook
         'John can do the cooking by himself.'

Otherwise it is routinely deleted by zero-pronominalization, as in:

(139) a. 'Ou te mafai 'ona alu taeao.
         I   uns can   Comp go tomorrow
         'I can go tomorrow.'

     b. Sā   tatau 'oia 'ona alu.
         past must he   Comp go
         'He had to go.'

Since sentences in which the copy has been deleted by zero-pronominalization are more frequent than sentences in which it has not, they make up the majority of examples in this subsection.

We now establish that Raising indeed operates as just described. As in previous subsections, this is done by arguing that the raised NP originates in the embedded clause, but is now the subject of the higher clause, to which it is attached in surface structure.

(a) The raised NP originates in the embedded clause, since it triggers several rules there that are clause-bounded.

For instance, Samoan has a Verb Agreement rule, governed by a class of intransitive verbs, which marks them as agreeing in number with their subjects. Agreement results in partial reduplication of verbs with dual or plural subjects; it is obligatory for most speakers, clause-bounded, and triggered only by subjects. The rule is regularly triggered in the embedded clause by the raised NP:

(140)   E   mafai e   tātou 'ona nonofo.
        uns can   Erg we   Comp stay=pl
        'We can stay.'

Samoan also has a rule of Quantifier Float, briefly mentioned in 3.4.4.4, which is clause-bounded. This rule can also be triggered within the embedded clause by the raised NP:

(141)   Sā   lātou 'āmata 'ona ōmai   'uma lava.
        past   they begin Comp come=pl all Emp
        'They began to all arrive.'

The ability of the raised NP to trigger both of these rules argues that it once occurred in the embedded clause, even though it no longer appears there in surface structure. This amounts to saying that it originates in the embedded clause, as will be shown further below.

159   Case Marking and Grammatical Relations

(b) The raised NP is the subject of the higher clause, since it undergoes rules there that are clause-bounded or restricted to subjects.

Thus, the raised NP can undergo Quantifier Float, a clause-bounded rule, in the higher clause:

(142) a. E   mafai 'uma lava e   'i lātou 'ona tautala
          uns can   all Emp Erg pl they Comp speak
          'They all can speak

          fa'a-Toga.
          Tongan
          Tongan.'

       b. 'Ua 'āmata 'uma e   lātou 'ona fa'aleaga le
          prf begin all Erg they Comp destroy the
          'They all began to tear down the

          fale.
          house
          building.'

It is also eligible for Clitic Placement, a clause-bounded rule which is restricted to pronominal subjects (see 1.4.2.2):

(143) a. Tātou te mafai 'ona nonofo.
          we   uns can   Comp stay=pl
          'We can stay.'

       b. 'Ua ia 'āmata 'ona a'oa'o-ina le tā-ina
          prf he begin Comp learn-Trans the play-Trans
          'He began to learn how to play

          o le organi.
          of the organ
          the organ.'

The raised NP can undergo Pronoun Preposing if the higher verb of the Raising structure has been nominalized. This rule, the nominal analogue of Clitic Placement, is restricted to pronominal subjects (see Chung 1973a):

(144)   'Ou te fefe   'ona   'o lo lātou mafai 'ona
          I   uns afraid because Pred their   can   Comp
          'I was afraid because of their being able to

         tautala fa'a-Toga.
         speak   Tongan
         speak Tongan.'

Finally, the case marking of the raised NP is often determined idiosyncratically by the higher verb. For instance, although Raising sentences involving <u>mafai</u> 'be able' and <u>tatau</u> 'be necessary' have identical derived structures, raised NPs associated with <u>mafai</u> always select ergative case marking, while those associated with <u>tatau</u> typically select the absolutive. Consider:

(145) a. E   mafai e   tātou 'ona nonofo.
          uns can   Erg   we   Comp stay=pl
          'We can stay.'

     b.   Pe-e   mafai e   se tasi 'ona ta'u mai le
          Q-uns can   Erg   a one Comp tell here the
          'Can anyone tell me the

          tali?
          answer
          answer?'

(146) a. E   tatau 'oia 'ona alu.
          uns must he   Comp go
          'He must go.'

     b.   E   tatau 'oia 'ona 'ave le tusi.
          uns must he   Comp take the letter
          'He must deliver the letter.'

(An alternative pattern of case assignment for raised NPs associated with <u>tatau</u> is described below.)

The contrast in case marking between (145) and (146) suggests that the case of the raised NP is lexically governed by one --or perhaps both-- of these higher verbs. Case assignment is, of course, a clause-internal phenomenon. Therefore, the ability of the raised NPs to have their case marking lexically governed by the higher verb argues that they are indeed members of the higher clause.

161 Case Marking and Grammatical Relations

In summary, the interaction of the raised NP with Quantifier Float and case marking argues that it occurs in the higher clause; its ability to undergo Clitic Placement and Pronoun Preposing argues that it is a higher clause subject.

(c) We have now only to reject the possibility that the raised NP originates in the higher clause and then triggers deletion of a coreferential target in the embedded clause. The idea that this NP instead starts out in the embedded clause and undergoes Raising is supported by the following.

First, Raising sentences --like their counterparts (136)-- exhibit the complementizer 'ona.

The complementizer 'ona introduces all embedded clauses that function as sentential subjects. Consider the following, in which 'ona occurs in the sentential subjects of several different higher verbs:

(147) a. E   sa   fo'i ona fai ni   upu vale.
          uns forbidden also Comp say some=pl word bad
          'It is also forbidden to use bad language.'
          (Stuebel 184)

     b.   E   seāseā 'ona 'ou fa'alogo.
          uns seldom Comp I   hear
          'It's seldom that I hear (that).'

     c.   E   faigofie 'i-āte a'u 'ona fai mea   sesē.
          uns easy   to-pro me Comp do thing wrong
          'It's easy for me to make mistakes.'

     d.   E   lelei ona ta   sosola.
          uns good Comp we=du run=pl
          'It is better that we run away.' (Stuebel 235)

'Ona is also restricted to sentential subjects; it does not occur in other embedded clauses, whether sentential objects or adverbial clauses:

(148) a. *Fai mai 'ona mamao tele le falema'i.
           say here Comp far   very the hospital
           ((They) said that the hospital is too far away.)

162   Case Marking and Grammatical Relations

  b. *Sā   alu 'oia 'ona 'aumai lona tinā.
    past go he   Comp bring his mother
    (He went to pick up his mother.)

 (149)a. Fai mai e   mamao tele le falema'i.
    say here uns far   very the hospital
    '(They) said that the hospital is too far away.'

  b. Sā   alu 'oia e   'aumai lona tinā.
    past go he uns bring his mother
    'He went to pick up his mother.'

This is true even when Equi has applied, as in:

 (150)a. *E   mana'o 'oia 'ona fa'afo'i tusi.
    uns want   he   Comp return   book
    (He wants to return the books.)

  b. E   mana'o 'oia e   fa'afo'i tusi.
    uns want   he uns return   book
    'He wants to return the books.'

Given this, the appearance of 'ona in Raising sentences argues that the embedded clause must have served as the sentential subject of the higher verb. Since the raised NP is now the subject, it follows that it did not always hold this function: it did not originate as the subject of the higher clause.

 Second, the raised NP in Raising sentences can trigger -Cia Insertion in the embedded clause.

 As described in 2.2.2.2, -Cia Insertion inserts the transitive suffix -Cia as a flag for certain types of missing subjects. In particular, it attaches the suffix to canonical transitive verbs whose subjects have undergone Clitic Placement:

 (151)a. 'Ou te tā-ina   le piano.
    I   uns play-Trans the piano
    'I play the piano.'

  b. Pe sā   'e faitau-ina le tusi?
    Q past you read-Trans the book
    'Did you read the book?'

The rule is triggered by cliticized subjects only when they have actually served as the subject of the verb in question. In (152), for instance, Equi has deleted a target in the embedded clause and its controller has undergone Clitic Placement in the higher clause. But since the controller has never served as the subject of the embedded clause, -<u>Cia</u> Insertion does not affect a canonical transitive verb in the embedded clause:

(152) a. 'Ou te mana'o e faitau le tusi.
       I   uns want   uns read the book
       'I want to read the book.'

   b. 'Aiseā le mea 'ua 'e mana'o ai e a'oa'o
      why? the reason prf you want   Pro uns learn
      'Why do you want to learn

      le gagana Sāmoa?
      the lg   Samoan
      the Samoan language?'

(The rule does not affect the higher verb in these examples because it is middle rather than canonical transitive.)

Now when the raised NP of a Raising structure has undergone Clitic Placement in the higher clause, -<u>Cia</u> Insertion applies to an embedded canonical transitive verb:

(153) a. Pe 'e te mafai 'ona tā-ina   le piano?
         Q you uns can Comp play-Trans the piano
         'Can you play the piano?'

   b. Tātou te fa'apea 'ona fai-a.
      we   uns thus   Comp do-Trans
      'We're going to do (it) like this.'

Sentences like (153) argue that -<u>Cia</u> Insertion can distinguish true controllers of Equi from raised NPs, and so Raising sentences are not derived by application of Equi. Further, the fact that the rule is triggered in the <u>embedded</u> clause by the raised NP argues that this NP once served as the subject of

164   Case Marking and Grammatical Relations

the embedded verb. That is, it originated in the embedded
clause and was only later promoted to the higher clause by
Raising.

Third, in Raising structures involving particular higher
verbs, the case marking of the raised NP can optionally be determined by its function in the embedded clause.

Like Tongan, Samoan has a case system which assigns different case marking to subjects depending on the transitivity of
the clause to which they are attached. Intransitive subjects
are unmarked; canonical transitive subjects are marked with
the ergative marker e:

(154) a. Sā   sola 'oia 'i le fale.
        past run he   to the house
        'He ran to the house.'

     b. E   iloa 'uma e   ia tali.
        uns know all Erg he answer
        'He knows all the answers.'

It is a trivial matter to show that the case marking of a subject is determined by the transitivity of its own clause, and
not any other clause. See the Equi sentences of 3.2.3 for
relevant examples.

Now in Raising structures, the case marking of the raised
NP is typically governed by the higher verb, in the manner
described above. But for structures involving some higher
verbs (e.g. tatau 'be necessary' and 'āmata 'begin', but not
mafai 'be able'), the case marking of this NP is not always
lexically governed, but can optionally be determined by the
transitivity of the embedded clause. Contrast examples (145)
and (146) above with the following:

(155) a. E   tatau 'oia 'ona alu.
        uns must he   Comp go
        'He must go.'

b. ??E   tatau e   ia 'ona alu.
      uns must Erg he Comp go
      (He must go.)

   c. E   tatau e   ia 'ona 'ave le tusi.
      uns must Erg he Comp take the letter
      'He must deliver the letter.'

Given that case marking is a clause-internal phenomenon, sentences like these argue that the raised NP must have once served as subject of the embedded clause, and only later been promoted to the higher clause. Only in this way can the role of the embedded clause in determining its case marking be accounted for satisfactorily.

Although case assignment of the type (155) appears not to be as frequent as the type (146), its existence is elegantly confirmed by nineteenth century texts. In these, raised NPs associated with __mafai__ 'be able' have their case marking governed by the transitivity of the embedded clause, as in:

   (156)a. Auā   ua le mafai le vaa   ona alu.
           because prf not can   the canoe Comp go
           '...since the boat could not move forward.'
           (Stuebel 168)

   b. E   mafai lava e   teine ma fafine ona si'a
      uns can   Emp Erg girl and woman Comp light
      'Girls and women can make their

      ai o   a latou afi.
      Pro Pred pl=their fire
      fires with it.' (Stuebel 166)

This contrasts with contemporary Samoan, in which such NPs are invariably in the ergative, their case marking being governed by __mafai__ instead. The contrast suggests that the case marking of raised NPs may well be changing from being determined by the embedded clause to being determined (idiosyncratically) by the higher verb.

In short, the facts of the __'ona__ complementizer, -__Cia__ Inser-

166 Case Marking and Grammatical Relations

tion, and case marking argue that the raised NP does not originate in the higher clause and then trigger Equi in the embedded clause. Rather, it originates in the embedded clause and is then turned into the subject of the higher clause by Raising. This rule has roughly the form: 'Raise an NP from the embedded clause to become the subject of the higher clause and leave behind a pronominal copy, subject to further conditions (described below)'.

3.3.3.2. <u>Raising as a Major Rule</u>. Samoan Raising has all of the properties of a major rule.

It corresponds to Raising in English, a cyclic rule.

It is also bounded: it cannot raise an NP across an intervening embedded clause to become the subject of the higher verb:

(157)a. *'Ua 'e fa'apea 'ona lelei tele 'ona fai-(a).
 prf you thus Comp good very Comp do-Trans
 (You are doing it better like it is.)

b. 'Ua fa'apea 'ona lelei tele 'ona 'e fai-a.
 prf thus Comp good very Comp you do-Trans
 'You are doing it better like it is (lit. It is like this that it is better that you are doing it).'

Finally, Raising is governed by a small class of modal, aspectual, and manner verbs whose membership exhibits some variation across speakers. The class includes <u>mafai</u> 'be able' and --for many speakers-- <u>tatau</u> 'be necessary', <u>'āmata</u> 'begin', and <u>fa'apea</u> 'be (done) thus', as well. <u>Taumafai</u> 'try' is also included in this class for a few speakers, although it is treated as governing Equi by others (see 3.2.3.2). All of these verbs trigger Raising optionally; in general, other higher verbs do not trigger it at all. Consider, for example:

(158) a. *E   lelei 'oia 'ona alu 'ese.
        uns good he   Comp go away
        (It is good for him to go away.)

     b. E   lelei 'ona alu 'ese 'oia.
         uns good Comp go away he
         'It is good for him to go away.'

3.3.3.3. Restriction to Subjects.

We now turn to Raising's major point of interest for this discussion; it is restricted to NPs that are subjects of the embedded clause.

Thus, the rule affects intransitive subjects:

(159) a. 'Ou te lē mafai 'ona tautala i le gagana
         I   uns not can   Comp talk   in the lg
         'I can't speak (in)

         Sāmoa.
         Samoan
         Samoan.'

     b. Sā lātou 'āmata 'ona ōmai   'uma lava.
         past they begin Comp come=pl all Emp
         'They began to all arrive.'

As well as subjects of canonical transitive clauses:

(160) a. E   lē mafai e   le falemeli   'ona meli
         uns not can Erg the postoffice Comp mail
         'The postoffice cannot deliver

         se tusi   pe'ā leai se stamp.
         a letter when not a stamp
         letters without stamps.'

     b. Sā   'āmata lava e   le tama'ita'i 'ona fafaga
         past begin Emp Erg the lady   Comp feed
         'The lady began to feed

         le tagata ma'i.
         the man   sick
         the sick man.'

     c. Sā   fa'apea e   ia 'ona fai-a   le fale.
         past thus   Erg he Comp do-Trans the house
         'He built the house like this.'

168   Case Marking and Grammatical Relations

       d. E   mafai e   le tama 'ona maua le tali.
           uns can   Erg the boy Comp catch the answer
           'The boy can come up with the answer.'

And subjects of middle clauses:

   (161)   E   tatau 'oia 'ona asiasi 'i ona   mātua.
          uns must he   Comp visit to pl=his parents
          'He has to visit his parents.'

But it does not affect absolutive direct objects:

   (162)a. *Sā   'āmata (e) le tagata ma'i 'ona fafaga
        past begin   Erg the man   sick Comp feed
        (The lady began to feed

        e   le tama'ita'i.
        Erg the lady
        the sick man.)

     b. *E   mafai (e) le tali   'ona maua e   le
        uns can   Erg the answer Comp catch Erg the
        (The boy can come up with the

        tama.
        boy
        answer.)

Direct objects of middle clauses:

   (163)a. *E   lē mafai e   tātou 'ona lātou mulimuli mai
        uns not can Erg we   Comp they follow   here
        (They can't follow us

        ai.
        Pro
        here.)

     b. *E   mafai e   Māria 'ona fesoasoani 'i ai se
        uns can   Erg Mary Comp help   to Pro a
        (Can anyone help

        isi?
        one
        Mary?)

Or oblique NPs:

   (164)a. *E   mafai e   Ioane 'ona galo   ai lana
        uns can   Erg John Comp forgotten Pro his
        (The book could be forgotten by

tusi.
book
John.)

b. *E   mafai (e)   le   lā'au 'ona 'ou tā-ina   'oe.
   uns can   Erg the stick Comp I   hit-Trans you
   (I can hit you with the stick.)

In order to capture this restriction, the structural description of the rule must mention subject explicitly.

Given that Samoan is an ergative language, the fact that its Raising rule picks out subjects regardless of their case marking argues that the integrated position is incorrect. It simultaneously supports the independent position, which claims that subject is one of two categories prominent in the syntax of Polynesian languages.

3.3.4. Summary

In summary, the Raising rules described above for Maori, Tongan, and Samoan differ in certain details: Maori Raising is governed by negative verbs; Tongan Raising is governed by a single modal verb; Samoan Raising is a copying rule. The three rules are united in that all pick out subjects, regardless of how these are morphologically marked. The fact that they refer to the category subject argues that the independent position is superior to the integrated one.

3.4. DIRECT OBJECT-REFERRING RULES

In addition to Equi and Raising, the three Polynesian languages investigated here have other major rules: Passive (in Maori), Promotion (in Maori), Object Incorporation, and Quantifier Float. This section surveys these rules and argues that they refer to direct object, or else to subject and direct object, where direct object includes direct objects of middle and canonical transitive verbs as well as locatives

170   Case Marking and Grammatical Relations

affected by the action of an underlyingly intransitive verb.
Direct objects do not form a unified category with respect to
case marking in any of the languages, given that direct objects of middle verbs and affected locatives have the case
marking of oblique NPs. Therefore, the fact that these NPs
are routinely picked out by major rules, regardless of their
case marking, argues against the integrated position and in
favor of the independent position.

   Given the number of rules to be covered, this section re-
stricts itself to describing one instance of each. 3.4.1
deals with Passive in Maori; 3.4.2, with Promotion in Maori;
3.4.3, with Object Incorporation in Samoan; and 3.4.4, with
Quantifier Float in Tongan.

3.4.1. **Passive in Maori**
Passive in Maori, an accusative language, supports the independent position as opposed to the integrated position.

3.4.1.1. **Basic Description**. As described in 2.2.1, the Maori
Passive relates sentences like (165) and (166):

   (165)   Ka   inu-mia   te wai   e   te tangata.
            uns drink-Pass the water Agt the man
            'The water is drunk by the man.' (Biggs 1969:
            32)

   (166)   Ka   inu   te tangata i   te wai.
            uns drink the man   Acc the water
            'The man drinks the water.' (Biggs 1969: 32)

This rule promotes a direct object to subject, turns the underlying subject into an oblique noun marked with e, and attaches the passive suffix -Cia to the verb.

   The fact that Passive alters grammatical relations was discussed in 2.2.1, where certain of its other characteristics

were also described. Here it is shown that the rule is a major rule and restricted to NPs that are direct objects.

3.4.1.2. <u>Passive</u> <u>as</u> <u>a</u> <u>Major</u> <u>Rule</u>. The fact that Passive is a major rule is established by the following.

The rule is the counterpart of Passive in English, which is cyclic (see Perlmutter and Soames, forthcoming).

It is also clause-bounded: it cannot take an embedded NP and promote it to subject in a higher clause.

Finally, Passive is governed, in that it is optional for the large majority of transitive verbs but obligatory for <u>roko</u> 'find, come upon' (Williams 1971: 345) and perhaps a few others:

(167)   Roko-hanga noa-tia atu kua tu   ano ki
        find-Pass vain-Pass away prf stand Emp to
        '(He) found to his surprise that (the tree) had

        runga.
        above
        stood up again.' (Grey 47)

It also exhibits other idiosyncracies. For instance, it exceptionally fails to attach the passive suffix to the compound verbs <u>hōmai</u>, <u>hoatu</u>, and <u>hoake</u>, which are formed from the verb stem <u>ho-</u> 'give' plus a directional particle (Biggs 1969: 116):

(168)   Kātahi ka hoatu e Hutu ko   tōna pounamu.
        then   uns give Agt Hutu Pred his greenstone
        'Then Hutu gave (her) his greenstone.' (Orbell
        4)

Despite the absence of passive suffixes in clauses like (168), the evidence indicates that they are passive rather than superficially transitive clauses governing an ergative type of case marking.

Thus, the deletion strategy for Relativization can affect

the underlying direct object of clauses of this type. Given
that the strategy is restricted to subjects (see 2.2.1.2),
this argues that the underlying direct object is a (derived)
subject:

(169)   He kai pērā me ērā   i   hoatu i te
        a food like with those past [give at the
        '(It) was like the food that (he) had given

        tuatahi rā.
        before that]
        (her) before.' (Orbell 74)

Further, the nonspecific article he can qualify the underlying direct object of clauses of this type. Since he occurs
only with subjects of intransitive clauses (see 2.2.1.3), its
ability to qualify the underlying direct object argues that
it is a (derived) intransitive subject:

(170)   Ka hoatu e   ngā   tamariki he ika tunu
        uns give Agt the=pl children a fish roasted
        'The children gave her a roasted

        māhana.
        for=her
        fish.' (Orbell 70)

Finally, Equi appears not to be able to delete either NP
of clauses like (168), consistent with the more general fact
that it does not delete targets in passive clauses (see
3.2.1.3). It can, however, delete the subject of the active
counterparts of such clauses, as shown by (171), in which the
direct object is marked accusative:

(171)   E   pai ranei koe ki te ho mai i   tetahi
        nonpast good Q   you Comp give   Acc one
        'Will you lend me a

        hereni?
        schilling
        schilling?' (Ngata 1953: 34)

The superficially passive character of clauses like (168)
thus seems undeniable.

Case Marking and Grammatical Relations

It can be concluded from all of this that Passive is a major rule.

3.4.1.3. <u>Restriction</u> <u>to</u> <u>Direct</u> <u>Objects</u>. Having shown this, we now ask whether Passive refers to any categories of NPs. The answer, first provided in detail by Mark (1970), is that it is restricted to direct objects.

Passive affects the direct objects of canonical transitive clauses, as amply demonstrated in 2.2.1.

In addition, it affects direct objects of middle clauses, whether marked with <u>i</u> or <u>ki</u> (see 2.1.2):

```
(172)a.  I    kite-a    e  ia ki Te Pukemore.
         past see-Pass Agt him to Te Pukemore
         'He saw (them) on Mt. Pukemore.' (Orbell 30)

     b.  E   mōhio-tia ana  te reo Māori e   te
         uns know-Pass prog the lg  Maori Agt the
         'The Maori language is known by the

         tangata.
         man
         man.' (Mark 1970: 17)

(173)a.  Kua kite atu  ia i   te wai   e   wiki ana.
         prf see  away he Acc the water uns ring prog
         'He saw the water making rings.' (Waititi 1969:
         133)

     b.  E   mōhio ana  te tangata ki te  reo Māori.
         uns know  prog the man    to the lg  Maori
         'The man knows the Maori language.' (Mark 1970:
         17)
```

It also affects locatives which are immediately or physically affected by the action of an underlyingly intransitive verb:

```
(174)a.  Ka  haere-tia te māunga   e   au.
         uns go-Pass   the mountain Agt me
         'The mountain has been walked on by me.' (Mark
         1970: 17)
```

b. Ka haere au i te māunga.
   uns go   I on the mountain
   'I walk on the mountain.' (Mark 1970: 17)

The rule does not, however, affect indirect objects, goals, instruments, or other oblique NPs. Consider (175), in which Passive has applied to a goal:

(175)a. *Ka haere-tia te māunga   e   au.
       uns go-Pass the mountain Agt me
       (The mountain has been gone to by me.) (Mark 1970: 17)

b. Ka haere au ki te māunga.
   uns go   I to the mountain
   'I go to the mountain.' (Mark 1970: 17)

Assuming that the affected locatives of (174) are surface direct objects of their associated, underlyingly intransitive verbs, the facts of (172-75) argue that Passive is restricted to NPs that are direct objects. It therefore refers to the category direct object and supports the independent position. The NPs picked out by the rule do not form a unified category with respect to case marking, since they include NPs marked with the accusative i but only a subset of those marked with the prepositions i 'at' or ki 'to' (i.e. direct objects of middle clauses and affected locatives, but not true oblique NPs). Passive therefore does not support the integrated position, at least not in the clear sense that it does the independent one.

3.4.2. Promotion in Maori

Promotion in Maori also supports the independent position, and may be interpreted as consistent with the integrated position as well.

175   Case Marking and Grammatical Relations

3.4.2.1. Background: Agent-Emphatic Sentences. Maori Promotion applies in structures of the type (176), which are known in the literature as 'agent-emphatic' sentences (see Williams and Williams 1950[1862]; Clark 1976):

(176)a. Ma rātou e   haere te haere.
         of them nonpast go the go
         'It is for them to manage it.' (Biggs 1969: 77)

     b. He tamaiti i   haere ki te tiki-wai, nā
         a child   past go   Comp fetch-water of
         'There was a child who went to fetch water; his

         ngā   mātua   i   tono.
         the=pl parents past send
         parents sent (him).' (Orbell 54)

     c. Ma wai e   haere? Ma Pita e   haere.
         of who? nonpast go   of Peter nonpast go
         'Who will go? Peter will go.' (Biggs 1969: 73)

     d. Kei whea rā   ngā   tāngata nā-na i
         at where? that the=pl people of-him past
         'Now where are the people who made

         tapuwae?
         make=footprint
         these footprints?' (Orbell 80)

Agent-emphatic sentences are two-clause structures in which one clause contains a predicate possessor and the other clause is embedded directly under it, serving as its sentential subject:

(177)
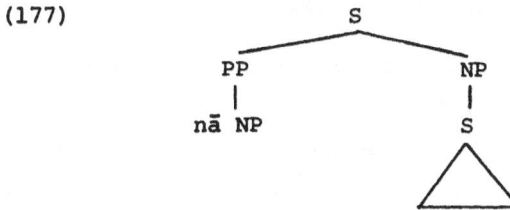

The predicate possessor is marked with the dominant possessive particle <u>a</u> (see 1.3.3), combined with the special tense prefixes m- 'nonpast' or n- 'past'. It corresponds to the subject of the embedded clause, which does not appear in that clause in surface structure.

The fact that agent-emphatic sentences have the biclausal structure of (177) is indicated by the following.

First, the predicate possessor of agent-emphatic sentences acts as a predicate for the purposes of negative selection. Maori has a number of negative verbs (see 3.3.1.1), selection of which is determined by the character of the clause embedded directly under them (i.e. the negated clause). If the clause contains a specific predicate nominal or certain types of predicate PPs, the negative ēhara is selected:[9]

   (178)a. Ēhara nā Pita te pukapuka.
           not   of Peter the book
           'The book isn't Peter's.'

       b. *Kāhore nā Pita te pukapuka.
           not   of Peter the book
           (The book isn't Peter's.)

If the clause contains a verb, several negatives can be selected, of which the most common is kāhore:

   (179)a. Kāhore i   patu-a   te poaka e Hōne.
           not   past hit-Pass the pig Agt John
           'John didn't kill the pig.'

       b. *Ēhara i   patu-a   te poaka e Hōne.
           not   past hit-Pass the pig Agt John
           (John didn't kill the pig.)

Ēhara and kāhore cannot be interchanged, as shown by the ungrammatical (178b) and (179b).

Now when agent-emphatic sentences are negated, the negative for predicate nominals or predicate PPs is selected, not the negative for clauses containing a verb:

   (180)a. Ēhara nā Hōne i   patu te poaka.
           not   of John past hit the pig
           'John didn't kill the pig.'

b. *Kāhore nā Hōne i   patu te   poaka.
   not   of John past hit the pig
   (John didn't kill the pig.)

This argues that agent-emphatic sentences have the predicate possessor as a higher predicate.

Second, the verb of agent-emphatic sentences is introduced by two of the tense-aspect-mood particles for embedded clauses: e 'nonpast' or i 'past' (see 1.2.1). Given that e occurs with nonstative verbs only in embedded clauses (while i occurs indifferently in matrix or embedded clauses), this argues that the verb of this sentence type is embedded.[10]

Facts like these provide the beginnings of a demonstration that agent-emphatic sentences are biclausal, their predicate possessors are higher predicates, and the rest of the sentence forms an embedded clause which serves as their sentential subject. This analysis is adopted in following paragraphs, although nothing crucial hinges on it and several of its details are left vague. For instance, it is unclear whether the predicate possessor of (177) originates as a higher predicate and later triggers deletion of the (coreferential) subject of the embedded clause; or it originates as the subject of the embedded clause and later achieves higher predicate status via an extraction rule.

Agent-emphatic sentences can involve embedded clauses that are underlyingly intransitive, as in (176c) and (176d), but it is more common for them to have embedded clauses that are underlyingly transitive. Structures of the latter type are the ones that undergo the rule referred to here as Promotion.[11]

3.4.2.2. **Basic Description**. Promotion applies to the embedded direct objects of agent-emphatic sentences to produce structures like:

(181) a. Ma rātou e   unahi ngā   ika.
        of them nonpast scale the=pl fish
        'They will scale the fish.' (Biggs 1969: 73)

    b. Nā Hōne i   patu te   poaka.
       of John past hit the pig
       'John killed the pig.'

This rule takes the direct object and turns it into the derived subject of the embedded clause. It appears to have no other morphological or syntactic consequences: no new morphology is attached to the verb, and the absence of the embedded underlying subject is a general feature of agent-emphatic sentences.

In order to establish that Promotion has the effect just described, we must show that it creates a derived subject but is distinct from the Passive rule of 3.4.1. The arguments for this include the following.

(a) The underlying direct object of structures like (181) is the derived subject of the embedded clause, for it has the lack of case marking of a subject. It is also eligible for several subject-referring rules.

Thus, the deletion strategy for Relativization can apply to the underlying direct object:

(182)   Ēhara i te poaka te mea   nā Hoani i   patu.
         not   ? the pig the thing [of John past hit]
         'The thing that John killed wasn't a pig.'

So can the chopping strategy for Clefting, which moves a focused NP to the left and marks it with the predicate particle ko (see 3.3.1.2):

(183)   Ko   te kūaha nā ngā   pirihimana i   pei.
         Pred the door of the=pl policeman past push
         'It is the door that the police pushed in.'

179 Case Marking and Grammatical Relations

Given that these strategies are restricted to subjects (see
2.2.1.2 and Chung 1977b), their ability to affect the underlying direct object argues that it has become a subject.

Further, the nonspecific article he can be attached to the
underlying direct object, as shown by:

(184) a. Nā Hōne i   hanga he whare.
          of John past build a   house
          'John built a house.'

      b. Mā-ku e   kōrero he tikanga.
          of-me nonpast tell   a advice
          'I will tell (you) what you must do (lit. I will
          give (you) a piece of advice).' (Orbell 8)

Since he is found only with intransitive subjects (see
2.2.1.3), its occurrence with the underlying direct object argues that it is the subject of a (derived) intransitive
clause.

Finally, Raising can affect the underlying direct object,
first turning it into the subject of the predicate possessor:

(185) a. Ma rātou ngā   ika e   unahi.
          of them the=pl fish nonpast scale
          'They will scale the fish.' (Biggs 1969: 73)

      b. Nā Hōne te poaka i   patu.
          of John the pig   past hit
          'John killed the pig.'

      c. Nā Hōne he whare i   hanga.
          of John a house past build
          'John built a house.'

And then reapplying to turn it into the subject of a higher
negative verb:

(186) a. Ēhara tēnei wahine nā Hōne i   patu.
          not   this woman of John past hit
          'This woman wasn't killed by John.'

      b. Ēhara rāua   nā te pirihimana i   wero.
          not   they=du of the policeman past stab
          'They weren't stabbed by the policeman.'

Although the issue of whether Raising figures in sentences like (185) is open to question, it has clearly affected the underlying direct object of negative sentences like (186). Since the rule is restricted to subjects, sentences like (186) offer further evidence that the underlying direct object has become a subject.

In short, Promotion turns the direct object of an agent-emphatic sentence into a derived subject.

(b) The effect of Promotion is similar to that of Passive in that both are subject-creating rules. However, some evidence suggests that the two should be considered distinct.

Passive triggers insertion of the passive suffix on the verb, but Promotion does not. So the following are ungrammatical:

(187) a. *Nā Hōne i   patu-a   te poaka.
          of John past hit-Pass the pig
          (John killed the pig.)

      b. *Nā ngā   pirihimana i   pei-a   te kūaha.
          of the=pl policeman past push-Pass the door
          (The police pushed in the door.)

Passive is also optional for the large majority of verbs which govern it (see 3.4.1.2). Promotion is generally obligatory, however:

(188)   *Nā Hōne i   patu i   te poaka.
          of John past hit Acc the pig
          (John killed the pig.)

The rule appears to be optional only when the embedded direct object is reflexive, as in:

(189) a. Nā Hera anō ia i   kākahu.
         of Sara Emp she past dress
         'Sara dressed herself.'

      b. Nā-u   anō i   kawe mai i   a   koe?
         of-you Emp past take here Acc pro you
         'Did you bring yourself here?' (Biggs 1969: 126)

Finally, Passive is governed by a wider range of verbs than seem to govern Promotion, a fact discussed further below.

Although evidence of this sort is not overwhelming, it does intimate that Promotion should be recognized as separate from Passive, and that is the approach taken here. The rule has roughly the form: 'Take the embedded direct object of an agent-emphatic sentence and turn it into the subject of the embedded clause, subject to further conditions (described below)'.

3.4.2.3. <u>Promotion as a Major Rule</u>. The small amount of data available on the topic suggests that Promotion is a major rule.

Promotion is the counterpart of Passive, a cyclic rule, if it is the counterpart of any syntactic rule of English.

Promotion also appears to be bounded, in that it operates only in the clause embedded directly under the predicate possessor.

Finally, Promotion is governed and exhibits lexical exceptions. It does not affect the direct object of <u>titiro</u> 'look at' and perhaps other middle verbs (but see below):

(190) a. *Nā Pita i titiro a ia.
 of Peter past look pro she
 (Peter looked at her.)

b. Mā-u...e titiro ki te rere-nga mai o
 of-you nonpast look to the rise-Nmlz here of
 'You...look towards the

 te rā.
 the sun
 sunrise.' (Orbell 46)

Further, it affects the affected locative of <u>moe</u> 'sleep' in the grammars of some speakers but not others:

(191) (*)Nā Hōne i   moe te moenga.
       of John past sleep the bed
       'John slept on the bed.'

3.4.2.4. <u>Restriction to Direct Objects</u>. Having suggested that Promotion is a major rule, we now turn to its major point of interest for this discussion: it applies only to NPs that are direct objects.

Thus, the rule affects direct objects of canonical transitive clauses:

(192) a. Ma rātou e   unahi ngā   ika.
         of them nonpast scale the=pl fish
         'They will scale the fish.' (Biggs 1969: 73)

    b. Nā wai koe i   hōmai ki taku taiwhenua?
       of who? you past bring to my   land
       'Who brought you to my land?' (Orbell 84)

As well as direct objects of some middle clauses:

(193)   Ka karanga atu tētahi wahine ki te   wahine
        uns call   away a   woman to the woman
        'One of them called to the woman

        nā-na i   kite taua poro rākau.
        of-her past see that piece wood
        who had found that piece of wood.' (Orbell 76)

For some speakers, it also affects locatives which are directly or physically affected by the action of an underlyingly intransitive verb, as in (191).

However, it does not apply to other NPs, including unaffected locatives:

(194)   *Nā Hōne i   oma te whare.
         of John past run the house
         (John ran in the house.)

Stative agents:

(195)   *Nā te hoariri i   mate te toa.
         of the enemy past die the warrior
         (The enemy died because of the warrior.)

183 Case Marking and Grammatical Relations

and other types of oblique NPs.

Assuming again that affected locatives count as derived direct objects of their associated, underlyingly intransitive verbs, these facts argue that Promotion picks out only direct objects. It thus refers to the category direct object and supports the independent position. The status of the rule with respect to the integrated position is less clear, due to the lack of data involving direct objects of middle clauses. Promotion fails to apply to at least one such direct object, namely the direct object of _titiro_ 'look at' in (190), which is marked with _ki_. Should it turn out that the rule fails to affect other direct objects marked with _ki_, then it could be claimed that the rule picks out a subset of NPs marked with the accusative _i_ or _i_ 'at'. In this sense it could be interpreted as consistent with the integrated position. Further study is needed before this question can be resolved. In the meantime, it should be noted that Promotion is either consistent with both positions, or else supports the independent position alone.

3.4.3. _Object Incorporation in Samoan_
A stronger argument in favor of the independent position is provided by Object Incorporation in Samoan, an ergative language.

3.4.3.1. _Basic Description_. Object Incorporation in Samoan is responsible for the surface difference between sentences like (196) and (197):

```
(196)    E    tausi-pepe  'oia.
         uns  care-baby   he
         'He takes care of babies.'

(197)    E    tausi e    ia pepe.
         uns  care  Erg he baby
         'He takes care of the babies.'
```

This rule applies to clauses with a frequentative or habitual sense; it takes a nonspecific common noun, strips it of any articles, and incorporates it into the verb.

Incorporation results in two major changes in the syntax of the clause. First, the incorporated noun is no longer a separate constituent but functions as part of the verb. So verbal modifiers like the pronominal copy <u>ai</u>, which would normally cliticize to the right of the verb, cliticize to the right of it instead. Compare (198), in which Incorporation has applied, with (199), in which it has not:

    (198) a. Po 'o   āfea e   tausi-tama ai 'oia?
             Q Pred when? uns care-child Pro he
             'When does he take care of babies?'
             'When does he babysit?'

        b. 'O   le   aso Tofi   e   tātā-lā'au ai 'oia.
           Pred the day Thursday uns chop-wood Pro he
           'On Thursdays he chops wood.'

    (199) a. Po 'o   āfea e   tausi ai e   ia tama?
             Q Pred when? uns care Pro Erg he child
             'When does he take care of the babies?'

        b. 'O   le   aso Tofi   e   tātā ai e   ia lā'au.
           Pred the day Thursday uns chop Pro Erg he wood
           'On Thursdays he chops wood.'

Second, clauses which have undergone Incorporation are detransitivized, and consequently take their subjects in the absolutive case rather than the ergative.

3.4.3.2. <u>Object Incorporation as a Major Rule</u>. Incorporation has all the properties of a major rule, with the possible exception of a cyclic counterpart in some other language: there is no counterpart to Incorporation in English or (to my knowledge) any other language in which the cycle is well-established.

Still, Incorporation is bounded, as shown by (200). It cannot take a noun from an embedded clause and incorporate it into a higher verb:

(200) *'Aiseā e māsani-malaga ai 'ona fai tagata?
why? uns usual-journey Pro Comp do person
(Why are people always going on trips?)

Compare the grammatical:

(201) 'Aiseā e māsani ai 'ona fai-malaga tagata?
why? uns usual Pro Comp do-journey person
'Why are people always going on trips?'
'Why is it usual for people to go on trips?'

Incorporation also exhibits lexical exceptions. In particular, it does not affect the direct objects of <u>iloa</u> 'know', <u>tago</u> 'touch', and <u>māfaufau</u> 'think about', among others:

(202) a. *E   iloa-tali   'oia.
         uns know-answer he
         (He knows answers.)

      b. *Sā   tago-teine 'oia.
         past touch-girl he
         (He kept touching girls.)

(203) a. E   iloa 'uma e   ia tali.
         uns know all Erg he answer
         'He knows all the answers.'

      b. Sā   tago 'oia 'i teine.
         past touch he to girl
         'He was touching the girls.'

The exact class of verbs which fail to govern Incorporation varies somewhat from speaker to speaker, and includes canonical transitive (202a) as well as middle verbs (202b); all are united, however, in that the action that they describe affects the direct object incompletely, if at all. It should be stressed that this property does not suffice to define the class of exceptions. Many verbs whose direct objects are less than completely affected do govern the rule, as will be shown below.

The available evidence, then, confirms that Incorporation is a major rule.

3.4.3.3. <u>Restriction to Direct Objects</u>. As might be expected by now, Incorporation is restricted to NPs that are direct objects.

The rule applies to direct objects of canonical transitive clauses:

(204) a. Sā   sogi-lā'au 'oia.
       past cut-tree   he
       'He was cutting down trees (all day).'

   b. Po 'o āfea e   tausi-tama ai 'oia?
      Q Pred when? uns care-child Pro he
      'When does he babysit?'

It also applies to direct objects of certain middle clauses:

(205) a. Sā   mulimuli-ta'avale le leoleo.
         past follow-car   the police
         'The policeman was following cars (all day).'

   b. Sā   tilotilo-teine 'oia.
      past watch-girl   he
      'He was girl-watching.'

   c. E   mana'o-tupe 'oia.
      uns want-money he
      'He is money-hungry.'

   d. E   fia matamata-tīfaga lātou.
      uns want watch-film   they
      'They like watching films.'

(206) a. Sā   mātou mulimuli i le ta'avale mūmū.
         past we   follow   at the car   red
         'We were following the red car.'

   b. Sā   tilotilo 'oia 'i le teine.
      past watch   he   to the girl
      'He was watching the girl.'

c. E   mana'o 'oia i aniani.
    uns want he at onion
    'He wants onions.'

d. 'E te matamata 'i le tīvī?
    you uns watch   to the television
    'Do you watch television?'

And to locatives which are directly or physically affected by the action of an intransitive verb:

(207)a. E nofo-nofoa le falesā?
        uns sit-chair the church
        'Does the congregation sit on chairs?'

b. Sā moe-fa'amalū   'oia.
    past sleep-mattress he
    'He was sleeping on a mattress.'

However, it cannot incorporate subjects, whether intransitive or transitive, semantically affected by the action or unaffected:

(208)a. *'O aso 'uma e mānunu'a-tagata ai.
         Pred day all uns hurt=pl-person Pro
        (People get hurt every day.)

b. *E fai-kāmuta   fale i aso 'uma.
    uns do-carpenter house at day all
    (Carpenters build houses every day.)

(209)a. 'O aso 'uma lava e mānunu'a ai tagata.
        Pred day all Emp uns hurt=pl Pro person
        'People get hurt every day.'

b. E   fai e kāmuta   fale i aso 'uma.
    uns do Erg carpenter house at day all
    'Carpenters build houses every day.'

And it also fails to incorporate oblique NPs. Thus in (210a), the rule has affected an oblique locative; in (210b), a goal:

(210)a. *Sā tamo'e-fale lātou.
         past run-house they
        (They were running around in houses.)

  b. *Sā alu-lotu 'oia i le aso Sā.
    past go-church he at the day Sunday
    (He went to church on Sundays.)

(211) a. Sā tamo'e lātou i le fale.
    past run they in the house
    'They were running around in the house.'

  b. Sā alu 'oia 'i le lotu i le aso Sā.
    past go he to the church at the day Sunday
    'He went to church on Sundays.'

  Assuming, as was done before, that affected locatives are the derived direct objects of their associated, underlyingly intransitive verbs, it appears that Object Incorporation picks out NPs that are direct objects. It therefore refers to the category direct object and supports the independent position. The rule does not support the integrated position, in contrast, because the NPs picked out by it do not form a unified category with respect to case marking. They include both a subclass of the NPs with absolutive marking and a subclass of those marked with the oblique prepositions i 'at' or 'i 'to'. Their morphological diversity reflects the fact that, in an ergative language like Samoan, direct objects are not picked out as a single category by the case marking rules. The fact that these NPs are nonetheless picked out by Incorporation argues that the independent position is to be preferred to the integrated position.

  A comparable argument for the independent position can be constructed from Object Incorporation in Maori; see Mark (1970) for a brief sketch. The question of whether such an argument can also be constructed from Incorporation in Tongan remains open. Although Tongan allows direct objects to incorporate, it also allows certain oblique NPs (including locatives and time phrases) to be incorporated into underlyingly intransitive verbs. Further study is needed to determine if

a single process is responsible for incorporating these two
types of NPs.

3.4.4. Quantifier Float in Tongan

Finally, Quantifier Float in Tongan, the last direct object-
referring rule to be described here, argues for the independent as opposed to the integrated position.

3.4.4.1. Background: Kotoa. Tongan Quantifier Float applies
to certain clauses containing an NP quantified by kotoa 'all'.

Kotoa is peculiar among nominal modifiers in that it is
unclear whether it occurs inside or outside the NP. On the
one hand, it occupies a standard position among the nominal
modifiers following the head noun:

 (212)a. Na'e manavahē 'a e kakai tangata kotoa.
    past leave Abs the people man   all
    'All the men left.'

   b. Na'e mahino 'a e fehu'i ki-a kinautolu
    past clear Abs the question to-pro them
    'Did all of them understand the question (lit.

    kotoa?
    all
    Was the question clear to all of them)?'

It also counts as part of the NP for the purposes of extraction rules. Thus, in (213), the quantified NP is removed
by Topicalization, and kotoa is removed along with it:

 (213) Ko ia kotoa pē na'e toki a'u   mai, kuo
    Pred that all Emp past just arrive here prf
    'All those who have just arrived, it is

    pau ke nau tu'u heni.
    must sbj they stand here
    necessary that they stand here.'

On the other hand, kotoa is treated as outside the NP by the
definitive accent, a morphophonemic shift in stress which af-

fects the last constituent of definite NPs (see 0.2). Consider (214), in which the definitive accent falls on the head noun **'asitalōnoma** 'astronomer' rather than on kotoa:

(214) Na'e ngāue fakataha 'a e kau 'asitalōnomá
past work together Abs the pl astronomer
'All the astronomers worked

kotoa.
all
together.' (C.M. Churchward 1953: 278)

Here it is assumed that kotoa originates within the NP and is subsequently moved outside it by a very late rule which precedes assignment of the definitive accent.

3.4.4.2. **Basic Description**. Quantifier Float relates sentences like (215) and (216):

(215) 'Oku vākē kotoa 'a e fanga patō.
prog make=noise all Abs the pl duck
'The ducks were all making noise.'

(216) 'Oku vākē 'a e fanga patō kotoa.
prog make=noise Abs the pl duck all
'All the ducks were making noise.'

This rule applies to certain clauses containing an NP quantified by kotoa; it removes the quantifier from its postnominal position and places it to the right of the verb, where it occupies a position among the normal verbal modifiers.

Quantifier Float appears not to be sensitive to the definiteness of the quantified NP. While the rule typically affects quantified NPs which are formally marked as definite, it sometimes affects ones that are not:

(217) Na'a ku sio kotoa 'i he fanga pato 'i he
past I see all at the pl duck in the
'I saw all the ducks in the

ahovai.
lake
pond.'

However, it is sensitive to other properties of the NP, as will be demonstrated further below.

3.4.4.3. Quantifier Float as a Major Rule.

Quantifier Float has all the properties of a major rule.

It is the counterpart of Quantifier Float in English, which can be shown to be cyclic.

It is also bounded: it cannot remove kotoa from an embedded NP and place it to the right of a higher verb:

(218) a. *'Oku ou 'ilo'i kotoa 'oku nau kei toe.
       prog I know all   prog they still remain
       (I know that they are all still here.)

   b. 'Oku ou 'ilo'i 'oku nau kei toe kotoa.
       prog I know prog they still remain all
       'I know that they are all still here.'

The rule, finally, exhibits lexical exceptions in the sense that it optionally applies to kotoa but does not affect any other quantifiers. Thus, (219) shows that it cannot move the quantifier taha 'one':

(219) a. *Na'e mate taha 'a e pēpē.
       past die one Abs the baby
       (One baby died.)

   b. Na'e mate 'a e pēpē 'e taha.
       past die Abs the baby uns one
       'One baby died.'

3.4.4.4. Restriction to Subjects and Direct Objects.

The major point of interest of Quantifier Float for this discussion is that it affects only certain types of quantified NPs: it is restricted to NPs that are subjects or direct objects.

Quantifier Float can be triggered by subjects of intransitive clauses:

192   Case Marking and Grammatical Relations

(220) a. Na'e manavahē kotoa 'a e   kakai tangatá.
        past leave   all Abs the people man
        'The men all left.'

     b. Na'e ngalo   kotoa 'a e lea faka-Tonga na'a
        past forgotten all Abs the lg Tongan   past
        'The Tongan that you taught me has all been

        ke ako'i ai au.
        you teach Pro me
        forgotten.'

As well as subjects of canonical transitive or middle clauses:

(221) a. Na'e tafulu'i kotoa 'e he kakai vaivai 'a
        past scold   all   Erg the people old Abs
        'The old people all scolded

        'Ālani.
        Alan
        Alan.'

     b. Na'e tafulu'i kotoa ia 'e he kakai vaivai.
        past scold   all   him Erg the people old
        'The old people all scolded him.'

     c. 'Oku lolotonga tafi kotoa 'a e   falikí 'e
        prog Prog   sweep all   Abs the floor Erg
        'The women were all sweeping the

        he finemātu'a.
        the women
        floor.'

(222) a. Pea nau sio kotoa ki ai.
        and they see all   to Pro
        'And they all looked at it.' (Gifford 47)

     b. Na'e 'a'ahi mai kotoa 'a e   tamaikí ki-ate
        past visit here all   Abs the children to-pro
        'The children all visited

        au.
        me
        me.'

It can also be triggered by absolutive direct objects:

(223) a. Na'a mau takai'i kotoa 'a e   'otu motu
        past we turn   all   Abs the row island
        'We toured all the islands

193 Case Marking and Grammatical Relations

```
            'o e     Pasifike.
            of the   Pacific
            of the Pacific.'

        b.  Kuo kai kotoa 'e   Mele 'a e   ngaahi fo'i
            prf eat all   Erg  Mary Abs the pl     one
            'Has Mary eaten all of those

            siainé?
            banana
            bananas?'
```

Direct objects of middle clauses:

```
    (224)a. Na'a ku 'a'ahi kotoa ki he    fanga ki'i tamaiki
            past I  visit  all   to the pl    small children
            'I visited all the children

            'i falemahaki.
            at hospital
            in the hospital.'

        b.  Na'a ku sio kotoa 'i he   fanga pato 'i he
            past I  see all   at the pl    duck  in the
            'I saw all the ducks in the

            ahovai.
            lake
            pond.'
```

And locatives directly or physically affected by the action of an underlyingly intransitive verb:

```
    (225)a. Na'a ku tangutu kotoa 'i he  sea    'i he  lokí.
            past I  sit     all   in the chair  in the room
            'I sat in all the chairs in the room.'

        b.  Na'a ku nofo kotoa 'i he   fale  'i Tonga.
            past I  stay all   in the house in Tonga
            'I lived in all the houses in Tonga.'
```

However, the rule is never triggered by other types of NPs, including indirect objects:

```
    (226)a. ?*'Oku mahino kotoa ki he   tamaikí 'a e   lea
            prog  clear   all   to the children Abs the lg
            (The children all understand Spanish (lit. The
```

194 Case Marking and Grammatical Relations

        faka-Sipeni.
        Spanish
        Spanish language is clear to all the children).)

   b. 'Oku mahino ki he tamaikí kotoa pē 'a e
      prog clear to the children all Emp Abs the
      'All the children understand

      lea faka-Sipeni.
      lg Spanish
      Spanish.'

Stative agents:

(227) a. *'Oku ilifia kotoa 'a e ta'ahiné 'i he
      prog afraid all Abs the girl Caus the
      (The girl is afraid because of all the

      tamaiki tangata.
      children man
      boys.)

   b. 'Oku ilifia 'a e ta'ahiné 'i he tamaiki
      prog afraid Abs the girl Caus the children
      'The girl is afraid because of all the

      tangatá kotoa.
      man   all
      boys.'

Or unaffected locatives:

(228) a. *Na'a mau takai kotoa 'i he 'otu motu 'o e
      past we turn all at the row island of the
      (We travelled in all the islands of the

      Pasifike.
      Pacific
      Pacific.)

   b. *Na'a ku tangutu kotoa 'i he fale 'i Tonga.
      past I sit   all in the house in Tonga
      (I sat in all the houses in Tonga.)

(229) a. Na'a mau takai 'i he 'otu motu kotoa 'o e
      past we turn in the row island all of the
      'We travelled in all the islands of the

      Pasifike.
      Pacific
      Pacific.'

b. Na'a ku tangutu 'i he   fale   kotoa pē   'i Tonga.
    past I sit   in the house all   Emp in Tonga
    'I sat in all the houses in Tonga.'

(The contrast between (228b) and (225a) shows that the degree to which a locative is physically affected is crucial in determining whether or not it can trigger Quantifier Float. Another revealing pair of examples is (228a) and (223a): in the former, the potential trigger is an unaffected locative, and so Quantifier Float does not apply. But in the latter, the trigger is the direct object of a derived canonical transitive verb, <u>takai'i</u> 'turn around in', and the rule is allowed.)

Assuming that the locatives of (225) are derived direct objects of their associated, underlyingly intransitive verbs, these facts argue that Quantifier Float is restricted to subjects and direct objects.

In addition to this, Quantifier Float has other restrictions which are at present poorly understood. For instance, the rule is triggered freely by direct objects of middle clauses if they are marked with <u>'i</u> 'at', but less freely if they are marked with <u>ki</u> 'to'. The choice of <u>'i</u> or <u>ki</u> for such direct objects is determined by lexical and semantic factors, and the restriction may ultimately be related to either or both of these (see 2.1.3). Further, Quantifier Float sometimes cannot move the quantifier across an intervening animate NP, as in the following:

(230)   *'Oku li'aki kotoa 'a Sione 'e he kakai
        prog leave all   Abs John Erg the people
        (The women are all abandoning

        fefiné.
        woman
        John.)

This suggests that linear order may be involved in the statement of the rule (cf. though (221b) and (221c)).

However, these other possible restrictions should not obscure the fact that Quantifier Float affects subjects and direct objects, but no other types of NPs. As such, it refers to the categories subject and direct object and supports the independent position. It does not support the integrated position, because the NPs picked out by it do not form a unified category with respect to case marking. In particular, they include not only ergative NPs (i.e. transitive subjects) and absolutive NPs (i.e. transitive direct objects and intransitive subjects), but also a subclass of NPs marked with oblique prepositions (i.e. direct objects of middle clauses and affected locatives). The fact that Quantifier Float picks out these NPs despite their morphological diversity argues that the integrated position is inferior to the independent one.

A comparable argument can be constructed from Quantifier Float in Samoan, which moves the quantifier 'uma 'all'. This rule can be triggered by subjects or direct objects regardless of their animacy or linear position; however, it is triggered by other NPs only when they are animate and occur to the immediate right of the verb (see Chung 1976a).

3.4.5. Summary

To sum up, the rules described in this section all refer to the category direct object, or else to subject and direct object. Maori Passive, Maori Promotion, and Samoan Object Incorporation pick out direct objects, while Tongan Quantifier Float is triggered by subjects or direct objects. Separately and together, the rules make a strong case for the existence of direct object in these languages. They therefore argue in favor of the independent position and against the integrated position.

3.5. OTHER MAJOR RULES

The correctness of the independent position is, finally, supported by the existence of two major rules which do not fall into the groups described above. These rules do not refer to subject or direct object, but --crucially-- do not refer to absolutive or ergative either; instead, they extend to all NPs regardless of syntactic category. As such, they are consistent with the claim that the major rules of these languages will pick out subjects and/or direct objects if they mention any categories of NPs.

The two rules of this type, zp-Equi in Tongan and māsani Raising in Samoan, are sketched briefly below. The arguments for their existence are roughly the same as for their subject-referring counterparts, Tongan Equi (see 3.2.2) and Samoan Raising (see 3.3.3), so little attempt is made here to motivate them explicitly.

3.5.1. Zp-Equi in Tongan

Zp-Equi in Tongan relates sentences like (231) and (232):

(231)   'Oku ke fiema'u ke nofo?
        prog you want   sbj stay
        'Do you want to stay?'

(232)   'Oku ke fiema'u ke ke nofo?
        prog you want   sbj you stay
        'Do you want for you to stay?'

This rule applies in certain two-clause structures in which one clause contains a verb of volition or effort and the other clause is embedded directly under it. It optionally deletes a target in the embedded clause under coreference with a controller in the higher clause, as shown in (231).

Zp-Equi can be motivated (and distinguished from zero-pronominalization, a free deletion rule) in basically the same way as the Equi of 3.2.2. It can also be shown to be a major rule.

In general, zp-Equi prefers to affect targets that are semantic agents or experiencers, particularly when the controller is a semantic agent itself. This is only a preference, however, and the rule otherwise affects any type of NP. It can delete intransitive subjects, as in (231), or transitive subjects:

(233) a. 'Oku sai'ia 'a Sione ke tā 'a e kakai
prog like Abs John sbj hit Abs the people
'John likes to hit the

fefiné.
woman
women.'

b. 'Oku sai'ia 'a Sione ke ne tā 'a e kakai
prog like Abs John sbj he hit Abs the people
'John likes for himself to hit the

fefiné.
woman
women.'

It can also delete direct objects:

(234) a. 'Oku ne manako ke ui 'e he 'eiki.
prog he like sbj call Erg the chief
'He likes to be called by the chief.'

b. 'Oku ne manako ke ui ia 'e he 'eiki.
prog he like sbj call him Erg the chief
'He likes for the chief to call him.'

Indirect objects:

(235) a. Na'e 'ikai ke feinga 'a e faiakó ke
past not sbj try Abs the teacher sbj
'The teacher didn't try

mahino 'a e lea faka-Tongá.
clear Abs the lg Tongan
to understand Tongan.'

199 Case Marking and Grammatical Relations

  b. Na'e 'ikai ke feinga 'a e faiakó ke
    past not sbj try Abs the teacher sbj
   'The teacher didn't try so that

   mahino ki ai 'a e lea faka-Tongá.
   clear to Pro Abs the lg Tongan
   Tongan would be clear to him.'

And other oblique NPs:

 (236)a. Na'e fiema'u 'e he tangatá ke ngalo
    past want Erg the man   sbj forgotten
   'The man wanted to forget

   'a e   tau.
   Abs the war
   the war.'

  b. Na'e fiema'u 'e he tangatá ke ngalo   ai
    past want Erg the man   sbj forgotten Pro
   'The man wanted for the war to be forgotten

   'a e   tau.
   Abs the war
   by him.'

In short, the rule not only fails to refer to subject or direct object, but is generally insensitive to the syntactic category of the target.

3.5.2. Māsani Raising in Samoan

Māsani Raising in Samoan relates sentences like (237) and (238):

 (237) Pe 'e te māsani 'ona 'e kuka-ina   mea'ai?
    Q you uns usual Comp you cook-Trans food
   'Do you usually cook dinner?'

 (238) Pe-e māsani 'ona 'e kuka-ina   mea'ai?
    Q-uns usual Comp you cook-Trans food
   'Do you usually cook dinner?'
   'Is it usual that you cook dinner?'

This rule applies in certain two-clause structures in which one clause contains the higher verbs māsani 'be usual, be used to' or sā 'be forbidden', and the other clause serves as its sentential subject. It raises an NP from the embedded clause to become the subject of the higher clause, at the same time leaving a pronominal copy of it in the embedded clause. The copy may surface, as in (237), but if it is a subject or direct object, it is generally deleted by zero-pronominalization:

>(239) Pe 'e te māsani 'ona kuka-ina mea'ai?
>Q you uns usual Comp cook-Trans food
>'Do you usually cook dinner?'

<u>Māsani</u> Raising can be shown to be a raising rule by exactly the same arguments given for Samoan Raising in 3.3.3. It can also be shown to be a major rule.

The rule differs from the Raising of 3.3.3 in affecting any syntactic type of NP. It can raise subjects of intransitive clauses:

>(240) E māsani 'i lātou 'ona ōmai.
>uns usual pl they Comp come=pl
>'They usually come.'

As well as subjects of canonical transitive or middle clauses:

>(241)a. Pe-e māsani e le tama 'ona tā so'o le
>Q-uns usual Erg the boy Comp hit often the
>'Does the boy usually hit the girl
>
>teine?
>girl
>often?'
>
>b. 'Ua sā 'uma lava tagata 'ona tago mai
>prf forbidden all Emp person Comp touch here
>'The people are all forbidden to touch
>
>'i-āte a'u.
>to-pro me
>me.'

It can also raise absolutive direct objects:

(242)a. E   māsani le pepe 'ona 'ou tausi-a   i le
         uns usual the baby Comp I   care-Trans in the
         'I usually take care of the baby in the

         afiafi.
         afternoon
         afternoon.'

    b.   E   māsani 'uma lava ipu 'ona tu'u 'ese e   ia
         uns usual all Emp cup Comp put away Erg she
         'She usually puts all the cups away

         i le taeao.
         in the morning
         in the morning.'

Direct objects of middle clauses:

   (243) Pe-e māsani 'oe 'ona asiasi pea   mai 'i ai
          Q-uns usual you Comp visit still here to Pro
          'Does So'otaga usually visit

          So'otaga?
          So'otaga
          you?'

Indirect objects:

   (244) E   māsani 'oia 'ona mātou 'ave-ina   'i ai
          uns usual he   Comp we   send-Trans to Pro
          'We usually send him

          tupe.
          money
          money.'

And other oblique NPs:

   (245)a. E   māsani luga o le fata 'ona tu'u ai e
            uns usual top of the shelf Comp put Pro Erg
            'She usually puts the cups on the

            ia ipu.
            she cup
            shelf.'

      b. E   māsani Ioane 'ona galo   ai lana tusi.
          uns usual John Comp forgotten Pro his book
          'His book is usually forgotten by John.'

Thus, while <u>māsani</u> Raising does not refer specifically to subject or direct object, it does not mention any NP categories at all.

3.5.3. <u>Summary</u>

To sum up, the two rules sketched above are insensitive to the syntactic category of the NP that they affect: zp-Equi in Tongan allows its target to be any NP, while <u>māsani</u> Raising in Samoan raises any NP. We can see in this further confirmation of the independent position. Because Tongan and Samoan are ergative languages, one might have expected them to have major rules which failed to refer to subject or direct object and referred to absolutive or ergative instead. However, the rules which meet the first of these criteria extend indifferently to any NP. They therefore argue that the major rules of these languages refer to subject or direct object if they pick out any syntactic categories of NPs.

3.6. CONCLUSION

This chapter has surveyed the major rules of Maori, Tongan, and Samoan and argued that they refer to the categories subject and/or direct object if they mention any categories of NPs. Equi and Raising rules in these languages refer to subject; Passive, Promotion, Object Incorporation, and Quantifier Float refer to direct object; and two remaining rules pick out no NP categories in particular. None of the rules mentions the putative categories absolutive or ergative, which appear not to figure in the major syntax of these languages at all.

The unanimity of these results is striking --even more so because they can be generalized to other Polynesian languages. Most if not all Polynesian languages have rules of Equi, Raising, Object Incorporation, and Quantifier Float, similar to those described above; many East Polynesian languages have rules of Passive and Promotion in addition. Although the available evidence bearing on these rules is less than conclusive, it nonetheless appears that they pick out subjects or direct objects if they refer to any categories of NPs.

This situation --which appears to be quite general in Polynesian-- leads to two conclusions.

First, since the major rules of Tongan, Samoan, and other ergative languages fail to refer to absolutive or ergative, the integrated position must be rejected for Polynesian:

(246) The Integrated Position:
In any given language, the NP categories picked out by the case marking rule(s) are exactly those to which other syntactic rules can refer.

In particular, the morphology and syntax of the ergative languages do not parallel each other in any important sense. There is thus no reason to expect the Polynesian languages to exhibit a deeper syntactic diversity, parallel to the diversity of case marking described in Chapter 2.

Second, since the major rules of Maori, Tongan, Samoan, and other languages refer to subject or direct object if they mention any categories of NPs, the independent position is vindicated:

(247) The Independent Position:
The NP categories picked out by the case marking rule(s) of a language may differ from the categories to which other syntactic rules refer. However, all languages have rules referring to subject and direct object, which are central to syntactic organization.

The independent position is borne out in a particularly satisfying way in that subject and direct object appear to be the only grammatical relations which major rules refer to in these languages. While the rules can also mention semantic roles (see 3.2.1.3, for instance) and perhaps linear order (see 3.4.4.4), they do not refer to categories like absolutive or ergative, referring instead to subject or direct object if they mention grammatical relations at all. The unanimity with which subject and direct object are picked out argues that these grammatical relations are present at the (deeper) level of structure at which major rules apply. In this sense, they can be said to organize the major syntax of Polynesian languages.

Finally, the presence of these categories in all Polynesian languages reveals a deeper syntactic unity running through the family, and suggests that subject and direct object may well be universal. The results of this chapter could thus be interpreted as supporting a theory of grammar, like relational grammar, in which grammatical relations are universal elements of clause structure. Certainly they establish the primacy of subject and direct object in Polynesian syntax, regardless of how these categories are formally defined.

NOTES

1. Some speakers allow the subject of <u>mate</u> 'die, be dead' to be a target of <u>ki te</u> Equi, although they do not allow this for subjects of other statives. The semantics of stative verbs and their interaction with the restriction described in the text deserve further study.
2. The interaction of Equi and zero-pronominalization should be mentioned here. In general, once the transitive subject of the embedded clause has been deleted by Equi, the tran-

sitive direct object can disappear through zero-pronominalization. Sentences like (a) are attested regularly in texts:

(a)   Na'a ne hiki 'a e   fine'eikí 'o   ha'aki
      past he lift Abs the woman   Comp throw
      'He picked up the woman and threw

      (ia) he   falikí.
           her the floor
      (her) on the floor.'

However, if the transitive subject of the embedded clause has not been deleted by Equi, the transitive direct object is usually not zero-pronominalized:

(b)   ?Na'a ne hiki 'a e   fine'eikí 'o ne ha'aki
      past he lift Abs the woman   Comp he throw
      'He picked up the woman and he threw

      he falikí.
      the floor
      (her) on the floor.'

To my knowledge, sentences like (b) do not occur in texts. Observe that the deletion of the direct object in (a) seems to require previous deletion of the subject. This argues that zero-pronominalization in Tongan is global (see also 1.4.3).

3. For some speakers, <u>galo</u> 'be forgotten' is not a stative, but rather a canonical transitive verb meaning 'forget' and governing ergative case marking. These speakers should refer to example (67), which illustrates deletion of the stative agent associated with <u>'uma</u> 'be done'.

4. It appears that embedded direct objects can be targets for zero-pronominalization in structures like (65), even though they are ineligible for Equi. Thus sentences like (64) are ungrammatical in isolation, but comparable sentences occur occasionally in texts:

(a) E   tau-a   tagata e   aumai e   ai o
     uns call-Trans   person uns bring uns eat Pred
     'The people who were brought for (the chief) to

     le   aso o   le Alii nei.
     the aso of the chief this
     eat were called the chief's aso.' (Stuebel 170)

5. Although sentences like (80) are ungrammatical in the reading given in the text, they are grammatical if interpreted as clefted sentences (e.g. 'It was a dog, not a cat, that bit Pipo'). In such a reading they would presumably have a biclausal structure consisting of a higher predicate, he kurī '(it was) a dog', followed by an embedded clause. See Reedy (1977) on the use of he to mark predicates. The grammaticality of the Clefting reading is irrelevant to the argument in the text.

6. Two points: (a) The ai of the examples is a copy of the extracted direct object that migrates to the higher clause, apparently by a rule of Clitic Climbing. (b) The constraint on extraction illustrated by (89) appears not to be limited to negated clauses, but to extend to all sentential subjects. The data available to me on this topic is limited, however.

7. Lava is sometimes associated with a lexical noun subject and an embedded clause introduced by ke, as in:

   (a) Te   nau lava pē   ke   totongi'i au kapau te
        uns   they can   Emp sbj pay   me if   uns
        'They could pay me if they

        nau   loto ki ai.
        they want to Pro
        wanted to.'

It can be shown that sentences like these do not involve Raising; rather, the lexical noun originates as the subject of lava and triggers zero-pronominalization in the embedded clause. Thus, the lexical noun is always in the absolutive case, regardless of the transitivity of the embedded clause:

(b) Na'e mei   lava pē ia ke kalofi au.
     past almost can Emp he sbj avoid me
     'He nearly managed to avoid me.'

Further, the NP of the embedded clause that it corresponds to need not be a subject:

(c) Te ke lava ke nau 'eva mai he Sāpate?
     uns you can sbj they visit here the Sunday
     'Can they visit you on Sunday?'

The raised NP of Raising structures does not have either of these properties, as will be shown in the text.

8. Some speakers allow absolutive direct objects to raise out of embedded clauses that are impersonal (i.e. have the generic agent as subject):

(a) Mahalo he 'ikai toe   lava ia 'o
     perhaps uns not   again can it Comp
     'Perhaps it cannot be

     fakalelei'i.
     repair
     repaired.'

This raising exhibits several curious properties. It is not allowed if the embedded clause has an overt or specified subject. It appears to raise some direct objects but not others, as can be seen by comparing (a) with:

(b) *Mahalo he 'ikai toe   lava 'a e   fale 'o
      perhaps uns not   again can Abs the house Comp
      (Perhaps the house cannot be

     fakalelei'i.
     repair
     repaired.)

Finally, it does not turn the raised NP into the subject of

the higher clause, since this NP cannot undergo Clitic
Placement:

    (c)   *Mahalo he 'ikai te ne toe lava 'o
            perhaps uns not uns it again can Comp
            (Perhaps it cannot be

            fakalelei'i.
            repair
            repaired.)

Whatever rule is responsible for promoting the direct object in (a), its failure to create a higher subject argues that it is distinct from the Raising described in the text.

9. As pointed out by Bruce Biggs, the construction illustrated in (178) occurs in contemporary Maori but not in the Maori of nineteenth century texts. In the latter, the negated clause of (178) would have the predicate possessive nā replaced by the locative possessive i a. A similar replacement would occur in the negated clause of (180), as shown in the following example, provided by Biggs:

    (a)   Ēhara i a Hōne i patu te poaka.
            not at prop John past hit the pig
            'John didn't kill the pig.'

10. The tense particle e 'nonpast' should not be confused with the discontinuous e...ana, which surrounds the verb and indicates progressive aspect. The latter occurs freely in matrix and embedded clauses.

11. Promotion is not involved in biclausal structures like (a-c), which resemble the agent-emphatic construction in certain respects:

    (a)   Nā Hōne i mate ai te tangata.
            of John past die Pro the man
            'Because of John, the man died.'

    (b)   Nā Hōne i tuku-na ai mātou e te
            of John past leave-Pass Pro we Agt the
            'Because of John, the policeman let us

pirihimana.
policeman
go.'

(c) Nā ērā i ngata ai te ngākau o taua
of those past satisfied Pro the heart of that
'With these treasures, the hearts of the fairy

iwi.
people
people were satisfied.' (Orbell 32)

In these structures, henceforth called indirect agent sentences, the predicate possessor corresponds to an indirect cause in the embedded clause, and is copied there by the pronominal copy ai.

Like agent-emphatic sentences, indirect agent sentences have a biclausal surface structure and appear to govern Raising. The two constructions are nonetheless derived in different ways, as shown by Hale (class lectures, 1969).

Hale's argument is based on the relative order of antecedents and pronominal anaphors in Maori. In general, antecedents precede their anaphors in surface structure --a generalization which holds in particular for agent-emphatic sentences. Thus the predicate possessor can serve as antecedent for the underlying embedded direct object, which has undergone Promotion and then Raising in (d):

(d) Nā Hera anō ia i kākahu.
of Sara Emp she past dress
'Sara dressed herself.'

But the embedded direct object (=surface subject) cannot serve as antecedent for the predicate possessor:

(e) *Nā-na anō a Hera i kākahu.
of-her Emp prop Sara past dress
(Sara dressed herself.)

In indirect agent sentences, however, not only can the

predicate possessor serve as antecedent for the underlying embedded subject:

(f) Nā Kare anō ia i mate ai.
of Kare Emp she past die Pro
'Because of Kare, (she) herself died.'

The embedded subject (=surface subject) can serve as antecedent for the predicate possessor, as well:

(g) Nā-na anō a Kare i mate ai.
of-her Emp prop Kare past die Pro
'Because of herself, Kare died.'

These facts argue that agent-emphatic sentences and indirect agent sentences are not derived in the same way, despite their surface similarity. Since the anaphor-antecedent order of (g) occurs in the output of other extractions (e.g. Clefting), it may be that the predicate possessor of indirect agent sentences originates in the lower clause and achieves its position via extraction, while the predicate possessor of agent-emphatic sentences originates as the predicate of a higher clause.

4. Case Assignment in the Ergative Languages

The preceding chapter argued that the major syntax of Polynesian languages is organized around the categories subject and direct object. In doing so, it provided an account of Equi, Raising, and other major rules in these languages, which either refer to subject and/or direct object or else do not mention any categories of NPs. This chapter returns to case marking in order to provide an account of the case assignment rules and determine whether their output plays any role in syntax. It deals with case marking in the ergative languages, since there the independence of grammatical relations from case morphology is most apparent.

4.1 presents two general proposals for case assignment and argues that the one phrased in terms of grammatical relations is superior. 4.2 discusses the case marking of middle clauses, which resembles that of intransitive clauses containing an oblique NP. It is argued that a special case assignment rule is required to account for these clauses. An alternative that would claim that middle clauses had been detransitivized by Antipassive is considered and rejected. Finally, 4.3 argues that case marking is referred to by several superficial rules and morphology rules in particular Polynesian languages. An account is suggested of why these types of rules are sometimes sensitive to case marking, but the major syntactic rules are not.

4.1. TWO PROPOSALS FOR CASE ASSIGNMENT

In this section two general proposals for case assignment are

put forth and applied to the ergative languages Tongan and
Samoan. The proposals are limited to the case marking of
subjects and direct objects, which, following Anderson (1976),
can be referred to as <u>direct case</u> NPs. Other NPs --i.e.
<u>oblique</u> NPs-- are assumed to have their case marking specified in underlying structure or else dealt with in some other
way.

4.1.1 describes a proposal of Anderson's (1976) which is
phrased in terms of linear order; 4.1.2 describes a proposal
phrased in terms of grammatical relations; and 4.1.3 compares
the two.

4.1.1. Linear Order

Anderson (1976) has proposed that a basic difference between
rules such as Equi, Raising, Reflexive, and Conjunction Reduction on the one hand, and case assignment rules on the
other, is that the former refer to grammatical relations
while the latter often refer to linear order. The second
half of this proposal is discussed here as the linear order
proposal.

In the linear order proposal, the relative order of subjects and direct objects within the clause is assumed to be
established at some point before case marking is assigned.
A general rule of case assignment is then posited for direct
case NPs in some accusative, and all ergative, languages.
The rule is:

(1)   When there are two direct-case NP in a clause,
       put a special mark on the one which comes first
       (or alternatively, on the one which comes second). (Anderson 1976: 19)

To see the effects of this rule, assume that subjects precede direct objects in the clause. Then, assignment of a special mark to the first NP would result in an ergative type of case marking, with transitive subjects being specially marked but not intransitive subjects or transitive direct objects. In contrast, assignment of a mark to the second NP would result in an accusative type of case marking, with direct objects being specially marked but not transitive or intransitive subjects. In this way two superficially different case systems would be produced by the same general rule.

The linear order proposal allows the case assignment rules of some accusative languages to refer to grammatical relations; however, it claims that case assignment in all ergative languages is accomplished by means of (1) (Anderson 1976). It would then be applied to Tongan and Samoan, both ergative languages, as follows.

Tongan would have the rule (2), a language-particular version of (1):

(2)   When there are two direct case NPs in a clause, mark the first one with 'e.

This would be followed by a rule optionally assigning 'a to all remaining unmarked NPs (see 2.1.3). The two rules would produce the correct case marking in intransitive and canonical transitive clauses.

Samoan would have the rule (3):

(3)   When there are two direct case NPs in a clause, mark the first one with e.

This would give the right case marking in intransitive and canonical transitive clauses, as well.

(The treatment of middle clauses in these languages is postponed to 4.2.)

4.1.2. Grammatical Relations

Although the linear order proposal is appealingly general, comparably general results can be achieved without having to refer to linear order. This subsection outlines an alternative proposal which is phrased in terms of grammatical relations.

The grammatical relations proposal assumes that the subject and direct object of a clause have been identified by the time that case marking is assigned. It then posits one universal rule of case assignment for direct case NPs:

(4)   When there are two direct case NPs in a clause, put a special mark on the subject (or, alternatively, on the direct object).

Depending on which option of (4) is chosen, an accusative or an ergative type of case marking will result, just as in the linear order proposal.

Applying the grammatical relations proposal to Tongan and Samoan, Tongan will have the language-particular rule:

(5)   When there are two direct case NPs in a clause, mark the subject with 'e.

This will be followed by the rule optionally assigning 'a to remaining unmarked NPs. Samoan will have the rule:

(6)   When there are two direct case NPs in a clause, mark the subject with e.

These give the right case marking for intransitive and canonical transitive clauses in their respective languages.

4.1.3. Comparison

A comparison of the two proposals reveals that they are equivalent in many respects.

Thus, both the linear order proposal and the grammatical relations proposal describe the same range of case marking and are able to account for the Tongan and Samoan systems in particular.

Both proposals posit one general case assignment rule and make two assumptions: that direct case NPs can be distinguished from oblique NPs, and subjects and direct objects can be distinguished from each other. (The linear order proposal invokes the latter assumption when it imposes a relative order on subjects and direct objects within the clause.)

Both proposals seem equally consistent with the larger generalizations that can be made about case morphology. For instance, not only in the ergative Polynesian languages but also in other ergative languages of the world, grammatical relations are independent of case marking (Anderson 1976). The linear order proposal expresses this by assigning case marking according to linear order; the grammatical relations proposal, by assigning it, in part, according to the number of direct case NPs in the clause. Further, in several languages of the world, the organization of the case system has changed from accusative to ergative, or vice versa. (For changes from accusative to ergative in Polynesian and in Indo-Iranian, see Chapter 6 of this book and Anderson (1977); for changes from ergative to accusative in Caucasian and in Australian, see Brathwaite (1970) and Hale (1970).) Both proposals allow for the apparently equal plausibility of these changes by assigning the two types of case marking through variants of a single rule.

This suggests that, in the absence of facts arguing strongly for one or the other, the proposal should be preferred whose case assignment rule refers to notions already referred to by other syntactic rules. In this way the overall coher-

216 Case Assignment in the Ergative Languages

ence of the syntax will be contributed to. Now it is clear from Chapter 3 that subject and direct object are referred to by syntactic rules in Polynesian languages, but it is not clear that the linear order of these NPs is.[1] This suggests that the grammatical relations proposal should be considered superior.

Ideally such a suggestion should be confirmed by arguments of a more empirical type; however, I know of no other types of facts bearing on this issue in Tongan, Samoan, or other languages. In their absence, it seems reasonable to conclude that the grammatical relations proposal is preferable to the linear order proposal.

4.2. CASE ASSIGNMENT IN MIDDLE CLAUSES

Both the grammatical relations proposal and the linear order proposal appear to have difficulty dealing with middle clauses in Polynesian languages, which are syntactically transitive but have the case marking of intransitive clauses containing an oblique NP. This section examines the properties of middle clauses in Tongan and Samoan and argues that a special case assignment rule is required to account for them.

4.2.1 reviews the facts of middle clauses, and 4.2.2 outlines two alternatives for describing their case marking. One of these posits a special case assignment rule for middle clauses, while the other would claim that they have been detransitivized by an Antipassive rule. 4.2.3 argues against the Antipassive alternative; 4.2.4 is a summary.

4.2.1. Middle Clauses in Tongan and Samoan

Middle clauses are clauses containing a middle verb, i.e. a verb describing an event that does not affect the direct object immediately (see 2.1.1). Such clauses have two notable characteristics, which are illustrated here for Tongan and Samoan.

First, middle clauses are syntactically transitive. This is shown by the ability of their direct objects to undergo major rules restricted to direct objects (or else subjects and direct objects), such as Tongan Quantifier Float (see 3.4.4), Samoan Object Incorporation (see 3.4.3), and Samoan Quantifier Float (see 3.4.4.4). It is also shown by the fact that their subjects count as transitive subjects for the governed restriction discussed for Samoan Equi in 3.2.3.2.

Second, middle clauses have the case marking of intransitive clauses containing an oblique NP. In Tongan, subjects of these clauses occur in the absolutive and their direct objects are marked with one of the oblique prepositions <u>'i</u> 'at' or <u>ki</u> 'to' (see 2.1.3):

Ton (7)a.   Na'e muimui 'a 'Ālani 'i-ate au 'aneafi.
            past follow Abs Alan at-pro me yesterday
            'Alan followed me yesterday.'

     b.   'Oku sio ki tahi 'a e sianá na.
            prog see to ocean Abs the man that
            'That man was looking at the ocean.'

In Samoan, subjects of these clauses are unmarked and their direct objects are marked with one of the prepositions <u>i</u> 'at' or <u>'i</u> 'to' (see 2.1.4):

Sam (8)a.   'Ua fa'ama'amulu Beni ma Liu i le galuega.
            prf give=up   Ben and Liu at the work
            'Ben and Liu gave up the work.'

     b.   Sā fa'afetai le teine 'i lona tinā.
            past thank   the girl to her mother
            'The girl thanked her mother.'

Given that clauses of this type are transitive, one might have expected them to undergo the general case assignment rule and emerge with an ergative case pattern. But they do not:

218   Case Assignment in the Ergative Languages

Ton   (9)a.   *'Oku sio 'e Mele 'a e   kakai tangatá.
                prog see Erg Mary Abs the people man
                (Mary sees the men.)

Sam   b.   *'Ua tago e ia le naifi.
                prf touch Erg he the knife
                (He touched the knife.)

Consequently, they pose a problem for the view of case assignment developed above.

4.2.2. Two Alternatives

Two alternatives suggest themselves for dealing with middle clauses within the general framework outlined above. These can be referred to as the case marking proposal and the Antipassive proposal.

Under the case marking proposal, case assignment is simply more complicated than was suggested in 4.1. This proposal posits a special case assignment rule for middle clauses, either a lexical redundancy rule which marks their direct objects with oblique prepositions in underlying structure, or else a syntactic rule with roughly the same effect. The special rule is ordered before the general case assignment rule, which is restated to mention <u>unmarked</u> direct case NPs.

Applying this proposal to Tongan and Samoan, each language will have the redundancy rule (10) or the rule (11), where i/ki represents the prepositions 'at' and 'to':

(10)   [+middle] → [+__Subj i/ki DO]

(11)   When there are two direct case NPs in a clause containing a middle verb, mark the direct object with i/ki.

They will also have a revised, general case assignment rule like (12), where e represents the ergative marker:

(12)   When there are two unmarked direct case NPs in
       a clause, mark the subject with e.

Under the Antipassive proposal, in contrast, middle clauses would have the morphology they do because they would be superficially intransitive. Such a proposal would posit an Antipassive rule to detransitivize middle clauses by demoting their direct objects to oblique NPs. This rule would be ordered before the general case assignment rule, so that middle clauses would first be detransitivized and hence be ineligible for ergative case marking. The demoted NPs would presumably have their case marking assigned by the mechanism which accounted for oblique NPs in general.

Applying such an alternative to Tongan and Samoan, each language would have an Antipassive rule like (13), where locative and goal refer to types of oblique NPs marked with i/ki:

(13)   Demote the direct object to a locative or goal.

As a clause-bounded rule governed by middle verbs, Antipassive would be a major rule. It would follow other major rules, such as Quantifier Float, Object Incorporation, and Equi, but precede case assignment.

One might at first be inclined to prefer the Antipassive proposal to the case marking proposal. For one thing, such a proposal would be plausible given the existence of Antipassive rules in other languages of the world (see Anderson 1976; Postal, forthcoming). For another, if Tongan and Samoan included an Antipassive rule, it would be possible to maintain for them the original case assignment proposal of 4.1.2.

However, if the Antipassive proposal were correct, one might well expect to find middle clauses treated as intransitive by rules besides case assignment; in particular, one would expect such clauses to be treated as transitive by

220   Case Assignment in the Ergative Languages

those rules which preceded the putative Antipassive rule, but as intransitive by those which followed it. The following subsection argues that these predictions are not borne out, and middle clauses in Tongan and Samoan are not detransitivized.

4.2.3. Arguments Against Antipassive

This subsection presents five arguments from Tongan and Samoan against an Antipassive proposal. The arguments are constructed around superficial rules, for two reasons: first, most major rules have already been claimed to precede the putative Antipassive rule; and second, an Antipassive proposal would have been strongly supported had major rules treated middle clauses as transitive, but superficial rules treated them as intransitive.

The first four arguments survey the superficial rules of Tongan and Samoan that are sensitive to transitivity. It is argued that none of these treats middle clauses as intransitive, and therefore no evidence exists for an Antipassive rule aside from case marking itself. The fifth argument shows that positing an Antipassive rule for Tongan would lead directly to an ordering paradox.

4.2.3.1. **Clitic Placement in Samoan**. Clitic Placement, the only superficial rule of Samoan which refers to transitivity, treats middle clauses as transitive rather than intransitive.

Clitic Placement relates sentences like (14) and (15):

(14)   'Ua mātou ōmai.
        prf we   come=pl
        'We have come.'

(15)   'Ua ōmai   mātou.
        prf come=pl we
        '<u>We</u> have come.'

221 Case Assignment in the Ergative Languages

This rule takes a nonemphatic, noncontrastive pronominal subject and attaches it to the right of the tense-aspect-mood particle of its clause, as described previously in 1.4.2.2.

Despite its clause-bounded character, Clitic Placement seems to qualify as a superficial rule. Its closest counterpart in more familiar languages is perhaps Clitic Placement in French, which is postcyclic (Kayne 1975), and it does not have lexical exceptions.

What is of immediate interest is that the rule exhibits a transitivity restriction for most speakers of Samoan: it does not affect third singular pronominal subjects if they are the subjects of intransitive clauses. Compare the third singular transitive subjects of (16):

(16) a. Sā   ia tipi-ina   le 'ulu   i   le naifi.
         past he cut-Trans the breadfruit with the knife
         'He cut the breadfruit with a knife.'

    b.   Ua ana iloa atu.
         prf he know away
         'When he recognized it...' (Stuebel 227)

(17) a. Sā   tipi-ina e ia le 'ulu   i   le
         past cut-Trans Erg he the breadfruit with the
         'He cut the breadfruit with a

         naifi.
         knife
         knife.'

    b.   'Ua iloa e   ia.
         prf know Erg he
         'He recognized it.'

With the intransitive subjects of (18):

(18) a. *Na   ia ala i le fitu.
          past he wake at the seven
          (He woke up at seven.)

    b.   *'Āfai na te toe   fo'i   mai...
          when she uns again return here
          (If she comes back...)

       c. *'Olo'o ia tautala lēmū.
           prog she speak soft
           (She is speaking softly.)

(19) a. Na ala 'oia i le fitu.
          past wake he at the seven
          'He woke up at seven.'

     b. 'Āfai e toe fo'i mai 'oia...
         when uns again return here she
         'If she comes back...'

     c. 'Olo'o tautala lēmū 'oia.
         prog speak soft she
         'She is speaking softly.'

Observe that the restriction holds regardless of whether the clause contains oblique NPs. This argues that transitivity, rather than the total number of NPs within the clause, determines whether or not Clitic Placement can apply.

    Significantly, Clitic Placement also affects third singular pronominal subjects of middle clauses, as shown by:

(20) a. 'Ua ia fiu lava i 'ai so'o.
          prf he tired Emp at eat often
          'He is tired of eating all the time.'

     b. Pe na te fiafia 'i le teine?
         Q he uns happy to the girl
         'Does he like the girl?'

     c. Na te lē māsani fo'i i-āte a'u.
         he uns not acquainted also at-pro me
         'He doesn't know me either.'

     d. Ua ia mana'o i ai.
         prf he want to Pro
         'He desires her.' (Stuebel 224)

(21) a. 'Ua fiu lava 'oia i 'ai so'o.
          prf tired Emp he at eat often
          '<u>He</u> is tired of eating all the time.'

     b. Pe-e fiafia 'oia 'i le teine?
         Q-uns happy he to the girl
         'Does <u>he</u> like the girl?'

223 Case Assignment in the Ergative Languages

    c.   E lē māsani   fo'i 'oia i-āte a'u.
         uns not acquainted also he at-pro me
         'He doesn't know me either.'

    d.   E mana'o 'oia 'i teine 'uma o le nu'u.
         uns want he to girl all of the village
         'He desires all the girls of the village.'

Therefore, for the purposes of the transitivity restriction, middle clauses count as transitive rather than intransitive.

There is some variation among speakers of Samoan in the way that the transitivity restriction on Clitic Placement is implemented. For some speakers, the restriction holds for all clauses, as in (18) (see also Neffgen 1903); for others, it holds in relative clauses but not in matrix clauses; for still others, it holds for third singular pronominal subjects represented by na, but not those represented by ia. However, for whatever domain the restriction holds, it treats subjects of middle clauses as transitive subjects rather than intransitive subjects. It thus argues that middle clauses are transitive at the time that Clitic Placement applies.

4.2.3.2. <u>Relativization in Tongan</u>. Relativization in Tongan, a superficial rule, treats middle clauses in this language as transitive rather than intransitive.

Relativization is responsible for the surface form of the relative clauses in:

    (22)a. Ko e   hā   'a e   me'a na'e hoko   ki he
           Pred the what? Abs the thing past happen to the
           'What (is the thing that) happened to the

           tamaikí   na'a ke tafulu'i?
           children [past you scold]
           children that you scolded?'

    b.   Meimei ko   e   'aho kotoa pē 'oku i ai   ha
         almost Pred the day all   Emp prog exist a
         'Almost every day there are

ni'ihi   'oku nau puke.
some=pl [prog they sick]
some who are sick.' (C.M. Churchward 1953: 205)

This rule has a deletion strategy and a pronominalization strategy, which were motivated in 1.4.3: the deletion strategy simply deletes the relative noun, while the pronominalization strategy pronominalizes it, to a clitic pronoun if possible.

Relativization has all the properties of a superficial rule. It is the counterpart of Relativization by deletion or pronominalization in English (i.e. with the complementizer that), which is postcyclic. It also operates over an essential variable and exhibits no lexical exceptions.

Significantly, the rule is sensitive to transitivity, in the following sense: it requires the deletion strategy for relative nouns which are third singular subjects of intransitive clauses, but not for other types of subjects. Compare the third singular intransitive subjects of (23), which must be relativized via the deletion strategy:

(23) a. Na'a ku fie lea   ki he siana kuo 'alú.
         past I want speak to the man [prf go]
         'I wanted to speak to the fellow who has gone.'
         (C.M. Churchward 1953: 70)

    b.   Ka e fēfē 'a e tamasi'i ia   na'e (*ne)
         but uns what? Abs the child   that [past he
         'And what about the child who

         mohe 'i hoku falé?
         sleep in my   house]
         fell asleep in my house?'

    c.   Na'a ke fe'iloaki mo e tamasi'i na'e
         past you meet   with the child   [past
         'Did you meet the boy who

         (*ne) lele holo 'i tu'á?
         he   run around at outside]
         ran around outside?'

And the third singular transitive subjects of (24), which can be relativized by either strategy:

(24) a. Tokaange ha tangata 'oku ne 'ilo hono 'uhingá.
doubtless a person [prog he know its meaning]
'There is someone, no doubt, who knows the meaning of it.' (C.M. Churchward 1953: 220)

b. Hono ai ha taha kuo 'ilo 'a e 'Otuá?
ironic be a one [prf know Abs the God]
'Is there anyone who knows God?' (C.M. Churchward 1953: 224)

Relativization therefore provides a test for transitivity if we limit ourselves to relative nouns that are third singular subjects.

Now if the relative noun is the subject of a middle clause, it is treated like a transitive subject for the purposes of this restriction. It can undergo the deletion strategy:

(25) a. 'Oku hangē ki-ate au na'a ku sio ki he
prog seem to-pro me past I see to the
'It seems to me that I saw the

ta'ahine 'oku 'ofa 'i-ate koe.
girl   [prog love at-pro you]
girl who is in love with you.'

b. Ko e tangata eni na'e sio ki he afi.
Pred the man this [past see to the fire]
'Here is the man who saw the fire.'

Or the pronominalization strategy:

(26) a. 'Oku ou 'ilo'i 'a e tokotaha na'a ne 'uma
prog I know Abs the one [past he kiss
'I know the person who kissed

ki-ate koe.
to-pro you]
you.'

b. Ko e tangata eni na'a ne sio ki he afi.
Pred the man this [past he see to the fire]
'Here is the man who saw the fire.'

226 Case Assignment in the Ergative Languages

Its ability to do so argues that it is a transitive subject, and middle clauses are transitive, at the time that Relativization applies.[2]

4.2.3.3. <u>Clefting and Topicalization in Tongan</u>. Clefting and Topicalization, two other superficial rules of Tongan that are sensitive to transitivity, also treat middle clauses as transitive rather than intransitive.

Clefting and Topicalization both produce relative clause-like structures, and can be motivated in ways similar to the way that Relativization was motivated in 1.4.3. Clefting moves a focused NP to the left and marks it with the predicate particle <u>ko</u>:

(27) a. Ko   Sione na'e 'alu 'aneafi.
         Pred John past go   yesterday
         'It is John who left yesterday.'

    b.   E   ikai, ke tufa ha taha; ko   au pe   te-u
         uns not   sbj allot a one   Pred I Emp uns-I
         'No one shall apportion; I only shall do

         tufa.
         allot
         the apportioning.' (Gifford 50)

Topicalization moves a topic NP to the left, marks it with the predicate particle <u>ko</u>, and separates it from the rest of the sentence by an intonation break:

(28) a. Ko   'eku tamasi'i 'aku ia, 'oku va'inga ia
         Pred my   child   mine that prog play   he
         'As for that child of mine, he is playing

         'i muí.
         at back
         in back.'

    b.   Ko   e   fo'i mo'oni kuo u toki lea   ki aí,
         Pred the one truth prf I just speak to Pro
         'The truth which I have just been speaking

227   Case Assignment in the Ergative Languages

> mou to͞ ia ki homou lotó.
> you=pl plant it to your=pl heart
> about, plant it in your hearts.' (C.M. Church-
> ward 1953: 101)

Each of these rules has a chopping strategy, which simply leaves a hole, and a copying strategy, which leaves behind a pronominal copy of the moved NP. The copying strategy of Clefting must leave behind a clitic if the appropriate form exists; the copying strategy of Topicalization does not exhibit this restriction.

Both Clefting and Topicalization qualify as superficial rules. They are the counterparts of English Clefting and Left Dislocation, respectively, which can be shown to be postcyclic. They are also unbounded and do not have lexical exceptions.

The two rules also exhibit transitivity restrictions of the following sort: they do not allow moved NPs which are third singular subjects of intransitive clauses to be copied by a pronominal clitic. For Clefting, this has the result that the copying strategy cannot affect these subjects at all:

> (29) a. Ko e   tamasi'i 'oku (*ne) va'inga 'i muí.
>   Pred the child   prog he   play   in back
>   'It is a child that is playing in back.'
>
> b. Pea mahino ki-a   Longopoa tā ko e fu'u
>   and clear to-prop Longopoa so Pred the tree
>   '...and then Longopoa realized that it was the
>
>   pukó pē 'oku leá.
>   puko Emp prog speak
>   puko tree itself that was speaking.' (C.M.
>   Churchward 1953: 280)

For Topicalization, it has the result that the copying strategy can apply only if it leaves behind an independent pronoun:

(30) a. Ko   'eku tamasi'i 'aku ia, 'oku (*ne) va'inga
         Pred my   child   mine that prog he   play
         'As for that child of mine, he is playing

         'i muí.
         at back
         in back.'

   b.   Ko   'eku tamasi'i 'aku ia, 'oku va'inga ia
         Pred my   child   mine that prog play   he
         'As for that child of mine, he is playing

         'i muí.
         at back
         in back.'

However, the rules allow moved NPs which are third singular subjects of transitive clauses to freely leave behind clitic copies. Consider the Clefting sentences:

(31) a. Ko   hoku tunga'ane na'e ma'u   'a e   fo'i
         Pred my   brother   past catch Abs the one
         'It is my brother who caught the

         pulú.
         ball
         ball.'

   b.   Ko   e   finemotu'a na'e 'ai 'eku tamasi'i 'o
         Pred the woman   past do my   child   Comp
         'It is that woman who made my child

         puke.
         sick
         sick.'

   c.   Ko   hoku tokoua 'oku ne haka 'a e   ika.
         Pred my   sibling prog he cook Abs the fish
         'It is my brother who is cooking the fish.'

And the Topicalization sentences:

(32) a. Ko   e   fefine ia, 'oku fai 'a e   fō.
         Pred the woman that prog do Abs the wash
         'As for that woman, she is doing the wash.'

   b.   Ko   Mele ia, na'a ne 'uma'i 'a Sione.
         Pred Mary that past she kiss Abs John
         'As for Mary, she kissed John.'

229   Case Assignment in the Ergative Languages

The rules can thus be used to test for transitivity, if only moved NPs that are third singular subjects are considered.

Now when the moved NP is the subject of a middle clause, it is treated like a transitive subject for the purposes of these restrictions: it is allowed to leave behind a clitic copy. Consider the Clefting sentences of:

(33) a. Ko   Mele 'oku fakamālō ki he tangatá.
         Pred Mary prog thank   to the man
         'It is Mary who was thanking the man.'

    b.   Ko   hai   na'a ne sio ki he'eku pení?
         Pred who? past he see to my   pen
         'Who has seen my pen?'

And the Topicalization sentences of:

(34) a. Ko   Mele ia, na'a ne 'uma ki-a   Sione.
         Pred Mary that past she kiss to-prop John
         'As for Mary, she kissed John.'

    b.   Ko   e   tangata Kalisitiané, 'oku totonu ke
         Pred the person Christian   prog right sbj
         'A Christian man ought to be kind to his

         ne 'ofa ki he'ene fanga manú.
         he love to his   pl   animal
         animals (lit. A Christian man, it is good for
         him to be kind to his animals).' (C.M. Churchward 1953: 101)

This property argues that subjects of middle clauses are transitive subjects, and middle clauses are transitive, at the time that Clefting and Topicalization apply.

4.2.3.4. Ordering Paradox. The preceding paragraphs examined the four superficial rules of Tongan and Samoan that refer to transitivity, and argued that they treat middle clauses as transitive rather than intransitive. There is thus no positive evidence for an Antipassive rule in these languages aside from case marking itself. This paragraph argues that positing an Antipassive rule for Tongan would lead directly to an ordering paradox.

The paradox would arise in the statement of Relativization and Clefting in Tongan. As discussed above, these rules treat middle clauses as transitive for the purposes of a restriction involving third singular subjects. Therefore, if an Antipassive rule were assumed to detransitivize middle clauses, Relativization and Clefting would have to be able to apply <u>before</u> it.

The restriction involving third singular subjects is not, however, the only restriction to which these rules are subject. In addition, Relativization requires the deletion strategy for direct objects:

(35)   Na'a mau fufuu'i 'a e   tamaiki fēfine ko
        past we hide   Abs the children women Pred
        'We hid the girls

        ia   na'a ne tuli (*kinautolu).
        that [past he chase   them]
        who he was chasing.'

And Clefting requires the chopping strategy for these NPs:

(36)   Ko   hai 'oku ke fiema'u (*ia) ke ne 'ave
        Pred who? prog you want   him sbj he take
        'Who do you want to take

        mama'o ho'o tīvī?
        far   your television
        your television away?'

Relativization requires the pronominalization strategy for obliques:

(37)   Na'e ngalo   kotoa 'a e lea faka-Tonga
        past forgotten all   Abs the lg Tongan
        '(I) forgot all the Tongan words

        na'a ke ako'i au ki ai.
        [past you teach me to Pro]
        that you taught me about.'

231 Case Assignment in the Ergative Languages

And Clefting requires the copying strategy for these NPs:

(38) Ko   hai 'oku mahino ki ai 'a e   lea
      Pred who? prog clear to Pro Abs the lg
      'Who understands the Tongan language (lit. To

      faka-Tongá?
      Tongan
      whom is the Tongan language clear)?'

Put more generally, the rules require the direct objects that they affect to leave a hole, and the oblique NPs to leave a copy.

Now when the direct objects of middle clauses undergo Relativization or Clefting, they are treated like oblique NPs for the purposes of these restrictions: they cannot leave a hole, but must leave behind a copy instead. Consider the Relativization sentences of:

(39)a. Ko   e   hā   'a e   me'a na'e hoko   ki he
       Pred the what? Abs the thing past happen to the
       'What (is the thing that) happened to the

       tamaikí   na'a ke 'ita *(ki ai)?
       children [past you angry to Pro]
       children who you were angry at?'

   b. Ko e hā   ha'o fakakaukau ki he lea
       Pred the what? your thought   to the speech
       'What is your opinion of the speech

       na'a ke toki fanongo ai?
       [past you just hear   Pro]
       that you just heard?'

And the Clefting sentences of:

(40)a. Ko e   lao kuo pau ke talangofua kotoa ki
       Pred the law prf must sbj obey   all   to
       'It is the law that everyone must

       ai.
       Pro
       obey.'

b. Ko   hoku tuofefiné 'oku nau manako *(ai).
   Pred my   sister   prog they like   Pro
   'It is my sister that they like.'

These facts show that the two rules do not treat these NPs like direct objects, but rather like oblique NPs. Therefore, if an Antipassive rule were posited to detransitivize middle clauses, Relativization and Clefting would have to be extrinsically ordered <u>after</u> it. The extrinsic ordering would be necessary to keep the ungrammatical versions of (39a) and (40b), with holes, from ever being derived.

In short, Relativization and Clefting would have to be allowed to precede the putative Antipassive rule for the purposes of one restriction, but prevented from ever doing so for the purposes of another. The orderings contradict each other, and a paradox arises.

There would seem to be no good way of avoiding the paradox within the Antipassive proposal. For instance, one could not simply appeal to intrinsic ordering, the cycle, or any other principle of rule application. This is because any ordering would have to state, explicitly or implicitly, whether or not Relativization and Clefting could precede the putative Antipassive rule. If so, then the ungrammatical versions of (39a) and (40b) would be produced; if not, then the copies in (26) and (33b) could never be generated.

Further, one could not successfully avoid the paradox by splitting Relativization and Clefting each into two rules: a rule for subjects, which could apply before Antipassive, and a rule for nonsubjects, which would be forced to apply after it. Such an attempt would lead to the situation outlined in (41):

(41)a. Subject Relativization/Subject Clefting UNORDERED WITH Antipassive

b. Antipassive PRECEDES Nonsubject Relativization/
Nonsubject Clefting

While able to describe the facts, such an approach would fail to account for the unity underlying the subject and nonsubject versions of each rule. For instance, both Subject and Nonsubject Relativization would have to involve a deletion strategy; both would have to involve a pronominalization strategy; and both would have to restrict the latter to produce clitic pronouns where possible. These shared characteristics argue that Relativization is a single process, and so the approach of (41) is not a viable one.

It follows from these considerations that an ordering paradox would be unavoidable if middle clauses in Tongan were assumed to be detransitivized by an Antipassive rule. But if Tongan has no such rule, then Relativization and Clefting do not have to interact with it, and no paradox arises. In this sense, the facts discussed here argue against the Antipassive proposal.

4.2.4. Two Case Marking Rules

The arguments presented above serve to establish two points. First, those superficial rules of Tongan and Samoan that refer to transitivity treat middle clauses as transitive rather than intransitive. There is therefore no evidence aside from case marking that middle clauses in these languages might be detransitivized. Second, a paradox would arise in the statement of Relativization and Clefting in Tongan if middle clauses were assumed to be detransitivized by an Antipassive rule, but not otherwise.

Both points argue that middle clauses in Tongan and Samoan are not detransitivized, and consequently the Antipassive proposal should be rejected for the case marking proposal of 4.2.2. The latter proposal claims that middle clauses in these languages are superficially transitive, but require a special case assignment rule, either (42) or (43):

(42)   [+middle] → [+__Subj i/ki DO]

(43)   When there are two direct case NPs in a clause containing a middle verb, mark the direct object with i/ki.

4.3. SOME RULES THAT ARE SENSITIVE TO CASE MARKING

Having defended a proposal for case assignment in Tongan and Samoan, we can now raise the question of what role (if any) case marking plays in the syntax of these languages. This section argues that case marking is not merely a morphological device but instead is referred to by several superficial rules and morphology rules.

4.3.1 deals with Relativization and Clefting in Tongan and Samoan; 4.3.2 briefly summarizes the situation for several morphology rules.

4.3.1. Relativization and Clefting in Tongan and Samoan

The question of the relevance of case marking to syntax is first raised by middle clauses in Tongan and Samoan. Above it was argued that these clauses are superficially transitive but take their direct objects in a special case. This proposal successfully accounts for a number of facts: for instance, the ability of middle clauses to host direct object-referring rules such as Samoan Object Incorporation, Samoan Quantifier Float, and Tongan Quantifier Float, as well as their ability to host subject-referring rules sensitive to transitivity, such as Samoan Equi and Samoan Clitic Placement. However, it provides only a partial account of the facts of Tongan Relativization and Clefting, discussed in 4.2.3.4.

Relativization and Clefting in Tongan treat the subjects of middle clauses like transitive subjects, but their direct objects like oblique NPs. Now if these rules were sensitive to transitivity alone, we would expect them to treat middle clauses as consistently transitive or intransitive. The fact that they appear not to suggests that they refer to some notion in addition to transitivity.

A comparable situation obtains for Relativization and Clefting in Samoan. Relativization in Samoan has a deletion strategy, which deletes the relative noun, and a pronominalization strategy, which simply pronominalizes it. The deletion strategy is required for direct objects:

(44) Na mātou tuli-ina   le teine lea sā
      past we   chase-Trans the girl that [past
      'We chased the girl who

      fasi (?'oia) e   le tama.
      hit her   Erg the boy]
      the boy hit.'

The pronominalization strategy is required for oblique NPs:

(45) 'O le ā   le aso o Mele e   alu *(ai)
      Pred the what? the day of Mary [uns go   Pro
      'Which day is Mary going to the store (lit.

      'i le fale'oloa?
      to the store]
      Which is Mary's day for (her) to go to the store)?'

Clefting has a chopping strategy, which moves the focused NP and leaves a hole, and a copying strategy, which moves the NP but leaves behind a pronominal copy. The chopping strategy is required for direct objects:

236   Case Assignment in the Ergative Languages

> (46)   'O   tamaiti nei na   (ia) maua (*lātou).
>   Pred children this past he catch them
>   'It is these children that he found.'

The copying strategy is required for oblique NPs:

> (47)   'O   le fale'oloa sā   'ou maua *(ai) Ioane
>   Pred the store   past I   catch Pro John
>   'It was in the store that I caught John
>
>   'o   gaoi niu.
>   Comp steal coconut
>   stealing the coconuts.'

Put more generally, these rules require affected NPs that are direct objects to leave a hole, and ones that are oblique to leave behind a copy.

Now when the direct object of a middle clause undergoes Relativization or Clefting, it is treated like an oblique NP for the purposes of these restrictions: it must leave behind a copy. Consider the Relativization sentence:

> (48)   'Āfai e   leai se tupe, e   leai se mea   e
>   when uns not a money uns not a thing [uns
>   'If there's no money, there is nothing to
>
>   popole ai.
>   worry Pro]
>   worry about.'

And the Clefting sentence:

> (49)   'O   ai   na   ia ьзaleaga 'i ai?
>   Pred who? past he mistreat to Pro
>   'Who did he mistreat?'

It can be shown that middle clauses in Samoan are treated as transitive by rules that apply before Relativization and Clefting (e.g. Quantifier Float) as well as ones that apply after it (e.g. Clitic Placement), so it is likely that they are transitive when they undergo Relativization and Clefting themselves. But then the fact that the latter rules treat

Case Assignment in the Ergative Languages

their direct objects like oblique NPs suggests that they refer not only to transitivity, but to some additional notion.

The identity of this other notion is revealed by a closer examination of the Tongan and Samoan facts: both languages require the direct objects of middle clauses to be relativized and clefted exactly like the oblique NPs whose case marking they share. Thus in Tongan, when middle objects marked with ki or oblique NPs marked with ki are relativized, both are pronominalized to ki ai; when middle objects marked with 'i or oblique NPs marked with 'i are relativized, both are pronominalized to ai. Similar observations can be made about Clefting in Tongan and Relativization and Clefting in Samoan.

This suggests that direct objects of middle clauses are relativized and clefted like oblique NPs because they look like them on the surface. The most general way to describe this would be to build a condition into Relativization and Clefting in these languages that mentions case marking directly, since it is the one salient characteristic shared by the NPs in question:

(50)   The pronominalization strategy/copying strategy is required for NPs with oblique case marking.

The entire set of restrictions on Relativization and Clefting can then be stated:

(51) a.   The pronominalization strategy/copying strategy is required for NPs with oblique case marking.

   b.   The deletion strategy/chopping strategy is required for direct objects.

   c.   In Tongan, the deletion strategy/chopping strategy is required for third singular intransitive subjects.

238   Case Assignment in the Ergative Languages

Restriction (51a) is extrinsically ordered before (51b). Except for the situations mentioned in (51), either strategy of the rules is allowed.

If the approach outlined above is correct, then Relativization and Clefting in Tongan and Samoan refer in part to case marking rather than structural configurations. In other words, their operation depends in part on the output of the case assignment rules.

4.3.2. Other Rules

The result just reached raises the question of whether other rules of Tongan or Samoan refer to case marking. Here two possible rules of this type are discussed, both of them morphology rules in Samoan.

The first rule is Possessor Marking, which assigns the possessive particles a 'dominant' or o 'subordinate' to the subject or direct object of a nominalization. The subject of the nominalization has either been moved to the left of the nominalized verb by Pronoun Preposing, the nominal analogue of Clitic Placement, or else appears to the right of it, in which case it would undergo case assignment (see 6.5.2.2).

Possessor Marking is sensitive to case marking in two respects. First, it is required for NPs in the unmarked (i.e. absolutive) case. Thus the rule must apply to intransitive subjects, middle subjects, and canonical transitive direct objects following the nominalized verb:

(52) a. le o'o   mai o le tala lelei 'i Sāmoa
         the arrive here of the news good to Samoa
         'the coming of the good news to Samoa'

     b. le kuka-ina   e   John o le i'a
         the cook-Trans Erg John of the fish
         'John's cooking of the fish'

It applies to preposed subjects, which are never marked for

case, either obligatorily (in formal Samoan) or optionally (in informal Samoan):

(53) a. l-o-na   'ave-ina   o le ta'avale
         the-of-him drive-Trans of the car
         'his driving of the car'

     b. le-na 'ave-ina   o le ta'avale
         the-he drive-Trans of the car
         'his driving of the car'

And it is optional for middle direct objects, which are marked with the prepositions <u>i</u> 'at' or '<u>i</u> 'to':

(54) a. l-o-na   mana'o o le teine
         the-of-him want   of the girl
         'his wanting of the girl'

     b. l-o-na   mana'o 'i le teine
         the-of-him want   to the girl
         'his wanting the girl'

Second, though available for preposed canonical transitive subjects (see (53a)), the rule does not affect such subjects if they appear to the right of the nominalized verb and are marked with the ergative <u>e</u>. Consider:

(55) a. *le faitau-ina a tātou o le nusipepa
          the read-Trans of us   of the newspaper
          (our reading of the newspaper)

     b. le faitau-ina e   tātou o le nusipepa
         the read-Trans Erg we   of the newspaper
         'our reading of the newspaper'

These facts argue that Possessor Marking should be restricted as follows:

(56) a. Possessor Marking is obligatory for NPs in the
         unmarked (absolutive) case.

     b. Possessor Marking is not allowed for NPs in the
         ergative case.

240   Case Assignment in the Ergative Languages

Both of the restrictions of (56) refer to case marking. See 6.5.3 for a proposed historical account of restriction (56b).

The second rule of Samoan which might be sensitive to case marking is -Cia Insertion, which was described in 2.2.2.2. This global rule attaches the transitive suffix to the verb as a flag for certain types of missing transitive subjects. It applies to canonical transitive clauses:

(57)   Sā 'e kiki-ina 'oia?
       past you kick-Trans him
       'Did you kick him?'

But not middle clauses:

(58)   Sā 'e mulimuli i lana ta'avale?
       past you follow   at his car
       'Did you follow his car?'

One way of handling this difference might be to state -Cia Insertion in terms of case marking:

(59)   Attach -Cia to the verb if the subject of the clause would have appeared in the ergative case, but (a) is the generic agent, or (b) has been moved or extracted by a superficial rule.

However, it should be emphasized that the rule could also be stated in other, perhaps simpler, ways, such as the statement in terms of canonical transitive verbs given in 2.2.2.2.[3]

In short, Possessor Marking in Samoan is sensitive to case marking, and -Cia Insertion may be as well. This suggests that morphology rules as well as superficial rules may refer to the output of case assignment.

4.4. ON THE ROLE OF CASE MARKING IN SYNTAX

The preceding two sections of this chapter have argued for two points. First, middle clauses in Tongan and Samoan cannot be subsumed under the general case assignment rule, but require a special case assignment rule of their own. Second, there are rules in each of these languages which are sensitive to case marking rather than grammatical relations or structural configurations.

These points lead to the conclusion that case marking in Tongan and Samoan interacts with the rest of the syntax --a conclusion that is rather surprising in view of recent work. Because case marking is realized morphologically, there has been some tendency to view it as a housekeeping rule with few, if any, syntactic consequences. Some linguists have proposed essentially that case marking serves to disambiguate subjects and direct objects; others have proposed that case marking should line up transparently with grammatical relations (see Chapter 3). The discussion of this chapter suggests instead that neither of these proposals is the whole story. If case marking were merely an anti-ambiguity device, it would be difficult to explain why two distinct types of case marking are exhibited by transitive clauses in Tongan and Samoan. If it were assumed to line up transparently with grammatical relations, it would be difficult to explain why some NPs with oblique case marking have the character of direct objects but others do not. In order to account for these facts and the ability of case marking to be referred to by other syntactic rules, some more sophisticated view of case assignment is called for.

While such a view will not be developed here, some preliminary steps can be taken in its direction by observing that case marking appears not to interact with the rest of the syntax entirely freely. In particular, case marking is referred to by superficial rules and morphology rules in Tongan and Samoan, but not by major rules in either of these languages.

We would like to be able to give an account of this limited interaction. One account which suggests itself would invoke ordering: if major rules are assumed to be extrinsically ordered before case assignment, then they will not have the opportunity to refer to case marking, case having not yet been assigned at the time that they apply. On the other hand, if superficial rules and morphology rules do not have this ordering, then they will be able to apply after case assignment and refer to its output.[4]

It can be tentatively suggested, then, that major rules are extrinsically ordered before case assignment, but superficial rules and morphology rules are not. Such a proposal has two desirable consequences. First, it accounts for the apparent generalization that rules other than superficial rules and morphology rules do not refer to case marking. To put it another way, while case marking does play a role in syntax, its role is relatively superficial. Second, in claiming that major rules have ordering properties not shared by the other types of rules, it suggests that the typology of major vs. superficial rules may have some basis in ordering. This brings the typology somewhat closer to the cyclic vs. postcyclic typology, which served as its original model.

NOTES

1. For arguments that subject and direct object are not defined in terms of linear order in Tongan or Samoan, see Anderson and Chung (1977) and Chung (1976a).
2. Although both strategies for Relativization are possible for subjects of middle and canonical transitive clauses, the frequency with which they are employed appears to vary. The deletion strategy seems more common than the pronominalization strategy for subjects of middle clauses;

the pronominalization strategy is far more common than the deletion strategy for subjects of canonical transitive clauses. The different frequencies remain unexplained within the proposal outlined in the text.
3. It might conceivably be proposed that -_Cia_ Insertion should be stated to refer to transitive subjects; if so, the rule would appear to treat middle clauses as detransitivized, since -_Cia_ is not inserted in them. While such an alternative is possible, it seems empirically indistinguishable from the alternatives suggested in the text.
4. To maintain the claim that major rules are extrinsically ordered before case assignment and describe the interaction of case marking with Raising in Tongan and Samoan (see 3.3.2.1 and 3.3.3.1), case assignment in these languages would have to be global. This is perhaps not surprising, given that morphology rules in other languages of the world are often global (see 3.1.3).

5. Previous Approaches to the History of the Case System

The diversity of case marking in Polynesian raises two historical questions, which form the topic of this and the following chapters. First, what was the case system of Proto-Polynesian? And second, how did the systems of the attested languages evolve from it?

Both questions follow naturally from the survey of case morphology given in Chapter 2, where it was observed that two generalizations hold for case marking throughout Polynesian. The case marking of canonical transitive clauses in the accusative languages resembles that of middle clauses in all Polynesian languages:

(1) Transitive case marking in accusative languages:
     Verb   Subj   _i_ DO
     Middle case marking throughout Polynesian:
     Verb   Subj   _i/ki_ DO

Further, the case marking of passive clauses in the accusative languages resembles that of canonical transitive clauses in the ergative languages:

(2) Passive in accusative languages:
     Verb-_Cia_   _e_ Agent   Subj
                    (=underlying   (=underlying
                    Subj)   DO)
     Transitive case marking in ergative languages:
     Verb   _e_ Subj   DO

These similarities argue that it would be wrong to reconstruct both types of case system for Proto-Polynesian. Rather, the two are descended from a single, original case system that has undergone a number of changes in the daughter languages.

Although it is logically conceivable that the original case system might have been a hybrid of the attested types, such a possibility has been largely ignored by previous approaches, which have adopted one of two stronger positions: either Proto-Polynesian was an accusative language, and the case systems of the ergative Polynesian languages are a later development; or else the proto-language was ergative, and the case systems of the accusative languages are a later development. These two positions have generated longstanding controversy in Polynesian linguistics (see Williams 1928 and S. Churchward 1928 for two early views).

This chapter reviews two recent positions on the history of the case system and offers commentary on each. 5.1 describes Hale's (1968, 1970) and Hohepa's (1969a) proposals that Proto-Polynesian was accusative; 5.2 describes Clark's (1973a, 1976) proposal that it was ergative. A separate proposal for the history of the case system is presented in Chapter 6.

5.1. PROTO-POLYNESIAN AS AN ACCUSATIVE LANGUAGE

The idea that Proto-Polynesian had an accusative case system was advanced recently by Hale (1968, 1970) and Hohepa (1969a) in several thought-provoking and controversial articles. Their proposals can be referred to jointly as the Hale-Hohepa proposal.

5.1.1. The Hale-Hohepa Proposal

The Hale-Hohepa proposal originated in Hale's (1968) review

of Hohepa's (1967) grammar of Maori. There Hale argued that Pronominalization in Maori preceded Passive --an ordering which he identified as crosslinguistically unusual. Hale's arguments for such an ordering, which themselves are controversial (see Clark 1973b), do not concern us here. What is of interest is that Hale used the ordering to suggest a possible scenario for the history of case marking in Polynesian, which runs as follows. Suppose that Proto-Polynesian, like Maori, had an accusative case system but ordered Pronominalization before Passive. After the split of the proto-language into daughters, various languages would change to eliminate the unusual ordering, either by reordering the rules or else by making Passive obligatory for transitive clauses. Changes of the first type would lead to accusative languages, such as Hawaiian; those of the second type would lead to ergative languages, such as Tongan. Although Hale claimed that Maori reflected the proto-case system and the original ordering of Pronominalization and Passive, he speculated (1968: 98) that its preference for Passive might indicate that it was "changing toward the ergative type".

Hale's proposal for Polynesian, and his similar proposal (1970) for Australian languages, were incorporated by Hohepa (1969a) into a proposal called 'the accusative-to-ergative drift'. Hohepa proposed that individual Polynesian languages have been undergoing a longterm change from accusative to ergative case marking. He suggested that such a change involves two stages: first, Passive is reanalyzed as an obligatory rule; and second, passive clauses are reanalyzed as active transitive clauses (1969a: 324). Hohepa outlined the status of a number of languages with respect to this change, which he speculated might eventually affect all of Polynesian.

Previous Approaches to the History of the Case System

Despite differences in approach, the two proposals are alike in claiming that Proto-Polynesian was accusative and that the case systems of the ergative languages have resulted from an obligatory Passive rule. These and other features of the Hale-Hohepa proposal are outlined below.

(3) The Hale-Hohepa Proposal:
   a. Proto-Polynesian had an accusative case system.
   b. Case marking in the ergative languages is the result of two changes:
      (i) reanalysis of Passive as obligatory;
      (ii) reanalysis of passive clauses as active transitive clauses.

   Hale's Proposal Only:
   c. Change (i) eliminates the ordering Pronominalization-precedes-Passive.

   Hohepa's Proposal Only:
   d. Changes (i) and (ii) are instances of syntactic drift.

5.1.2. Commentary

The Hale-Hohepa proposal gives an elegant account of the history of the case system, and in this sense is initially appealing. However, objections can be raised to the claim that the ergative Polynesian languages have, at some point in their history, reanalyzed Passive as an obligatory rule.

To begin with, the motivation for such a change would not be entirely clear. Hale hypothesized that Passive might have become obligatory in order to eliminate an unusual ordering of Passive and Pronominalization. But, as observed by several people (Hale, class lectures, 1969; Clark 1973b), there is no firm evidence that Pronominalization ever preceded Passive in Maori or other Polynesian languages.

Further, if Passive were obligatory in one of the attested languages, we might expect subjects of intransitive clauses and underlying direct objects of transitive clauses to form a unified category for the purposes of major rules (see Chapter 3). But, as far as I know, such a situation does not obtain in any Polynesian language.

For these reasons, the Hale-Hohepa proposal will not be considered further. In Chapter 6, however, I will argue for a proposal that resembles it in claiming that Proto-Polynesian was accusative.

5.2. PROTO-POLYNESIAN AS AN ERGATIVE LANGUAGE

The Hale-Hohepa proposal has been criticized by Clark (1973a, 1976), who offers the alternative hypothesis that Proto-Polynesian had an ergative case system.

5.2.1. Clark's Proposal

Clark's proposal is based on two assumptions about the nature of syntactic reconstruction, discussed in some detail in Clark (1976). First, it is assumed that the optimal reconstruction will be the simplest, in the sense of positing the most plausible proto-situation and the fewest and most natural changes from it. Second, it is assumed that reconstructions are based on distributional facts. Clark (1976: 25) illustrates his use of these assumptions with a hypothetical example:

> If, in a family with several daughter languages and no evidence of subgrouping, a large majority of the languages share a feature X and only a small number have Y, this counts as evidence in favor of the hypothesis that

249   Previous Approaches to the History of the Case System

> the proto-language had X. This is not an extension of
> political democracy to the linguistic realm....The X hy-
> pothesis involves postulating only a few independent
> changes of X to Y, whereas the Y hypothesis involves a
> large number of independent changes from Y to X.

He goes on (1976: 25) to describe another hypothetical example involving a proto-language, PA-G, which splits into two independent daughter languages plus a subgroup, PC-G, with a number of members:

> Things are more complicated where subgrouping does exist,
> but the principle remains the same....Here a majority
> of the daughter languages have the feature X. However,
> they all belong to a single subgroup, while two indepen-
> dent daughter languages have Y. The hypothesis PA-G=X
> involves a minimum of two independent changes from X to
> Y, but the Y hypothesis requires only a single change
> Y>X between PA-G and PC-G. Hence in this case distribu-
> tional evidence is in favor of the Y hypothesis.

Applying these assumptions to Polynesian, Clark observes that three surface case patterns are found for underlyingly transitive clauses in Polynesian languages:

(4)   Clark's Case Patterns for Transitive Clauses:
        Pattern I: Verb   Subj   i/ki DO
        Pattern II: Verb-Cia   e Subj   DO
        Pattern III: Verb   e Subj   DO

He then characterizes their distribution as follows. Pattern III is found in the Tongic and Samoic-Outlier subgroups and occurs sporadically in the East Polynesian subgroup.[1] Pattern II is also found in Tongic and Samoic-Outlier and is used for passives in East Polynesian. But Pattern I occurs for canonical transitive clauses only in East Polynesian, although it is found for middle clauses in all three subgroups. Schematically:

250   Previous Approaches to the History of the Case System

(5)   Distribution of Clark's Case Patterns:

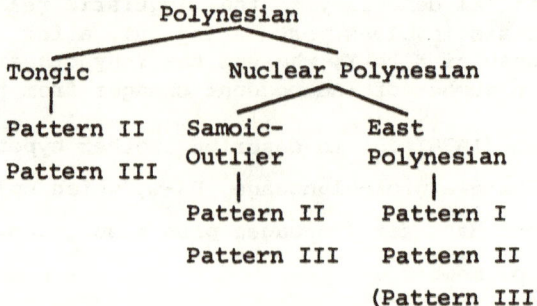

Such a distribution leads Clark (1973a: 586) to conclude that "by elementary reconstructive reasoning, the simplest hypothesis is that the Tongic-Samoic system prevailed" in Proto-Polynesian. He proposes that Proto-Polynesian used Patterns II and III for canonical transitive clauses but Pattern I for middle clauses --in our terms (see 2.1.1), it had an ergative case system.

Clark's proposal for the development of case marking in East Polynesian languages is presented most explicitly in Clark (1973a), where the following is suggested. In Proto-East Polynesian, Pattern I was generalized to all transitive clauses as a "marked imperfective construction" (1973a: 589). In addition, the -Cia suffix became obligatory for Pattern III, so that this pattern fell together with Pattern II. Later, in individual East Polynesian languages, the 'imperfective' Pattern I became the norm for transitive clauses, and the 'perfective' II-III were reinterpreted as passive. Clark speculates that the majority of East Polynesian languages have undergone all of these changes, but Maori has stopped at the perfective/imperfective stage.

The salient points of Clark's proposal are outlined below:

(6)   Clark's Proposal:
        a. Proto-Polynesian had an ergative case sys-

tem.
b. Case marking in the East Polynesian languages is the result of four changes:
- (i) generalization of the middle case pattern to transitive clauses that are imperfective;
- (ii) generalization of -Cia to transitive clauses that are perfective;
- (iii) reanalysis of the imperfective pattern as the normal case pattern for transitive clauses;
- (iv) reanalysis of perfective clauses as passive clauses.

5.2.2. Commentary

Clark's proposal has been viewed favorably by many Polynesian linguists, in large part because it invokes the comparative method and considers the internal and external relationships of Polynesian languages. The methodology of the proposal and the evidence supporting it therefore merit close attention.

5.2.2.1 deals with the emphasis laid on distributional facts in Clark's reconstruction; 5.2.2.2, with the requirement that changes be plausible; and 5.2.2.3, with the external evidence and its significance.

5.2.2.1. Distributional Facts and Reconstruction.

Although Clark (1976: 25) notes only that distributional facts are among "the types of evidence most commonly used" in reconstruction, in practice his proposal appears to hold to the stronger position that reconstructions are based primarily (if not totally) on distributional facts. Thus, the proposed reconstruction of the Proto-Polynesian case system outlined

252 Previous Approaches to the History of the Case System

in 5.2.1 relies primarily on distributional evidence. Clark
also suggests that his proposal may be superior to the Hale-
Hohepa proposal in positing changes which happened only once
in the history of Polynesian, thereby avoiding an appeal to
parallel development. As he says:

> In the remainder of this chapter I will discuss a hypoth-
> esis that avoids the problem of parallel development by
> proposing that P[roto-]P[oly]N[esian] had a structure
> more like TON[gan] or SAM[oan], and that the major inno-
> vation took place once, in P[roto-]E[ast] P[olynesian]...
> (1976: 70)
>
> ..."drift" is not part of the hypothesis....Samoic and
> Tongic languages have not expanded the domain of pattern
> I significantly from P[roto-]P[oly]N[esian], and the
> theory makes no prediction that they will do so....All
> the changes postulated took place once within a single
> language. (1976: 81)

The idea that parallel development should be avoided,
where possible, can be traced to the assumption that reconstructions should reflect the distributional facts as closely
as possible. On this view, if related languages happen to
share a feature, it should be reconstructed for a language
ancestral to them. Such a view implies that parallel but independent changes should be posited within a language family
only under unusual circumstances --for instance, when the
parallelism can be attributed to a specific, overriding "mo-
tive force" (Clark 1973a: 588).

However, linguistic change is probably more complex than
such a view suggests. As recognized as early as Schmidt
(1872), the wide distribution of a linguistic feature within
a family is often due to changes postdating the dissolution
of the parent language. It can be speculated that these parallel but independent changes arise in two general ways. On
the one hand, changes may arise independently in particular
languages if they result in more highly valued grammars from

Previous Approaches to the History of the Case System

the point of view of linguistic theory. On the other hand, parallel but independent changes in related languages may have their origins in their common ancestor. The latter possibility is perhaps not surprising. Assuming that a parent language, like other languages, is continually in the process of change, one might expect some changes to have been implemented only partially, or just begun, at the time that the language splits into its daughters. The continuation and conclusion of such changes in individual daughter languages represents one type of parallel development. Changes of this type are usual rather than remarkable --a point made ably by Meillet (1966[1925]: 48-49):

> Les changements ultérieurs sont largement commandés par l'état de la langue commune et par la façon dont elle se brise. Il suit de là que des changements identiques ou semblables ont lieu même après la séparation et le commencement de la différenciation des langues issues de la "langue commune". Ce fait est souvent méconnu. Les traités de grammaire comparée procèdent souvent comme si tous les faits superposables des divers représentants d'une même "langue commune" remontaient à l'époque d'unité....Or, rien n'est moins conforme à la réalité.

This conception of linguistic change introduces a parallel complexity to the theory of reconstruction; namely, reconstructions should not be based entirely or even primarily on distributional facts. Instead, they should be supported wherever possible by more reliable evidence of the age of the feature in question, such as morphological relics surviving in the attested languages (see Chapter 6). The appeal to other types of evidence is necessary if reconstruction is to approximate the parent language as closely as possible; otherwise, it merely provides a summary of correspondences among attested languages. The failure of Clark's proposal to take this into account could be interpreted as a methodological difficulty. At any rate, the fact that the proposal does not posit parallel changes cannot be counted as a clear point in its favor.

5.2.2.2. **Plausibility**. Clark's proposal also assumes that reconstructions should be evaluated according to plausibility --both of the reconstructed system and of the changes required to relate it to the attested systems. This assumption is standard in comparative historical linguistics, and will also be adopted here. What is unclear is whether some of the changes posited within Clark's proposal are, in fact, possible.

Consider, for instance, the reanalysis of perfective clauses as passive suggested by Clark (1973a) for many East Polynesian languages, and schematized below:

(7)   Reanalysis of Perfective Clauses as Passive:
   a. Verb-Cia   e Subj   DO   (perfective)
              → reanalyzed as →
   b. Verb-Cia   e Agent   Subj
                   (=underlying   (=underlying
                    Subj)   DO)

According to recent literature on the mechanisms of change (e.g. Andersen 1973), reanalyses are the product of ambiguities in surface data: they occur when a given surface structure can be analyzed in more than one way, and a new generation of speakers chooses an analysis different from that of preceding generations. For (7) to be a possible reanalysis, then, we might expect the surface structure of the stage (7a) to have two possible analyses, one of which is represented by the stage (7b).

However, the structure of (7a) does not seem to be ambiguous in this sense. In particular, the unmarked NP serves as direct object, and the e NP as subject, at all levels of derivation --a fact which makes it difficult to see how they might have been reinterpreted as surface subject and agent, respectively.

Some further motivation is therefore necessary in order for (7) to count as a possible change. In Clark (1973a: 589-90), it is suggested that such a motivation might have been provided by clauses with unspecified subjects or direct objects:

> It would seem that the basis for this re-interpretation was present from the earliest times, in sentences with subject or object unspecified:
>
> (67) PPN *e kai te ika
>   'The fish is eating'
>
> (68)   *e kai-na te ika
>   'The fish is being eaten'
>
> As a by-product, as it were, of its function of indicating transitivity (presence of a specific object), the suffix in such sentences served to indicate the case relation of the lone unmarked noun phrase, which of course represented the point-of-view of the sentence. Thus, in some way which I find it difficult to formulate precisely, this type of sentence may have been the pivot around which the whole system swung from perfective-imperfective to passive-active.

This passage is open to several interpretations, one of which might be that the reanalysis in question involved a shift of topic. On this view, the direct object of 'perfective' clauses would have first been reanalyzed as a topic, on the model of clauses like Clark's example (68), in which the subject is unspecified and the direct object is topic by default. This NP would then have been reanalyzed further as a surface subject, producing a situation in which topics and surface subjects would coincide.

Such a view predicts that topics and surface subjects should coincide in all languages which have undergone the proposed reanalysis --in other words, all languages in which

256   Previous Approaches to the History of the Case System

the clause type (7) is superficially passive. But this prediction is not borne out in particular East Polynesian languages. In Maori, for instance, (7) is superficially passive (see 2.2.1), but its topic is usually the surface agent (=underlying subject) rather than the surface subject (=underlying direct object). See Clark (1973b), and Chung and Timberlake (1974) for relevant examples.

In short, it appears that the reanalysis in (7) could not have involved a shift of topic, and so the question must be raised again of whether (7) as it stands could be a possible change. The view of reanalysis sketched above suggests that (7) may not be possible --a conclusion which presents another type of difficulty for Clark's proposal.

5.2.2.3. <u>External Evidence</u>. We turn finally to the evidence from the larger Eastern Oceanic family, which is said to be "strongly against" the Hale-Hohepa proposal (Clark 1976: 82) and in favor of Clark's.

(8) sketches the position of Polynesian within the Eastern Oceanic family, whose existence has been argued for by Pawley (1972):

(8)

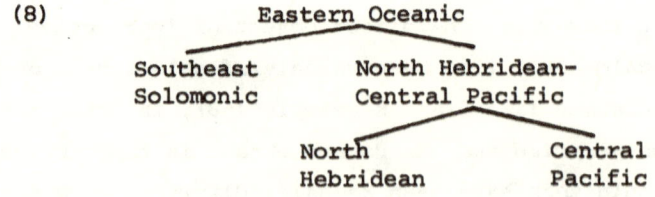

Following Pawley (1972) and Clark (1973a), it is possible to reconstruct the following details of the surface syntax of Proto-Eastern Oceanic. The basic word order of Proto-Eastern Oceanic was SVO; transitivity was indicated by a suffix *-<u>Ci</u>

257   Previous Approaches to the History of the Case System

attached to the verb. Subject and direct object were copied
by pronominal elements that were incorporated into the verb
complex, which is enclosed in brackets below:[2]

(9)   Intransitive and Transitive Clauses:
         Subj [SubjPro Verb]
         Subj [SubjPro Verb-Ci ObjPro] DO

The pronominal copy for third singular direct objects was *-a:

(10)   Transitive Clauses with Third Singular Objects:
         Subj [SubjPro Verb-Ci-a] DO

In many respects, such a system is equally far removed from Clark's proposal and the Hale-Hohepa proposal for Proto-Polynesian. In particular, both Clark's and Hale-Hohepa's proposals reconstruct Proto-Polynesian as having verb-initial word order, but Proto-Eastern Oceanic had the word order SVO. Both proposals reconstruct a system of prepositional case marking for Proto-Polynesian, but Proto-Eastern Oceanic did not have case markers for subjects or direct objects.

Perhaps the only respect in which one proposal might appear closer than the other to the Proto-Eastern Oceanic system involves the form *-Cia, which in Proto-Eastern Oceanic represented the transitive suffix plus a third singular direct object. Since Clark's proposal reconstructs Proto-Polynesian *-Cia as a transitive suffix, but the Hale-Hohepa proposal reconstructs it as a passive suffix, it might be supposed that Clark's reconstruction was closer in function to Proto-Eastern Oceanic *-Ci-a, and thus to be preferred.

The situation is more complicated, however, since Proto-Eastern Oceanic seems also to have had *-Ci-a forms with a rather different function from that sketched above. As pointed out by Andrew Pawley, a number of Eastern Oceanic languages give evidence of having (or having had) a suffix -a which forms adjectives from nouns and passive adjectives from verbs. In the latter use -a is attached to the transitive form of the verb, producing a derivative with the shape Stem-Ci-a and the meaning of a passive participle or adjective. Consider the following, from the Solomons language Nggela:

(11)   Na halili t-e   aho-ri-a   tua.
       the hook tns-it fasten-Trans-Suff ?
       'The hook is fixed.' (Fox 1950: 147; cf. aho
       'fasten')

According to Fox (1950), the -a suffix is mildly productive in Nggela and more productive in two other Solomons languages, Arosi and Lau. Although -a appears not to derive passive adjectives in Fijian, it nonetheless forms adjectives from nouns in that language; consider gelegele-a 'dirty', from gele 'dirt'.

If *-a can indeed be reconstructed as an adjectival suffix in Proto-Eastern Oceanic, and *-Ci-a as the suffixal morphology of passive adjectives derived from verbs, then the latter would seem closer to Hale-Hohepa's passive suffix than to Clark's transitive suffix. The full range of Eastern Oceanic evidence concerning *-Cia would thus seem to be indifferent between the two proposals.[3]

The external evidence is similarly unhelpful on the issue of the Proto-Polynesian case markers. As hinted above, the use of prepositional case markers for subjects and direct objects appears to have been a Proto-Polynesian innovation, and so *i, *ki, and *e cannot be reconstructed with these functions in the larger Eastern Oceanic family, although they can be identified with oblique prepositions there. For instance, Proto-Polynesian *i is identified by Pawley (1972) as a reflex of Proto-Eastern Oceanic *i 'locative'; and Proto-Polynesian *ki, as a reflex of Proto-North Hebridean-Central Pacific *ki 'dative-instrumental'. Although *e has no exact cognates outside Polynesian, it is identified by Pawley (1973a) and Clark (1973a) as an irregular reflex of Proto-Eastern Oceanic *i 'locative', which was extended to sources and causes in Proto-Central Pacific.

Conceivably, had some of these markers reflected case markers for subjects or direct objects in Proto-Eastern Oceanic, but others reflected oblique prepositions, there might have been a basis for choosing between Clark's and Hale-Hohepa's proposals. But the evidence indicates that all of the markers were originally oblique. Further, both *i and *e -- the prime candidates for nonoblique case markers in Proto-Polynesian-- can ultimately be traced to the same oblique preposition in Proto-Eastern Oceanic. This situation is not very revealing as far as Polynesian is concerned, and there appears to be no clear sense in which it argues for either proposal over the other.

5.3. SUMMARY

This chapter has examined two recent approaches to the Proto-Polynesian case system and its history: the Hale-Hohepa proposal that Proto-Polynesian was accusative, and Clark's proposal that it was ergative. It was argued that neither proposal is superior to the other as far as the evidence from the larger Eastern Oceanic family is concerned. The Hale-Hohepa proposal involves the questionable assumption that Passive became obligatory in some Polynesian languages, while Clark's proposal posits a reanalysis which may not be a possible change.

NOTES

1. Clark (1976: 71) suggests that Pattern III occurs in Easter Island, but notes in another place (1973a: 575) that the case system of that language has evolved "to the point where it is of little use in comparative reconstruction". It might appear that Pattern III also occurs, optionally, in Maori clauses introduced by the optative particle me:

   (a)   Me tua e   koe te rākau.
         opt fell Agt you the tree
         'You better fell the tree.'

   However, clauses of this type are better analyzed as passive clauses without the passive suffix (see 3.4.1.2) than as superficially transitive. Their underlying direct objects can, for instance, be qualified by the nonspecific article he, which occurs only with intransitive subjects (see 2.2.1.3).

2. Proto-Eastern Oceanic also had a transitive suffix *-Caki, used when the direct object had a semantic relation such as instrument or benefactive. See Pawley (1973b) for discussion. The Proto-Eastern Oceanic system is reflected in Fijian with slight differences, the most important of which is that the subject has shifted to the right and so the basic word order is VOS. See Pawley (1975) for discussion of the Fijian transitive suffix and the third singular copy -a.

3. A transitive suffix *-Ci should probably be reconstructed for Proto-Polynesian (see Clark 1973a); however, its existence does not bear directly on the question of the case system. Reflexes of *-Ci in individual Polynesian languages select whatever is the normal case marking for canonical transitive clauses, whether accusative (as in Maori) or ergative (as in Tongan).

6. The Passive-to-Ergative Reanalysis

This chapter presents a new approach to the history of the case system. It is argued that the Proto-Polynesian case system was accusative, and in this respect resembled the systems of many East Polynesian languages. It is argued further that the ergative case systems of Tongic and Samoic-Outlier languages arose through a reanalysis of passive clauses as active transitive clauses.

The arguments used to support this approach are those typically used for reconstructions within the comparative method. First, facts of the attested Polynesian languages argue that the proto-case system was accusative. Second, the reconstructed system can be related to the attested systems by means of possible types of change.

6.1 outlines the proposal for the history of the case system and comments on its plausibility; 6.2 discusses the strategy for reconstruction. 6.3 through 6.5 reconstruct the functions of Proto-Polynesian *-Cia, *i, and *e, which figured prominently in the case and voice morphology of that language. It is argued that Proto-Polynesian *-Cia was a passive suffix, *i was a marker of direct objects, and *e was an oblique preposition. These conclusions combine to argue that the proto-case system was accusative. 6.7 presents a more detailed scenario for the rise of ergative case marking. 6.8 is a conclusion.

6.1. A NEW PROPOSAL

6.1.1. Outline

The proposal discussed in this chapter claims that Proto-Polynesian had an accusative case system. Subjects were unmarked; direct objects of canonical transitive clauses were marked with *i; direct objects of middle clauses were marked with the oblique prepositions *i 'at' or *ki 'to':

(1) Proto-Polynesian Case Marking:

Verb	Subj		(intransitive)
Verb	Subj	i DO	(canonical transitive)
Verb	Subj	i/ki DO	(middle)

Proto-Polynesian also had a Passive rule which promoted the direct object to subject, turned the underlying subject into an oblique noun marked with *e, and attached the passive suffix *-Cia to the verb. This rule produced the structure:

(2) Proto-Polynesian Passive:

Verb-Cia   e Agent   Subj
              (=underlying   (=underlying
               Subj)   DO)

It is claimed further that Passive applied more often than not to canonical transitive clauses. This situation may have resulted, as it does in Maori, from a requirement like (3) applying fairly close to the surface:

(3) Apply Passive to clauses containing an affected direct object.

The high frequency of Passive had the result that the rule was relatively opaque, in a sense of this term like that proposed for phonology by Kiparsky (1971, 1973). Passive clauses sometimes lacked the semantic and discourse properties most typically associated with Passive in the languages of the world. This made the rule difficult to learn, in that it was hard for new speakers to figure out the semantic and discourse conditions governing it, and hard to predict when the rule should or should not apply. As a result, it was correspondingly hard to recover the underlying structure of underlyingly transitive clauses from their surface structure. After the split of Proto-Polynesian into daughter languages, this opacity was decreased by two subsequent developments.

In a number of East Polynesian languages (e.g. Hawaiian, Tahitian), condition (3) on Passive was lost, leaving the active as the more common surface construction for canonical transitive clauses.

In Tongic and Samoic-Outlier languages, passive clauses were reanalyzed as active transitive clauses: their underlying subject was reinterpreted as a surface subject, and their underlying direct object, as a surface direct object:

(4)   The Passive-to-Ergative Reanalysis:

Verb-<u>Cia</u>   e Agent   Subj
                (=underlying   (=underlying
                Subj)   DO)

→ reanalyzed as →

Verb-<u>Cia</u>   e Subj   DO

This change, referred to here as the <u>passive-to-ergative</u> reanalysis, eliminated Passive; at the same time, it created a new type of case marking for transitive clauses which identified the direct object (not the subject) with the subject of an intransitive clause. In most languages this ergative pattern replaced the older accusative pattern for canonical transitive clauses, resulting in the ergative case systems found today.

The proposal resembles the Hale-Hohepa proposal in claiming that Proto-Polynesian was accusative, but differs in claiming that ergative case marking arose directly through the reanalysis of (4). It thus avoids the difficulties of an intermediate stage involving an obligatory Passive. It differs from Clark's proposal in claiming that the proto-case system was accusative rather than ergative.

6.1.2. Plausibility

For the proposal of 6.1.1 to be considered seriously, it should be shown that the claims made by it are allowed within linguistic theory and the theory of language change. This subsection gives the outlines of such a demonstration, starting from two familiar assumptions about what is possible. First, it is assumed that a linguistic feature is de facto possible if it is found in some attested language. (This is, obviously, a sufficient but not a necessary condition for a possible linguistic feature.) Second, it is assumed that a linguistic change is possible if it is allowed within the theory of change summarized by King (1969), which recognizes five types of change: rule addition, rule loss, rule simplification, rule reordering, and reanalysis.

The features posited for Proto-Polynesian in 6.1.1 are fragments of possible linguistic systems, since they occur in a number of attested languages. The case system of (1) and the Passive of (2) are found in several East Polynesian languages (e.g. Maori, Hawaiian, Tahitian) and have parallels in other languages of the world. Passive rules with high frequencies are found in Maori and may be characteristic of the larger Austronesian family, since they also occur in languages such as Indonesian and Tagalog. Finally, condition (3) was proposed in 2.2.1.5 as a condition on Passive in Maori.

The changes posited for the subsequent history of Polynesian appear to be allowed within the theory of change. The loss of condition (3), which was hypothesized for several East Polynesian languages, can be viewed as a simplification of Passive. Further, the passive-to-ergative reanalysis of (4) qualifies as a possible reanalysis, in the following sense.

The Passive-to-Ergative Reanalysis

According to recent literature on the mechanisms of change (e.g. Andersen 1973), reanalyses are products of ambiguities in surface data; they occur when a given surface structure can be analyzed in more than one way, and new speakers choose an analysis different from that of the preceding generation. The passive-to-ergative reanalysis conforms to this definition in that passive clauses like (2) have two possible analyses. In terms of surface structure they are intransitive clauses with an oblique NP and a subject; in terms of underlying structure they are transitive clauses with a subject and a direct object. The change of (4) consists of the underlying analysis winning out over the surface analysis: the underlying subject is reinterpreted as a surface subject, and the underlying direct object, as a surface direct object.

Finally, we turn to the motivation proposed for these changes --that they decrease the opacity of Passive.

The notion of opacity is due to Kiparsky, who states (1973: 79) that it is "intended as a measure of...the 'distance' between what the rule says and the phonetic forms in the language of whose grammar the rule is a part". His definition (1973: 79) runs as follows:

> A process P of the form A → B/C_D [is] <u>opaque</u> to the extent that there are phonetic forms in the language having either
>
> (i)   A in env. C_D
>
> or...
>
> (iia) B <u>derived by the process P</u> in env. other than C_D
> (iib) B <u>not derived by the process P</u>...in env. C_D.

According to Kiparsky (1971), opacity adds to linguistic complexity and so can be used to predict the direction of certain types of change. In particular, it is proposed that if rules are reordered, the new ordering will minimize opacity.

Although Kiparsky's discussion is limited to phonology, the definition of opaque rules can be extended in a direct way to syntax. Further, assuming that semantic and discourse conditions form part of the environment of a syntactic rule, and there are universal expectations about the conditions attached to particular rules, then the Passive reconstructed for Proto-Polynesian can be identified as relatively opaque. Because of condition (3), passive clauses appeared in contexts lacking the typical semantic and discourse conditions associated with Passive; the rule was therefore opaque in sense (iia) of the definition quoted above. The two subsequent changes posited for Polynesian decrease this opacity, either by eliminating (3) or else doing away with Passive altogether. The motivation proposed for these changes thus appears to be a possible motivation for change, assuming that the idea that change works generally to decrease opacity is correct.

6.2. ON RECONSTRUCTION

The proposal of 6.1.1 is supported by evidence that the Proto-Polynesian case system was accusative. Before turning to this, some remarks should be made about the framework in which the reconstruction of the case system will be conducted.

It has been observed by Watkins (1976) that the kinds of facts relevant for syntactic reconstruction are rather different from those most important in constructing a synchronic grammar. Very generally, the former kinds of facts are exceptional or restricted, the latter are regular or general. The observation implies that syntactic reconstructions often build on the results of internal reconstruction in attested languages. That is, one first uses facts internal to a particular language to reconstruct the grammar of an earlier stage of it, and then compares grammars of different languages.

The Passive-to-Ergative Reanalysis

The facts relevant for internal reconstruction can be referred to as relics or archaisms. These are constructions that are unmotivated or restricted synchronically, but can be explained as survivors of motivated or general constructions from an earlier stage of the language. In other words, they are exceptions that cease to be exceptional when placed in the context of a historical proposal. Though this definition is not particularly rigorous, it approximates the working definition used with success within the comparative method, and will be adopted here.

The reconstruction of the case system follows this approach in relying on internal reconstruction, and on archaisms in particular. Distributional facts are not relied on as heavily, for reasons given in Chapter 5. The reconstruction further assumes the theory of change summarized by King (1969) and mentioned in 6.1.2. Such a theory is necessary because the other half of reconstruction consists of relating the reconstructed system to the attested systems by means of possible types of change. The role of this in the proposal of this chapter is discussed further in 6.7.

Finally, the reconstruction is conducted against the following background. Morphologically, it is clear from the attested languages that a surface pattern like (5) should be reconstructed for intransitive clauses in Proto-Polynesian:

(5)   Verb   NP

It is also clear that two surface patterns should be reconstructed for underlyingly transitive clauses: an accusative or middle pattern:

(6)   Verb   NP   _i_ NP

And a passive or ergative pattern:

(7)   Verb-(_Cia_)   _e_ NP   NP

268 The Passive-to-Ergative Reanalysis

The question of whether the proto-case system was accusative or ergative can then be reformulated as two questions. First, was (6) limited to middle verbs or available for all transitive verbs? And second, was (7) superficially transitive or not?

These questions can be answered by reconstructing the functions of *-_Cia_, *_i_, and *_e_, which distinguish (6) from (7) morphologically. The following sections examine the functions of these morphemes in attested Polynesian languages and argue that *-_Cia_ was a passive suffix, *_i_ was a direct object marker, and *_e_ was an oblique preposition.

6.3. PROTO-POLYNESIAN *-_Cia_

This section reconstructs the function of Proto-Polynesian *-_Cia_ after first applying internal reconstruction to the -_Cia_ suffixes of several Tongic and Samoic-Outlier languages. It is shown that there are several -_Cia_ suffixes with distinct functions in these languages: one type serves as a kind of inflectional suffix attached to canonical transitive verbs, and another type occurs in lexical derivation. The latter, lexical suffix argues that -_Cia_ originally marked Passive.

6.3.1 describes Tongan -_Cia_; 6.3.2, Niuean -_Cia_; and 6.3.3, Samoan -_Cia_. 6.3.4 discusses their implications for Proto-Polynesian.

6.3.1. Tongan -_Cia_

Until recently, Tongan appears to have had two distinct -_Cia_ suffixes.

First, -_Cia_ served as a 'durational' suffix attached to canonical transitive verbs to indicate duration (C.M. Churchward 1953: 242). The most frequent form of this suffix was

-a, and it could apparently be attached to the large majority of canonical transitive verbs (see C.M. Churchward 1959).[1] The durational -Cia is not allowed by my Tongan consultants, however, and I am unable to provide convincing sentence examples of it from more recent grammars (Shumway 1971) or texts (Fanua 1975). See Clark (1976: 74) for a similar experience. It is hypothesized here that the durational suffix existed formerly but has disappeared in contemporary Tongan.

Second, -Cia serves as a formative in three types of lexical derivation, both in contemporary Tongan and the Tongan described by C.M. Churchward (1953, 1959). These are:

(a) -Cia is attached to nouns to form derived adjectives or stative verbs. This type of derivation is productive with the forms of the suffix -a or -'ia and nonproductive otherwise:

(8) a. Ha'u ki tu'a   na'a ke 'ahu-ina.
        come to outside lest you smoke-Suff
        'Come outside or you will be overpowered by the
        smoke.' (C.M. Churchward 1959: 544; cf. 'ahu
        'smoke')

    b. Ko e   motu   feke-'ia   'a Mango.
        Pred the island squid-Suff Abs Mango
        'Mango is an island where there are lots of
        squid.' (Shumway 1971: 572; cf. feke 'squid')

(b) -Cia is attached to adjectives or other intransitives to form derived adjectives or intransitive verbs with an evaluative meaning. These formations are sometimes mildly productive, as is the case for evaluative verbs formed with -'ia, but generally not:

(9) a. 'Oku ou moko-sia.
        prog I cold-Suff
        'I feel cold.' (cf. momoko 'cold (of things)')

    b. 'Oku ou faingata'a-'ia pea 'oku 'ikai te u
        prog I difficult-Suff and prog not   uns I
        'I find it troublesome and I can't sit

ma-nofo.
can-sit
still.' (cf. _faingata'a_ 'difficult')

(c) Finally, -_Cia_ is attached to transitive verbs to form derived verbs of various syntactic and semantic types. This type of derivation is nonproductive:

(10) a. Na'a ku afuhi-a   'i   he 'uhá.
         past I spray-Suff Caus the rain
         'I was sprinkled by the rain.' (C.M. Churchward 1959: 2; cf. _afuhi_ 'spray (something)')

    b.   Na'a ku länga'i-a 'eku fie 'alu.
         past I jog-Suff my   want go
         'I felt a desire to go.' (cf. _langa'i_ 'jog, move')

Only the last type of derivation, in which -_Cia_ is attached to transitive verbs, bears directly on the reconstruction of the suffix in pattern (7), and so only it is examined below. However, many of the properties described below are shared by the other two types of derivation, suggesting that no great distortion is introduced by limiting the discussion in this way.

6.3.1.1 describes the formation of derivatives of type (c) (henceforth -_Cia_ verbs) in greater detail. 6.3.1.2 describes their semantic properties, and 6.3.1.3, their syntactic properties. 6.3.1.4 presents an internal reconstruction.

6.3.1.1. _Formation of_ -_Cia_ _Verbs_. The formation of -_Cia_ verbs from transitive stems is fairly straightforward. A form of the -_Cia_ suffix is attached which is lexically selected by the stem. This form is -_a_ or -_na_ if the stem has itself been derived by means of the 'transitive' or 'executive' suffixes -_Ci_ or -_Caki_ (see C.M. Churchward 1953: 240-41, 243-44); otherwise it may be any one of a number of lexically selected alternants:

(11)
Stem:		Derivative:	
teke	'push'	teke-na	'be pushed, fall'
misi	'suck'	misi-kia	'be sucked in'
inu	'drink'	inu-mia	'consume by evaporation'
tutu	'set on fire'	tū-ngia	'set on fire, catch fire'
a'u-si	'reach, arrive at'	a'u-si-a	'have attained'

The initial consonant of the -Cia suffix is usually the same as the initial consonants of other suffixes selected by the stem (namely, -Ci, -Caki, -Canga). This is not always the case, however; compare the -Cia verb fue-sia 'bear the burden of' and the executive transitive verb fua-'i 'carry', both from fua 'carry'.

The formation of -Cia verbs from transitive stems is nonproductive, and there is speaker variation regarding the acceptability of some derivatives. For instance, Tongan speakers interviewed by me rejected a number of -Cia verbs cited by C.M. Churchward (1959) and volunteered other -Cia verbs not listed by him. The generalizations holding for this type of derivation are independent of this, however, and so the examples below are taken both from C.M. Churchward (1959) and my field research.

6.3.1.2. Semantics of -Cia Verbs. The semantics of -Cia verbs is only partially predictable, in that no single semantic difference, or set of differences, holds between every derivative and its stem. Instead, three major types of differences obtain; these are lexically selected by particular stems.[2]

Some -<u>Cia</u> verbs differ from their stems in focusing on the completion or results of the event. Compare the derivatives of (12) with the corresponding stems of (13):

(12) a. Na'a ne kapa-sia   au mei hoku ngaahi filí.
         past he protect-Suff me from my pl   enemy
         'He protected me (successfully) from my enemies.'

  b. 'Aho lelei 'eni he   na'e tosi-a   'eku
      day good this because past nibble-Suff my
      'It's a good day because I caught a lot of
      māta'u.
      hook
      fish (lit. It's a good day because my hook has been (successfully) nibbled at).'

(13) a. Na'a ku fie kapa   hoku kaume'a.
         past I want protect my   friend
         'I wanted to protect my friend (but I didn't carry through with it).'

  b. Tosi   'e he iká 'a e   māta'u.
      nibble Erg the fish Abs the hook
      'The fish nibbles at the hook.'

The completive sense of these derivatives as opposed to their stems is brought out when both are embedded under a higher verb like <u>feinga</u> 'try', which requires the embedded clause to be completive:

(14) a. Na'a ku feinga ke u kapa-sia   hoku kaume'á.
         past I try   sbj I protect-Suff my   friend
         'I tried to protect my friend.'

  b. ??Na'a ku feinga ke u kapa   hoku kaume'á.
      past I try   sbj I protect my friend
      (I tried to protect my friend (but I didn't do anything about it).)

Other -<u>Cia</u> verbs indicate duration, either of the event or its resulting state. Although derivatives of this type are semantically similar to transitive verbs inflected with the

273 The Passive-to-Ergative Reanalysis

durational suffix, they are typically intransitive rather than transitive (see 6.3.1.3). Compare the derivatives of (15) with the corresponding stems of (16):

(15) a. Ko e fuamelié 'oku olo-ngia 'i he va'a
Pred the mulberry prog rub-Suff Caus the branch
'The mulberry branch is all the time being

pīsí.
peach
rubbed by (or is rubbing against) the peach branch.' (C.M. Churchward 1959: 393)

b. 'Oku tositosi-a 'a e   mounú 'e he iká.
prog peck-Suff Abs the bait Erg the fish
'The fish kept nibbling at the bait (without taking the hook).' (C.M. Churchward 1959: 497)

c. Na'e hilifaki-a 'a e vaká 'i he funga hakau.
past place-Suff Abs the ship on the top reef
'The ship was stranded on the reef (for several days).'

(16) a. Na'a ne olo hono va'e.
past he rub his foot
'He rubbed his foot.'

b. Na'e tositosi 'e he moá 'a e koané.
past peck   Erg the chicken Abs the corn
'The chicken pecked the corn.'

c. Na'a ku hilifaki 'a e pepa 'i he funga
past I place   Abs the paper on the top
'I placed the paper on the

puhá.
shelf
shelf.'

The durative sense of these derivatives is brought out in examples like (17), in which the durative <u>hilifaki-a</u> 'be accidentally caught' is incompatible with the adverbial phrase <u>he taimi si'i</u> 'a little while':

(17)   Na'e hilifaki-a 'a e fo'i pulu 'i he funga
past place-Suff Abs the one ball on the top
'The ball was accidentally caught in the

'akau (*'i he taimi si'i).
tree at the time small
tree (*for a little while).'

Finally, still other -*Cia* verbs indicate that the event is not controlled by a canonically human or specific agent; in other words, they indicate lack of agency. Derivatives of this type usually impose additional selectional or subcategorization restrictions on the (transitive) subject. For instance, if transitive, the derivatives may require their subjects to be nonhuman or inanimate. Compare the derivatives of (18) and the corresponding stems of (19):

(18) a. Na'e fangu-na   au 'e he nanamu 'o e
         past awaken-Suff me Erg the smell of the
         'I was awakened by the smell of the

         kakalá.
         flower
         flower.' (C.M. Churchward 1959: 142; <u>fangu-na</u>
         'be awakened (by something)')

    b.   'Oku hanga 'e he kulī 'o kei-na   'a e
         prog do   Erg the dog Comp eat-Suff Abs the
         'The dog is eating the

         puaka mata.
         pig   raw
         dead pig.'

    c. *'Oku hanga 'e Sione 'o kei-na   'a e
         prog do   Erg John Comp eat-Suff Abs the
         (John is eating the

         puaka mata.
         pig   raw
         dead pig.)

(19) a. Na'e fafangu kinautolu 'e Sione.
         past awaken them   Erg John
         'John awakened them.' (C.M. Churchward 1959: 19)

    b.   Na'e kai 'e he tangatá 'a e iká.
         past eat Erg the man   Abs the fish
         'The man ate the fish.'

The Passive-to-Ergative Reanalysis

Or they may require their subjects to be generic. Compare (20) and (21):

(20) a. 'Oku fai-tokoni-a 'eku ngāué 'e he kakaí.
prog do-help-Suff my work Erg the people
'My work is helped by the people (in general).'
(C.M. Churchward 1959: 22)

b. *'Oku fai-tokoni-a 'eku ngāué 'e Sione.
prog do-help-Suff my work Erg John
(My work is helped by John.) (C.M. Churchward 1959: 22)

(21) Na'a ne ha'u heni ke tokoni mai ki-ate au.
past he come here sbj help here to-pro me
'He came here to help me.'

Finally, they may not allow a transitive subject at all, but may be intransitive and imply that the event was spontaneous or accidental. Consider (15c) and (17) as well as the derivative of (22) and the corresponding stem of (23):

(22) a. Na'e teke-na atu 'a e ki'i ta'ahine he
past push-Suff away Abs the small girl the
'The little girl fell in the

loto 'ata'ata.
inside open=space
field.'

b. *Na'e teke-na 'e 'Ālani 'a e ki'i
past push-Suff Erg Alan Abs the small
(Alan pushed the little

ta'ahine he loto 'ata'ata.
girl the inside open=space
girl in the field.)

(23) 'Oua te ke teke 'a Sandy.
don't uns you push Abs Sandy
'Don't you push Sandy!'

The lack of agency conveyed by <u>teke-na</u> 'fall' makes it anomalous in the coordinate sentence (24), in which the falling is caused by an overt agent:

(24) *Na'e teke au 'e 'Ālani pea na'a ku teke-na
      past push me Erg Alan and past I push-Suff
      (Alan pushed me and I fell

      atu ki tu'a.
      away to outside
      outside.)

In summary, the semantic properties that differentiate -Cia verbs from their stems are:

(25) Completion
      Duration
      Lack of agency

6.3.1.3. <u>Syntax of -Cia Verbs</u>. The syntax of -Cia verbs is not fully predictable, in that some of the derivatives are intransitive and others are transitive.

The large majority of -Cia verbs differ from their stems in being intransitive rather than transitive. Compare the derivatives of (26), which are subcategorized for one direct case NP, with the stems of (27), which are subcategorized for two:

(26)a. Na'e (*ku) hilifaki-a 'a e fo'i pulú.
        past I   place-Suff Abs the one ball
        'The ball was caught (*by me).'

   b.   Na'e tanu-mia 'a e kapa.
        past bury-Suff Abs the can
        'The can was covered over (*by someone).'

(27)a. Na'a ku hilifaki 'a e   pepa 'i he funga
        past I place   Abs the paper on the top
        'I placed the paper on top of the

        puhá.
        shelf
        shelf.'

   b.   'Oku 'ikai te tau tanu 'a e kapa.
        prog not uns we bury Abs the can
        'We aren't burying the can.'

The single direct case NP associated with intransitive derivatives like (26) invariably has the following properties. Semantically, it has the same selectional restrictions as the direct object of the corresponding stem; it also has the same semantic role as the direct object of the stem, i.e. it is a semantic patient. Syntactically, it is a subject, as shown by its eligibility for subject-referring rules (Clark 1976: 75). It can serve as the target for Equi (see 3.2.2):

(28)   Na'a ne 'alu 'o   tūki-a   he va'akaú.
        past he go   Comp strike-Suff the stick
        'He went and tripped on the stick.'

And undergo Clitic Placement (see 1.4.2.1):

(29)   Na'a ne tanu-mia.
        past he bury-Suff
        'He was covered over (by accident).'

It is marked with the 'a possessive particle by Possessor Marking if the -Cia verb has been nominalized (see 3.3.2.1):

(30)   'ene vāe-a
        its split-Suff
        'its coming apart' (C.M. Churchward 1959: 528;
        'ene is an 'a possessive pronoun)

If third singular, it must be relativized via the deletion strategy --a fact which confirms that it is the subject of an intransitive clause (see 4.2.3.2):

(31)   Na'a mau keli hake 'o   fakahaofi 'a   e
        past we dig up   Comp save   Abs the
        'We dug up and saved the

        tamasi'i na'e (*ne) tanu-mia 'i he
        child   [past   he bury-Suff Caus the
        boy who was buried by the

        mofuike.
        earthquake]
        earthquake.'

A minority of -Cia verbs are transitive and therefore subcategorized for two direct case NPs. However, many of these differ from their stems in imposing more stringent selectional restrictions on the subject (see 6.3.1.2), and a few others --curiously-- do not pass all of the tests for transitivity.

One such test is provided by two-clause structures containing the higher verb <u>hanga</u> 'do', which governs obligatory, subject-controlled Equi in the embedded clause (see 3.2.2.2). <u>Hanga</u> emphasizes the agency of its subject in the event described by the embedded clause:

(32)   'Oku ou hanga 'o   fakaava 'a e   matapā.
        prog I do   Comp open   Abs the door
        'I am opening the door.'

Clauses embedded directly under <u>hanga</u> exhibit a restriction which appears in part to involve transitivity. These clauses cannot contain intransitive verbs:

(33)a. *Na'a ku hanga 'o   'alu ki 'api.
         past I do   Comp go   to home
         (I went home.)

    b. *'Oku ou hanga 'o   hela'ia 'i   he'eku ngāué.
         prog I do   Comp tired   Caus my   work
         (I am tired because of my work.)

Or middle verbs:

(34)a. *Na'a ku hanga 'o   'a'ahi ki-ate ia.
         past I do   Comp visit to-pro him
         (I visited him.)

    b. *Na'e hanga 'e 'Ana 'o   sio he tā   'eku
         past do   Erg Anna Comp see the picture   my
         (Anna looked at the pictures of my

        pēpē.
        baby
        baby.)

They can, however, contain canonical transitive verbs, whether they describe an action, a mental process, or an act of communication:

(35) a. Na'e hanga 'e Sione 'o   fana'i 'a e   hōsí.
         past do   Erg John Comp shoot Abs the horse
         'John shot the horse.'

   b.   Na'a nau hanga 'o   'ilo 'a e   me'a kotoa
        past they do   Comp know Abs the thing all
        'They know

        pē.
        Emp
        everything.'

   c.   Na'a ne hanga 'o   tala mai ki-ate kimautolu
        past he do   Comp tell here to-pro us
        'He told us

        'o   kau   ki ai.
        Comp concern to Pro
        about it.'

The only further requirement is that the subject and direct object of the embedded clause cannot be coreferential:

(36) a. *Na'a ne hanga pē 'e ia 'o   taa'i ia.
          past he do   Emp Erg he Comp hit   him
         (He hit himself.)

   b.   Na'a ne hanga pē 'e ia 'o   taa'i ia.
        past he do   Emp Erg he Comp hit   him
        'He hit him.'

It thus appears that <u>hanga</u> imposes a restriction on the embedded clause to the effect that it must be canonical transitive and nonreflexive.

Curiously, although some -<u>Cia</u> verbs that are canonical transitives can be embedded under <u>hanga</u> (see (18b)), others cannot. Consider <u>hūfi-a</u>, a completive derivative formed from <u>huufi</u> 'enter (in order to open officially)':

(37) a. Na'e hūfi-a   hoku falé 'e he tu'i.
         past enter-Suff my   house Erg the king
         'The king finally entered my house.'

b. Na'e huufi 'a e falelotú 'e Tupou IV.
past enter Abs the church Erg Tupou IV
'Tupou IV entered the church (to open it officially).'

Both derivative and stem are canonical transitive verbs, as shown by the fact that they govern ergative case marking. Only the stem can occur in a clause embedded under *hanga*, however:

(38) a. *Na'e hanga 'e he tu'i 'o hūfi-a hoku
past do Erg the king Comp enter-Suff my
(The king finally entered my

fale.
house
house.)

b. Na'e hanga 'e he tu'i 'o huufi 'a e
past do Erg the king Comp enter Abs the
'The king entered the church (to

falelotu.
church
open it officially).'

The inability of *hūfi-a* to occur in this context remains somewhat mysterious. On the face of it, though, sentences like (38a) suggest that not all transitive -*Cia* verbs pass all of the tests for transitivity.

In summary, the syntactic properties that can be exhibited by -*Cia* verbs are:

(39) Typically intransitive
If intransitive, the subject has the semantic role/selectional restrictions of the direct object
If transitive, may not pass all of the tests for transitivity

6.3.1.4. *Internal Reconstruction*. We are now in a position to compare the two -*Cia* suffixes attached to transitive verbs in Tongan: the -<u>Cia</u> of the lexical derivation just described, and C.M. Churchward's durational suffix.

The lexical -<u>Cia</u> and C.M. Churchward's durational suffix exhibit several types of overlap: both serve (or can serve) to indicate duration and occur in similar morphological patterns. The lexical -<u>Cia</u> forms derived verbs that are either intransitive or canonical transitive, suggesting a pattern like:

(40)   Verb-<u>Cia</u>   (<u>e</u> NP)   NP

The durational suffix was attached as a kind of inflection to canonical transitive verbs, so it occurred in the pattern:

(41)   Verb-<u>Cia</u>   <u>e</u> NP   NP

These formal and functional similarities argue that the two suffixes are descended from a single, earlier -<u>Cia</u>.

Where the two suffixes differ is in their productivity and their predictability. The lexical -<u>Cia</u> is nonproductive and restricted to a somewhat arbitrary class of transitive stems. But the durational suffix, to judge from C.M. Churchward (1959), could be attached to the large majority of canonical transitive verbs. Further, the effects of the lexical -<u>Cia</u> are not available across the board, but instead are determined idiosyncratically by the stem: some derivatives indicate completion while others indicate lack of agency; some are transitive while others are intransitive. In contrast, the effects of the durational suffix appear to have been invariant, since the suffix merely indicated duration.

These differences suggest that the durational suffix has a straightforward synchronic description, but the lexical -<u>Cia</u> is a relic: the restrictions on it are not synchronically motivated, but instead appear to reflect some earlier function of the suffix that has become lexicalized. Given that the two suffixes can be traced to the same earlier suffix, it follows that the function of that earlier suffix can be better determined through the lexical -<u>Cia</u> than through the durational suffix.

We can then ask what earlier function is reflected by the lexical -<u>Cia</u>. The answer is suggested by the full range of effects of this suffix as they were described above. Semantically, the lexical -<u>Cia</u> can indicate the completive, durative, or agentless character of the event described by the stem. Syntactically, it creates a derived verb that is typically intransitive and selects a subject corresponding to the direct object of the stem. Finally, even when the suffix creates a derived verb that is transitive, the derivative may not pass all of the tests for transitivity.

These effects are strikingly similar to those traditionally associated with Passive rules in the languages of the world. As traditionally conceived, Passive turns the underlying direct object into a subject and the underlying subject into an oblique noun, thereby detransitivizing the clause. The underlying subject is often unknown or obvious from context and therefore not overt (Jespersen 1924: 167). Accompanying these syntactic effects are several familiar semantic characteristics: emphasis on completion (<u>He was dismissed on Tuesday</u>) or the results of the event (<u>The museum is closed for repairs</u>), on duration-repetition of the event (<u>Foreign names are easily forgotten</u>), or on lack of agency (<u>They were hurt in an accident</u>). See Jespersen (1970[1931]: 98-107) for further examples.

Where the lexical derivatives of 6.3.1.2 and 6.3.1.3 differ from a true Passive is in the distribution of their semantic and syntactic effects, which are not invariably present but instead are lexically selected by the stem. However,

283 The Passive-to-Ergative Reanalysis

since lexicalization often results in arbitrary restrictions of this sort, we are justified in looking beyond them to the full range of effects. These argue that -Cia verbs were passive verbs, and the -Cia suffix indicated Passive, at an earlier stage of Tongan or some language ancestral to it.

6.3.2. Niuean -Cia

Niuean, the other Tongic language, does not have an inflectional -Cia suffix attached to transitive verbs. However, it does employ -Cia in several types of lexical derivation, including one type which affects transitive verbs.

The derivation of -Cia verbs from transitive stems is nonproductive, and the derivatives can differ from their stems in several semantic and syntactic respects. Semantically, they can indicate completion of the event:

(42)   Taha nī   e sipunu lahi, ua   laka-fia.
        one only a spoon   large don't cross-Suff
        'One large spoonful, not more (lit. One large
        spoonful, not to be exceeded).' (McEwen 1970:
        144; cf. laka 'cross over')

Duration:

(43)   Kua piki-tia   a   ia he   ngangao pata.
        prf touch-Suff pro he the sickness fever
        'He is infected with filariasis.' (McEwen 1970:
        274; cf. piki 'touch')

Or lack of agency:

(44)   Kia fiti-kia mai he kauafo.
        impv flip-Suff here the fishing=line
        'May he be entangled in a line.' (McEwen 1970:
        51; cf. fiti 'flip (something) over')

Syntactically, they are usually intransitive and select a subject corresponding to the direct object of the stem:

(45)   Ka e   ponoti-a   e   hala i   a   Manā.
         but tns close-Suff the road Caus prop Mana
         'But the road was blocked by Mana.' (McEwen
         1970: 280; cf. ponoti 'stop up, close')

These effects are not available across the board, but appear to be lexically determined by the stem. Taken together, they argue that Niuean -Cia reflects an earlier passive suffix.

6.3.3. Samoan -Cia

Samoan has two distinct -Cia suffixes, referred to in Chapter 2 as the transitive suffix and the transitivizing suffix.

The transitive suffix, whose usual surface forms are -a and -ina, was discussed in 2.2.2. Although this suffix can be attached in principle to any canonical transitive verb, in practice it serves as a kind of flag for missing transitive subjects, occurring most frequently when the subject has been removed by certain superficial rules or is not overt because it is generic. Secondarily, it appears to serve as a marker of unrealized mood.

The transitivizing suffix has a number of surface forms that are lexically selected by the stem. It is attached to middle verbs to form derived verbs that are typically canonical transitive (i.e. govern ergative case marking):

(46) a. Sā   pā'i-a   e   a'u le nofoa.
         past grope-Suff Erg I   the chair
         'I groped for the chair.'

     b. Sā   vala'au-lia mai a'u e   ia.
         past call-Suff   here me Erg he
         'He invited me.'

(47) a. Sā   pa'i   a'u 'i le nofoa.
         past grope I   to the chair
         'I groped for the chair.'

     b. Sā   vala'au mai   'oia 'i-āte a'u.
         past call   here he   to-pro me
         'He called me.'

The Passive-to-Ergative Reanalysis

This type of derivation is not fully productive, but instead extends to a small majority, or perhaps minority, of middle verbs.

Derivatives formed by means of the transitivizing suffix can exhibit several semantic or syntactic characteristics, the choice of which is lexically determined by the stem. Semantically, they can indicate completion of the event:

    (48) a. 'E te lavā-tia le 'āvega lea?
            you uns able-Suff the load that
            'Can you manage this load?' (Milner 1966: 103;
            cf. <u>lavā</u> 'be able')

        b. 'Ou te lē mana'o 'i-āte ia e fa'amālosi-a
            I uns not want to-pro him uns encourage-Suff
            'I don't like him to force

            a'u e tautala fa'a-Sāmoa.
            me uns speak Samoan
            me to speak Samoan.' (cf. <u>fa'amālosi</u> 'encourage')

Duration:

    (49) a. 'Ua alofa-gia 'i-tātou e le nu'u.
            prf love-Suff pl-us Erg the village
            'We are well-treated by the village.' (Milner 1966: 17; cf. <u>alofa</u> 'love')

        b. 'Ua 'ou ofo i le tago-fia o lona
            prf I surprised Caus the touch-Suff of her
            'I was surprised by his massaging of

            ulu e ia.
            head Erg he
            her head.' (cf. <u>tago</u> 'touch')

Lack of agency, or remoteness of the agent:

    (50) a. 'Ua pa'i-a lona mata.
            prf touch-Suff his eye
            'His eye was (accidentally) touched.' (Milner 1966: 172; cf. <u>pa'i</u> 'touch')

        b. 'Ua mana'o-mia 'oe (e le fale-fa'amasino).
            prf want-Suff you Erg the house-investigate
            'You are wanted (by the court).' (cf. <u>mana'o</u> 'want')

Syntactically, the derivatives are usually canonical transitive, but a few are intransitive and select a subject corresponding to the direct object of the stem:

(51)   'Ua 'ite-a   mauga o Manu'a.
       prf see-Suff hills of Manua
       'The hills of Manua are in sight.' (Milner
       1966: 88; cf. **'i'ite** 'foresee' from Proto-Polynesian ***kite** 'see')

When combined with the syntactic properties of the few derivatives of the type (51), the semantic properties of the transitivizing suffix argue that it is the relic of an earlier passive suffix. Interestingly, a similar argument can be made for the transitive suffix of 2.2.2. As observed by Cook (1978), the transitive suffix resembles a passive suffix in indicating that the underlying transitive subject of the clause has been removed. In particular, it shows up when the underlying subject is unknown or generic, and hence not overt. This partial overlap can be taken to suggest that the transitive suffix is descended from an earlier passive suffix. If so, then both -**Cia** suffixes argue for the existence of a passive suffix -**Cia** at an earlier stage of Samoan or some language ancestral to it.

6.3.4. Passive Suffix

Returning to the question of Proto-Polynesian, we can make three general observations. First, the -**Cia** suffixes employed in lexical derivation in Tongan, Niuean, and Samoan are relics of earlier passive suffixes that occurred in a clause type like (52), having the syntax and semantics of a typical Passive:

(52)   Verb-**Cia**   (**e** NP)   NP

Second, the passive function of -**Cia** is older than its func-

287   The Passive-to-Ergative Reanalysis

tion as a durational suffix (in recent Tongan) or a transitive suffix (in Samoan), both of which have a relatively straightforward synchronic description. Finally, there appears to be no evidence of an earlier <u>transitive</u> function for -<u>Cia</u>, either in these languages or the East Polynesian languages, which now employ -<u>Cia</u> in the output of Passive. These observations combine to argue that Proto-Polynesian *-<u>Cia</u> functioned as a passive suffix, and the clause type in which it occurred was superficially passive.[3]

6.4. PROTO-POLYNESIAN *<u>i</u>
This section reconstructs the function of Proto-Polynesian *<u>i</u> after first applying internal reconstruction to the <u>i</u> case markers of two Samoic-Outlier languages. It is argued that *<u>i</u> was not restricted to direct objects of middle clauses, but instead was used to mark direct objects of canonical transitive clauses.

  6.4.1 deals with <u>i</u> in Rennellese; 6.4.2, with <u>i</u> in the Tokelauan dialect of Ellicean. 6.4.3 presents the reconstruction.

6.4.1. <u>Rennellese i</u>
6.4.1.1. <u>Basic Description</u>. Rennellese, a Samoic-Outlier language, uses <u>i</u> as a case marker for certain types of direct objects.

  Rennellese has an ergative case system with many of the familiar characteristics described in 2.1.1. Subjects of intransitive clauses are unmarked:

  (53) a.   A'u   Pingikoke.
           come Pingikoke
           'Pingikoke came.' (Elbert and Monberg 164)

       b.   O   'oti kinai te kai pegea o Mugaba
            Comp done Pro   the eat person of Rennell
            '...and thus was ended cannibalism here on

nei.
this
Rennell.' (Elbert and Monberg 250)

Subjects of middle clauses are unmarked; their direct objects are preceded by one of the oblique prepositions i 'at' or ki 'to':

(54) a. Hitangi atu i te baka o Iba.
         wait   away at the canoe of Eight
         'Wait for Eight's canoe.' (Elbert and Monberg 164)

     b. Ma te 'agoha ake ki-nai a   tena ugūgu.
         and the love up to-Pro prop his wife
         'And his wife felt compassion for him.' (Elbert and Monberg 229)

Subjects of canonical transitive clauses are marked with e:

(55) a. Sa'u ake e   Sinakibi te tokangua kongoa.
         bring up Erg Sinakibi the two   tapa
         'Sinakibi brought out two tapas.' (Elbert and Monberg 73)

     b. O   sengesenge ai e   ia te mata.
         Comp operate   Pro Erg she the eye
         'And she operated on the eye with it.' (Elbert and Monberg 69)

     c. O   tā   e   kigatou te tokatogu pegea o
         Comp beat Erg they   the three   person Comp
         '...and they beat three people to

         mamate.
         die=pl
         death.' (Elbert and Monberg 232)

Rather unusually, direct objects of canonical transitive clauses exhibit two types of marking: common nouns are unmarked, as in (55), but pronouns or proper nouns are marked with i. Consider the pronominal-proper direct objects of:

(56) a. Ma te sa'u   e   'Iti'iti i-a   Ekeitehua.
         and the bring Erg 'Iti'iti DO-prop Ekeitehua
         'And 'Iti'iti picked up Ekeitehua.' (Elbert and Monberg 82)

b. O   hai ake a   Tauha'ugua ke tā   i-a
    Comp say up prop Tauha'ugua sbj kill DO-prop
    'And Tauha'ugua said (he) would kill

    Gauatana.
    Gauatana
    Gauatana.' (Elbert and Monberg 355)

c. Ka te hai nei e   koe i-a te au o   ina.
    but the do this Erg you DO-pro me Comp see
    'But you treated me and (I can) see.' (Elbert
    and Monberg 69)

d. Ma te tengeu'ake a   Tekungu ke manga tā
    and the think   prop Tekungu sbj tns   kill
    'And Tekungu thought he would

    e   ia i-a te ia.
    Erg he DO-pro him
    kill himself.' (Elbert and Monberg 379)

Accompanying the direct objects of (56) is the pronominal-proper article a, which has the form a te before pronouns. This article is obligatory for pronouns or proper nouns preceded by i or ki, and optional for pronouns or proper nouns in the unmarked case (see 1.3.2).

6.4.1.2. <u>Case Marker or Oblique Preposition?</u>. The phonological shape of the direct object marker i suggests two synchronic analyses for it. One would claim that the marker is the oblique preposition i 'at', used exceptionally to mark certain direct objects of canonical transitive clauses; the other claims that it is a distinct case marker for direct objects only accidentally homophonous with the oblique preposition. Two arguments are presented here that support the second analysis and show that the direct object i and the oblique i 'at' should be considered distinct. These involve the Rennellese Clefting rule and the transitive suffix -<u>Cia</u>.

Rennellese has a Clefting rule that moves a focused NP to the left and marks it with the predicate particle ko. This rule has a chopping strategy, which simply leaves behind a hole, and a copying strategy, which leaves behind a pronominal copy of the moved NP. The chopping strategy is required for intransitive subjects and canonical transitive direct objects. Compare (57a), in which the direct object has been clefted, with (57b), in which the direct object has not:

(57) a. Ko   te tinana kua kai e   te tamana.
       Pred the mother prf eat Erg the father
       'The father had eaten the mother (lit. It was
       the mother who the father had eaten).' (Elbert
       and Monberg 351)

   b. Kai e   kigāua   te tinana o Patikoge.
       eat Erg they=du the mother of Patikoge
       'They ate the mother of Patikoge.' (Elbert and
       Monberg 76)

The copying strategy is required for NPs with oblique case marking --in particular, for NPs which are marked with the oblique i 'at':

(58) a. Ko   ba'i 'aso e   ta'anga hano ai au ki mouku.
       Pred each day   tns tns   go   Pro I to bush
       'Every day...I come up here to the bush.' (Elbert and Monberg 98)

   b. Kae kakabe hakahoki iho ki Niupani i te
       and take   back   down to Niupani in the
       '(They) took (him) back to Niupani in the

       taha'ata.
       morning
       morning.' (Elbert and Monberg 413)

The copying strategy is required for all NPs with oblique case marking, whether they are direct objects or genuinely oblique. Thus in (59), the copying strategy has affected a middle direct object marked with i 'at':

(59)   Ko   koe a'u   ai au, kau kakabe-'ia.
       Pred you reach Pro I   I   take-Trans
       'I have come for you and will take (you) away.'
       (Elbert and Monberg 347)

291   The Passive-to-Ergative Reanalysis

This suggests that the choice of strategies is governed by two ordered conditions:

(60) a. The copying strategy is required for NPs with oblique case marking.

b. Otherwise, the chopping strategy is required for intransitive subjects and transitive direct objects.

Now if the *i* marking the pronominal-proper direct objects of (56) were oblique, then the copying strategy should be required for these NPs as well. But when these NPs are clefted, they do not leave behind a copy but are chopped instead, as shown by:

(61) a. Ko Moesabegubegu na   kai e   Guatupu'a.
         Pred Moesabegubegu past eat Erg Guatupu'a
         'Moesabegubegu was eaten by Guatupu'a.' (Elbert and Monberg 74)

b. Ka ko   au na   kakabe e   te ahenga.
    but Pred I past take   Erg the gods
    '...for I was taken away by the parading gods.'
    (Elbert and Monberg 327)

c. Namā hati ni   ngangu susungu, ko   au he'e
    when break some=pl wave   white   Pred I not
    'When white waves break, he has not

    tā   e   ia.
    kill Erg he
    killed me.' (Elbert and Monberg 137)

The failure of these NPs to select the copying strategy shows that the direct object *i* is not an oblique preposition; in particular, it is distinct from the oblique *i* 'at'.

Rennellese also has a transitive suffix -Cia which is attached to canonical transitive verbs. This suffix, whose usual surface form is -'ia, seems to be attached to the verb obligatorily if a transitive subject has been cliticized:[4]

(62) Kau kakabe-'ia.
I take-Trans
'I...will take (you) away.' (Elbert and Monberg 347)

And optionally if the transitive subject has been removed by zero-pronominalization, or is not overt because it is generic:

(63) a. Kua he'e kite-a   i   te kua a'u a
       prf not see-Trans Caus the prf come prop
       '(He) did not find (it) because Tebaghoghu

       Tebaghoghu.
       Tebaghoghu
       had come.' (Elbert and Monberg 332)

    b. Ma te to'o-'ia   tona ngongo ki Ngotuma.
       and the take-Trans his news   to Ngotuma
       'This news of him was taken to Ngotuma.' (Elbert and Monberg 379)

What is of immediate interest is the cooccurrence restrictions involving this suffix and other morphological elements of the clause. Whereas the oblique *i* 'at' can surface in the same clause as the transitive suffix:

(64) a. Te tagatupu'a ki-a   Ngatonga, na
       the story   to-prop Ngatonga past
       'The story of Ngatonga, who

       tā-'ia   i Tuhugago.
       kill-Trans at Tuhugago
       was killed at Tuhugago.' (Elbert and Monberg 247)

    b. Mano   tona ugūgu kua tā-'ia   i na
       perhaps his wife prf kill-Trans at the=pl
       'Perhaps his wife had been killed among

       ta'u takotonga.
       crowd buried
       those buried.' (Elbert and Monberg 400)

the direct object *i* cannot. Consequently, when the verb is suffixed with -*Cia*, a pronominal-proper direct object is not marked with *i* but is, exceptionally, unmarked:

The Passive-to-Ergative Reanalysis

(65) a. Kau pipiki-'ia ngā koe.
         I   keep-Trans that you
         'I'm going to keep you.' (Elbert and Monberg 68)

   b.   Kau go u'u-'ia   ai koe.
        I   tns bite-Trans Pro you
        'I'm going to bite you with them!' (Elbert and Monberg 120)

   c.   Tā-'ia   ai a   Tagosia ma Tagitonga ma
        beat-Trans Pro prop Tagosia and Tagitonga and
        'Tagosia and Tagitonga and Manugei were

        Manugei.
        Manugei
        beaten.' (Elbert and Monberg 232)

   d.   Manga hakakata-'ia   Tehu'aigabenga.
        tns   make=laugh-Trans Tehu'aigabenga
        'And Tehu'aigabenga laughed (lit. (It) made
        Tehu'aigabenga laugh).' (Elbert and Monberg 339)

Since the restriction illustrated in (65) affects the direct object i but not the oblique i 'at', it provides a second argument that the markers are distinct. At the same time, it suggests that the case assignment rule for direct objects in Rennellese is roughly: 'Mark the direct object of a canonical transitive clause with i if (a) it is a pronoun or proper noun, and (b) the verb is not suffixed with -Cia'.

6.4.1.3. <u>Internal Reconstruction</u>. Closer examination of Rennellese i suggests that it may well reflect an earlier case marker with a less restricted distribution.

The case assignment rule formulated above is synchronically restricted in that it requires the direct object to be a pronoun or proper noun. While such a requirement may not be crosslinguistically unusual, it is surprising from the standpoint of Polynesian. Case assignment rules limited to pronouns and proper nouns are rare in other Polynesian languages and cannot be reconstructed for Proto-Polynesian. Further, the rule is restricted in that it requires that the verb of the clause not be suffixed with -Cia --a requirement that is rather anomalous. Both in Polynesian and in other languages of the world, case assignment is rarely contingent on the absence of a particular element of verb morphology. In this sense, the Rennellese rule is synchronically unmotivated.

We can, however, construct a historical account of these restrictions by observing that Rennellese -Cia is descended from Proto-Polynesian *-Cia, which was a passive suffix (see 6.3). As such, it appeared in clauses lacking a surface direct object, and would never have cooccurred with a case marker for direct objects. This suggests that the second restriction on the case assignment rule is a relic from an earlier stage at which -Cia indicated Passive, and i marked direct objects of canonical transitive clauses, as it does now. The account of the restriction to pronouns and proper nouns is perhaps less clear; however, it may well be a relic from an earlier stage at which i marked all direct objects of canonical transitive clauses. It thus appears that Rennellese i reflects an earlier direct object marker, assigned by the rule: 'Mark the direct object of a canonical transitive clause with i'. This rule applied at the same, or some of the same, stages at which -Cia functioned as a passive suffix.

6.4.2. Tokelauan i

The Tokelauan dialect of Ellicean appears to use i to mark certain direct objects and intransitive subjects, in a manner unusual enough to suggest that it is the relic of an earlier, less restricted case marker. The facts discussed below are taken from a lecture on Tokelauan syntax delivered by Peter

Sharples at the University of Auckland in 1971. He is, of course, not responsible for my interpretation of them.

Tokelauan has an ergative case system. Subjects of intransitive clauses and direct objects of canonical transitive clauses are unmarked, except as described below; subjects of canonical transitive clauses are marked with e. Consider the intransitive clauses of (66) and the canonical transitive clauses of (67):

(66) a.   Na   fano kitā i   te vaka.
          past go   we=du in the canoe
          'We went in the canoe.'

     b.   Na   fano te tino i te vaka ki te akau.
          past go   the man in the canoe to the reef
          'The man went in the canoe to the reef.'

(67) a.   Na   kave e   au te hua   ki te teine.
          past take Erg I the coconut to the girl
          'I took the coconut to the girl.'

     b.   Na   kite-a   kitā e   te teine.
          past see-Suff us=du Erg the girl
          'The girl saw us.'

(Kite-a 'see' is a derived canonical transitive verb formed by attachment of the -Cia suffix.)

Curiously, subjects of intransitive clauses and direct objects of canonical transitive clauses exhibit a different case marking if they are pronominal and separated from the verb by another NP: they are not unmarked but rather marked with i, followed by the pronominal-proper article a:[5]

(68) a.   Na   fano i te vaka   i a   kitā.
          past go   in the canoe pro we=du
          'We went in the canoe.'

     b.   Na   kite-a   e   te teine i a   kitā.
          past see-Suff Erg the girl pro us=du
          'The girl saw us.'

296 The Passive-to-Ergative Reanalysis

This marking is obligatory:

(69) a. *Na   fano i   te   vaka kitā.
         past go   in the canoe we=du
         (We went in the canoe.)

  b. *Na   kite-a   e   te   teine kitā.
         past see-Suff Erg the girl   us=du
         (The girl saw us.)

The contrast of (68) and (66-67) argues that Tokelauan has a case assignment rule of the form: 'Mark an unmarked NP with i if (a) it is a pronoun, and (b) it is separated from the verb by another NP'. This rule follows the ergative case assignment rule.

The second restriction on Tokelauan i is synchronically rather bizarre, and suggests that this marker may well be the relic of an earlier, less restricted case marker. Now in Tokelauan, as elsewhere in Polynesian, the subject of an intransitive clause typically occurs to the immediate right of the verb; the direct object of a canonical transitive clause typically follows the subject and so is separated from the verb by another NP. This suggests that, at an earlier stage of Tokelauan or some language ancestral to it, i may have been restricted to those NPs which were normally separated from the verb by another NP; namely, direct objects of canonical transitive clauses. Although the significance of the restriction to pronouns is less clear, it can be viewed as a relic from an earlier stage at which i marked all direct objects, not just those that were pronouns. Combining these observations, it appears that Tokelauan i reflects an earlier direct object marker, assigned by a rule which said roughly: 'Mark the direct object of a canonical transitive clause with i'.

6.4.3. Direct Object Marker

The discussion of the preceding subsections suggests the following conclusions. First, Rennellese i and Tokelauan i are relics of earlier case markers that were assigned to all direct objects of canonical transitive clauses. In Rennellese, this earlier, more general function of i can be reconstructed for roughly the same period at which -Cia functioned as a passive suffix --in other words, the period around Proto-Polynesian. Second, in their present, restricted function, Rennellese i and Tokelauan i are competing with the unmarked (i.e. absolutive) case, which now serves generally to mark direct objects of canonical transitive clauses. Since the absolutive has a more straightforward synchronic description than i, i is older as a marker of direct objects in these languages.

Finally, those East Polynesian languages that now employ i in canonical transitive clauses appear to give no evidence that it had any earlier function other than accusative marker. We can therefore reconstruct *i as a marker of all direct objects of canonical transitive clauses --that is, an accusative marker-- in Proto-Polynesian.

6.5. PROTO-POLYNESIAN *e

This section reconstructs the function of Proto-Polynesian *e, using evidence from nominalizations discussed at greater length in Chung (1973a). It is argued that *e was not a direct case marker but rather an oblique preposition.

Although the reconstruction of *e as oblique is consistent with the facts of nominalizations in at least fifteen Polynesian languages (see Chung 1973a), the evidence presented below is abbreviated severely and only two languages, Maori and Samoan, are considered in detail. 6.5.1 describes the general structure of nominalizations, and 6.5.2, the rule of Possessor Marking. 6.5.3 presents the reconstruction.

6.5.1. Structure of Nominalizations

The nominalizations found in Polynesian are noun phrases having much of the internal structure of clauses and the syntax-semantics of sentential NPs. Semantically, they indicate the simple occurrence of the event described by the corresponding clause; syntactically, they are regularly used for several types of embedded clauses (e.g. adverbial clauses of time). It is assumed here that nominalizations are derived from clauses directly dominated by NP by a combination of three rules which are described in this subsection and found, with minor variations, in all Polynesian languages.

The Nominalization rule turns the verb of the embedded clause into a derived noun and replaces the tense-aspect-mood particle of the clause with a specificity article. Consider (70), which is related to (71) by this rule:

Sam (70) le kuka-ina
the cook-Trans
'the cooking (of it)'

(71) 'Ua kuka-ina.
prf cook-Trans
'(He) cooked (it).'

In East Polynesian languages and a few Samoic-Outlier languages, the Nominalization rule also attaches some alternant of the nominalizing suffix -Canga to the verb:

Mao (72) te kōrero-tanga
the speak-Nmlz
'the speaking' (Waititi 1969: 76)

(73) Ka kōrero.
uns speak
'(She) speaks.'

The Possessor Marking rule marks an NP associated with the nominalized verb with the possessive particles <u>a</u> 'dominant' or <u>o</u> 'subordinate', which are also used to mark possessors of lexical nouns (see 1.3.3). In general, Possessor Marking affects only one NP associated with the nominalized verb, typically the one closest to it:

Sam (74)a. le ōmai   o misionare
            the come=pl of missionary
            'the coming of the missionaries'

     b. le sau a le ta'avale a leoleo
         the come of the car   of police
         'the coming of the police car'

Finally, the Possessor Preposing rule optionally moves possessors to the immediate right of the specificity article and incorporates them with it to form possessive pronouns. This rule is available for possessors of nominalizations as well as possessors of lexical nouns, as shown by:

Mao (75)a. t-ō-na   puta-nga mai ki waho
            the-of-her come-Nmlz here to outside
            'her coming outside' (Orbell 6)

     b. ā-na   mea-tanga
         pl=of-him do-Nmlz
         'all the things he did (lit. his doings)' (Orbell 6)

     c. t-ō-na   whare
         the-of-her house
         'her house'

In Tongic and Samoic-Outlier languages, Possessor Preposing is restricted to possessors which are pronouns, and the rule is the nominal analogue of Clitic Placement in an obvious sense.

Facts of the attested languages argue that some version of Nominalization, Possessor Marking, and Possessor Preposing should be reconstructed for Proto-Polynesian (see Chung 1973a). One aspect of Possessor Marking in the attested languages is dealt with immediately below.

6.5.2. Possessor Marking

The Possessor Marking rules of Polynesian languages differ from one another in their assignment of the particles _a_ and _o_, and in whether or not they apply obligatorily to unmarked NPs. However, they are remarkably uniform as regards the total class of NPs that they can affect. In East Polynesian languages, Possessor Marking is restricted to subjects and direct objects of the nominalized verb; in Tongic and Samoic-Outlier languages, it is restricted to these NPs with one consistent exception. The restrictions are illustrated here for Possessor Marking in Maori, an East Polynesian language, and Possessor Marking in Samoan, a Samoic-Outlier language.

6.5.2.1. Maori.

In Maori, an accusative language, Possessor Marking affects the NP to the immediate right of the nominalized verb. The rule is available for subjects and direct objects of the nominalization but no other types of NPs.

Because the word order of nominalizations is not particularly free, subjects are usually to the immediate right of the nominalized verb when Possessor Marking applies. They undergo the rule obligatorily, apparently because they are in the unmarked (i.e. nominative) case. Subjects of intransitive nominalizations and of some middle nominalizations are marked with _o_:

(76)a. te   tae-nga   o Hutu ki raro
        the arrive-Nmlz of Hutu to below
        'When Hutu arrived in the underworld,...'
        (Orbell 4)

    b. Ko   te kite-nga   o taua wahine i   te upoko
        Pred the see-Nmlz of that woman Acc the head
        'When the woman saw the head,

        kātahi ka oma.
        then   uns run
        (she) ran.' (Biggs, Hohepa, and Mead 36)

Subjects of canonical transitive nominalizations are marked with a:

(77) a. te whakamau-tanga a Hata i   te taura
         the fasten-Nmlz   of Hata Acc the rope
         'Hata's fastening the rope' (Waititi 1969: 143)

     b. Ka rua a-na   pātai-nga atu, i   haere mai
         uns two pl=of-her   ask-Nmlz away past go   here
         'Twice she asked, where do

         koe i   whea?
         you from where?
         you come from?' (Biggs, Hohepa, and Mead 46)

In (77b), the subject has first undergone Possessor Marking and then Possessor Preposing.

Alternatively, the subject can undergo an Agent Postposing rule (called Extraposition in Chung 1973a) which turns it into an oblique noun marked with e and optionally moves it to the right. This rule is available for subjects of middle or canonical transitive nominalizations, and renders them ineligible for Possessor Marking:

(78) a. te tiro-hanga mai e   te pā
         the look-Nmlz here Agt the people
         'When the people saw (it)...' (Biggs, Hohepa, and Mead 38)

     b. te epa-nga   i   te kupenga e   te tangata
         the throw-Nmlz Acc the net   Agt the man
         'the throwing the net by the man'

     c. te whakataka-nga   e   Ngāti-Rarua i   a
         the surround-Nmlz Agt Ngati-Rarua Acc pro
         'Because Ngati-Rarua surrounded us

mātou i Whakatū
us   at Whakatu
at Whakatu...' (Biggs, Hohepa, and Mead 143)

If the (former) subject has been moved to the right by Agent Postposing, the direct object is to the immediate right of the nominalized verb when Possessor Marking applies. It optionally undergoes the rule, and is marked with o:

(79) a. te epa-nga   o te kupenga e   te tangata
         the throw-Nmlz of the net   Agt the man
         'the throwing of the net by the man'

     b. I te kai-nga o te kurī mōkai rā   e Toi
         at the eat-Nmlz of the dog pet that Agt Toi
         'When Toi and his friends ate the pet dog,

         mā,   i a   wai te nui-nga?
         associates at prop who? the big-Nmlz
         who got the biggest share?' (Biggs, Hohepa, and Mead 44)

The Agent Postposing rule resembles one half of Passive in demoting a transitive subject to an oblique noun marked with e; therefore, it might be supposed that nominalizations of the type (79) were simply formed from passive clauses (Biggs 1969). However, several facts argue that Agent Postposing is distinct from Passive and the nominalizations of (79) are not passive nominalizations.

First, Passive promotes the direct object to subject, but Agent Postposing appears not to have this effect, since direct objects of nominalizations which have been affected by it can still be marked with the accusative i (see (78)). Second, Passive attaches some alternant of the passive suffix -Cia to the verb, but Agent Postposing does not.[6]

The relevance of this second fact is increased when we consider an Agreement rule in Maori which appears to spread the feature [+passive] from a passive verb to certain verbal modifiers, with the result that they surface with passive suf-

303   The Passive-to-Ergative Reanalysis

fixes of their own (see Biggs 1969). Consider:

(80) a. Whati-ia   poro-tia   i   waenganui.
         break-Pass strike-Pass at middle
         '(He) was completely broken off in the middle.'
         (Grey 2)

   b. I   tanu-mia   ora-tia   a   Te Heuheu rātou
       past bury-Pass   alive-Pass   prop Te Heuheu they
       'Te Heuheu was buried alive, together with

       ko   tōna iwi.
       Pred his people
       his people.' (Biggs 1969: 115)

The passive suffixes of the modifiers may differ from those attached to the verb, a fact which argues that it is the feature [+passive] that is copied, rather than the surface form of the -Cia suffix per se.

Now if the nominalizations of (79) were formed from passive clauses, we would expect the nominalized verb to be marked [+passive] and to trigger Agreement, even if some independent constraint prevented the nominalized verb from surfacing with the -Cia suffix itself. However, nominalized verbs of this type do not trigger Agreement, as shown by the absence of the passive suffix on the verbal modifier of:

(81)   Kāore e   makere i   ngā   ngutu-nga
       not   nonpast   lost   Caus the=pl   talk-Nmlz
       '(They) are not forgotten, because (people)

       kōrero o   te hūmārie-tanga.
       say   of the beautiful-Nmlz
       still talk of (her) beauty.' (Biggs, Hohepa, and Mead 73)

It thus appears that Agent Postposing is distinct from Passive and the nominalizations of (79) are not formed from passive clauses. Instead, they contain a demoted subject and a direct object which undergoes Possessor Marking.

Possessor Marking does not affect NPs other than subjects

or direct objects, regardless of their position with respect to the nominalized verb. Thus in (82), the oblique NPs retain their original case marking even though they appear to the immediate right of the nominalized verb in surface structure:

(82) a. te   tae-nga   ki ngā   kupu whakamutunga o
         the arrive-Nmlz to the=pl word concluding   of
         'When (he) came to the last words of

   te   haka
   the dance
   the dance...' (Biggs, Hohepa, and Mead 153)

b. te   hinga-nga i Te Whetū-matarau
    the fall-Nmlz at Te Whetu-matarau
    '(their) defeat at Te Whetu-matarau' (Biggs, Hohepa, and Mead 97)

The condition on the rule is therefore: 'Possessor Marking affects a subject or direct object to the immediate right of the nominalized verb'.

The availability of Possessor Marking for subjects and direct objects, but no other types of NPs, is repeated in other East Polynesian languages, which also resemble Maori in having an accusative case system. See Chung (1973a) for discussion.

6.5.2.2. <u>Samoan</u>. In Samoan, an ergative language, Possessor Marking affects NPs to the right or the immediate left of the nominalized verb, in a fashion described below. The rule is available for subjects and direct objects with one consistent exception.

Possessor Marking applies to the output of Pronoun Preposing, a rule which moves nonemphatic pronominal subjects of nominalizations across the nominalized verb and attaches them to the immediate right of the specificity article. This

The Passive-to-Ergative Reanalysis

rule, which also extends to the pronominal possessors of lexical nouns, is the nominal equivalent of Clitic Placement in an obvious sense. It differs from Clitic Placement only in failing to exhibit the restriction on third singular pronouns discussed in 4.2.3.1. Consider:

(83) a. le-na 'ave-ina o le ta'avale
    the-he drive-Trans of the car
    'his driving of the car'

   b. le-na ta'avale
    the-he car
    'his car'

Possessor Marking is obligatory (in formal Samoan) or optional (in informal Samoan) for NPs occurring to the immediate left of the nominalized verb. These NPs have acquired their position by virtue of Pronoun Preposing, and they are marked with a or o depending on semantic considerations irrelevant here. Consider the intransitive subject of (84a), the middle subject of (84b), and the canonical transitive subjects of (84c) and (84d):

(84) a. l-o lātou ōmai 'i Sāmoa
    the-of them come=pl to Samoa
    'their coming to Samoa'

   b. l-o-na va'ai 'i le teine
    the-of-him see to the girl
    'his seeing the girl'

   c. Sā 'ou ofo i l-a-na kuka-ina
    past I surprised Caus the-of-him cook-Trans
    'I was surprised at the way he cooked

    o le i'a.
    of the fish
    the fish.'

   d. 'Ua 'ou ofo i l-o-na tīa'i o
    prf I surprised Caus the-of-him discard of
    'I was surprised that he threw out the

The Passive-to-Ergative Reanalysis

le i'a, 'ina 'ua 'uma 'ona kuka.
the fish Comp prf done Comp cook
fish, after (it) was cooked.'

Possessor Marking also affects NPs to the right of the nominalized verb, obligatorily if they are in the unmarked (i.e. absolutive) case and optionally otherwise. Thus, the rule is required for subjects of intransitive or middle nominalizations, which occur to the immediate right of the nominalized verb if they have not been preposed. These NPs are marked with a or o:

(85) a. le o'o   mai o le tala lelei 'i Sāmoa
       the arrive here of the news good to Samoa
       'the coming of the good news to Samoa'

   b. 'O le sau a le ta'avale a leoleo 'ou te
      Pred the come of the car   of police I   uns
      'When the police car came, I

      lē mālamalama 'i ai.
      not understand to Pro
      wasn't aware of it.'

   c. le tago a le teine 'i lona ulu
      the touch of the girl to his head
      'the girl's touching his head'

The rule is also required for direct objects of canonical transitive nominalizations, regardless of their linear position. These NPs are marked with o, as shown by (84c), (84d), and:

(86) a. le kuka-ina   o le i'a e   John
       the cook-Trans of the fish Erg John
       'John's cooking of the fish'

   b. le kuka-ina   e   John o le i'a
      the cook-Trans Erg John of the fish
      'John's cooking of the fish'

   c. Ua tiga le vavao e   i laua   o le tama.
      prf hurt the forbid Erg pl they=du of the boy
      'They forbade the child in vain.' (Stuebel 234)

The Passive-to-Ergative Reanalysis

Finally, the rule is optional for direct objects of middle nominalizations if they occur to the immediate right of the nominalized verb, the subject having been removed by Pronoun Preposing. These NPs are marked with o:

(87) a. l-o-na   va'ai o le teine
         the-of-him see   of the girl
         'his seeing of the girl'

   b. l-o-na   mana'o o le teine
       the-of-him want   of the girl
       'his desiring of the girl'

   c. Afai e tiga-ina   se tasi i   le fa'atali
       if   uns hurt-Trans a one   Caus the wait
       'If anyone is annoyed because of (his) waiting

       o se mea...
       of a thing
       for something...' (Stuebel 234)

Compare (88), in which Possessor Marking has not applied:

(88)   l-o-na   va'ai 'i le teine
       the-of-him see   to the girl
       'his seeing the girl'

The idea that the nominalizations of (87) are formed from middle clauses rather than derived canonical transitive clauses (see 6.3.3) is supported by several facts. First, the nominalizations of (87) do not allow their subjects to appear in the ergative case. In this respect they contrast with canonical transitive nominalizations, such as (86):

(89)   *le mana'o e   Ioane o le teine
        the want Erg John of the girl
        (John's desiring of the girl)

Second, the middle nominalizations of (87) do not allow their direct objects to undergo Possessor Marking unless they occur to the immediate right of the nominalized verb. In this respect they contrast with canonical transitive nominaliza-

308   The Passive-to-Ergative Reanalysis

tions, whose direct objects must undergo Possessor Marking regardless of linear position:

(90) a.   *le   mana'o o   Ioane o   le   teine
          the   want   of John   of the girl
          (John's desiring of the girl)

     b.   le   mana'o o   Ioane 'i le   teine
          the   want   of John   to the girl
          'John's desiring the girl'

Third, alongside (87), there are nominalizations formed from derived canonical transitive clauses which do exhibit all of the relevant properties. These involve verbs derived from middle verbs by attachment of the transitivizing suffix -Cia:

(91) a.   l-o-'u   va'ai-a o   le   manufe'ai
          the-of-me see-Suff of the monster
          'my watching of the monster'

     b.   le   mana'o-mia e   ia o   se ofuvae fou
          the want-Suff Erg he of a   shoe   new
          'his wanting of new shoes'

In conclusion, the nominalizations of (87) are middle nominalizations whose direct objects have undergone Possessor Marking.

Possessor Marking does not apply to NPs other than subjects or direct objects, regardless of their linear position. Thus, the oblique NPs of (92-93) retain their original case marking, despite the fact that they occur to the immediate right of the nominalized verb in surface structure:

(92) a.   *le   nofo 'umi o   fafo
          the   sit   long of outside
          (sitting outside for a long time)

     b.   *l-o   lātou ōmai   o   Sāmoa
          the-of them   come=pl of Samoa
          (their coming to Samoa)

(93) a.   le   nofo 'umi i   fafo
          the   sit   long at outside
          'sitting outside for a long time'

b. 'O le tīfaga e fa'atatau 'i l-o   lātou
    Pred the film   uns about   to the-of them
    'The film is about their

    ōmai   'i Sāmoa.
    come=pl to Samoa
    coming to Samoa.'

Ignoring the complications introduced by linear order and case marking, on which see 4.3.2, it appears that the rule exhibits a condition of the form: 'Possessor Marking is available for subjects and direct objects of a nominalization'.

This condition exhibits a curious exception, however; Possessor Marking cannot apply to canonical transitive subjects if they occur to the right of the nominalized verb and are marked with e. Compare (94) with (95), in which Possessor Marking has not applied:

(94) a. *le fasi o le tagata o lona to'alua
         the beat of the man   of his wife
         (the man's beating of his wife)

     b. *le faitau-ina a tātou o le nusipepa
         the read-Trans of us   of the newspaper
         (our reading of the newspaper)

     c. *'Ua 'ou ofo   i   le tīa'i   o Ioane
         prf I   surprised Caus the discard of John
         (I was surprised that John threw out

         o le i'a, 'ina 'ua 'uma 'ona kuka.
         of the fish Comp prf done Comp cook
         the fish, after (it) was cooked.)

(95) a. le fasi e   le tagata o lona to'alua
         the beat Erg the man of his wife
         'the man's beating of his wife'

     b. le faitau-ina e   tātou o le nusipepa
         the read-Trans Erg we   of the newspaper
         'our reading of the newspaper'

     c. 'Ua 'ou ofo   i   le tīa'i   e Ioane
         prf I   surprised Caus the discard Erg John
         'I was surprised that John threw out

o le i'a, 'ina 'ua 'uma 'ona kuka.
of the fish Comp prf done Comp cook
the fish, after (it) was cooked.'

Crucially, not all canonical transitive subjects are ineligible for Possessor Marking, but only those marked with e. Canonical transitive subjects regularly undergo the rule if they have been moved to the left by Pronoun Preposing and would not be marked with e, as shown by (84c) and (84d). Further, not all direct case NPs with overt marking are ineligible for the rule, but only subjects marked with e. Direct objects of middle nominalizations, which are marked with i 'at' or 'i 'to', can undergo Possessor Marking, as shown by (87).

These facts argue that the condition on Possessor Marking should be amended to read: 'Possessor Marking is available for the subject and/or direct object of a nominalization, except for canonical transitive subjects marked with e'. This condition is repeated in other Tongic and Samoic-Outlier languages, which also resemble Samoan in having an ergative case system.[7] See Chung (1973a) for discussion.

6.5.3. Oblique Preposition

Why should subjects marked with e fail to undergo Possessor Marking? There seems to be no good synchronic answer to this question. We can, however, begin to provide a historical rationale by observing that Possessor Marking can be reconstructed for Proto-Polynesian as affecting subjects and direct objects, but no other types of NPs. This, plus or minus the exception referring to e, is the situation that now obtains for the Possessor Marking rules of all Polynesian languages.

The reconstruction suggests an account of the failure of

subjects marked with e to undergo Possessor Marking; namely, this failure is a relic from an earlier time at which e was an oblique preposition, and so NPs marked with it could not undergo the rule. Such a proposal accounts for the fact that e NPs are ineligible for Possessor Marking, and contrasts like (94) versus (84c-d) obtain, in almost every ergative Polynesian language.

It can be hypothesized, then, that e was an oblique preposition at an earlier stage of the Tongic and Samoic-Outlier languages. Since e now serves as an oblique preposition for passive agents in the East Polynesian languages, and no evidence from these languages suggests that it had any other, earlier function, it can be concluded that Proto-Polynesian *e was an oblique preposition, and the NPs marked with it were oblique NPs.

6.6. THE PROTO-POLYNESIAN CASE SYSTEM

The preceding sections used facts from attested Polynesian languages to reconstruct the functions of Proto-Polynesian *-Cia, *i, and *e. It was argued that *-Cia was a passive suffix, *i was a case marker for direct objects of canonical transitive clauses, and *e was an oblique preposition.

These points combine with the morphological patterns reconstructed in 6.2 to reveal the organization of the Proto-Polynesian case system. Recall that pattern (96) can be reconstructed for intransitive clauses:

(96)   Verb   Subj

Further, since *i functioned as a case marker for canonical transitive direct objects, pattern (97) must have been used for canonical transitive clauses:

(97)   Verb   Subj   i DO

312   The Passive-to-Ergative Reanalysis

Finally, since *-_Cia_ functioned as a passive suffix, and *_e_ as an oblique preposition, pattern (98) must have been superficially passive rather than transitive:

(98)   Verb-_Cia_   _e_ Agent   Subj
                    (=underlying   (=underlying
                    Subj)   DO)

It follows from all of this that Proto-Polynesian subjects formed a unified morphological category as opposed to direct objects. In other words, the proto-case system was accusative, and clauses of type (98) were derived by a Passive rule. The reconstructions therefore support the proposal for the history of the case system presented in 6.1.1.

6.7. THE RISE OF ERGATIVE CASE MARKING

Another type of evidence supporting the proposal of 6.1.1 consists of a demonstration that the reconstructed system can be related to the attested systems by means of possible types of change. This demonstration is presented here.

It is hypothesized that all Tongic and Samoic-Outlier languages underwent the passive-to-ergative reanalysis, by means of which passive clauses were reanalyzed as active transitive clauses. As a result of this change, Passive was eliminated and an ergative case assignment rule was added to the grammar: this rule marked subjects of canonical transitive clauses with _e_ and simultaneously attached the -_Cia_ suffix to the verb.

Then, in some but not all Tongic and Samoic-Outlier languages, two further changes occurred.

First, the -_Cia_ suffix was reanalyzed as two suffixes: a 'transitive' suffix attached as a kind of inflectional suffix to canonical transitive verbs, and a less productive, passive-like suffix used in lexical derivation. The reanalysis may have occurred at the same time as, or immediately after, the passive-to-ergative reanalysis, although for ease of exposition the latter possibility is adopted here. The change was made possible by the fact that some -Cia suffixes, but not others, had the semantics and discourse properties associated with Passive (see 6.1.1). As a result, the ergative case assignment rule was simplified so that it no longer inserted -Cia, and two new rules were added to the grammar: a word formation rule for -Cia derivatives, and a rule attaching -Cia more generally to canonical transitive verbs.

Thus in Tongan, ergative case assignment was simplified and two -Cia rules were added: one rule forming lexical derivatives with -Cia, and another rule attaching the durational -Cia more generally to canonical transitive verbs. Both rules appear in the Tongan recorded by C.M. Churchward (1953, 1959), but the second has been lost in contemporary Tongan.

In Samoan, ergative case assignment was simplified and two -Cia rules were added: one rule forming lexical derivatives from middle verbs, and another rule attaching -Cia more generally to canonical transitive verbs to indicate a missing subject. The first rule employs the transitivizing suffix of 6.3.3; the second, the transitive suffix of 2.2.2.

In Niuean, ergative case assignment was simplified and may well have been replaced by two -Cia rules. However, only one of them --that forming lexical derivatives-- is attested today.

Second, the accusative case assignment rule inherited from Proto-Polynesian, which marked direct objects of canonical transitive clauses with *i*, was either lost, restricted, or reanalyzed.

Thus in Tongan and Samoan, the rule was simply lost.

In Rennellese, the rule was restricted to pronouns and

proper nouns and came to apply conjunctively with the ergative case assignment rule; it retained its former avoidance of the -<u>Cia</u> suffix as an idiosyncratic restriction.

In Tokelauan, the rule was restricted to pronouns, came to apply conjunctively with the ergative case assignment rule, and was reanalyzed as affecting all unmarked NPs separated from the verb by another NP.

Finally, in Kapingamarangi, the accusative and the ergative case patterns were reanalyzed as derived by a single rule of the form 'Mark the subject with <u>e</u> and the direct object with <u>i</u>', followed by another rule optionally deleting any case marker. These rules left Kapingamarangi with an accusative case system (see 2.1.5).

The changes affecting the -<u>Cia</u> suffix and the accusative case pattern may well have occurred separately in each of the languages mentioned above. Although the passive-to-ergative reanalysis is posited for all Tongic and Samoic-Outlier languages, no claims have been made about its chronology relative to the split of Proto-Tongic or Proto-Samoic-Outlier --an omission which is deliberate. Regardless of when or how often it occurred, the reanalysis is motivated by the fact that it is a possible type of change, and, more specifically, by the idea that Passive in Proto-Polynesian was relatively opaque. Given this, the change can be viewed as one type of attempt to simplify the original situation. Its recurrence in two or more languages merely reflects the fact that all Polynesian languages are descended historically from the same source.

6.8. CONCLUSION

This chapter has argued that the Proto-Polynesian case system was accusative, and the case systems of the ergative Polyne-

sian languages have arisen through a reanalysis of passive
clauses as active transitive clauses. Although these conclusions bear on the syntactic history of a single language family, they suggest several more general remarks.

First, there are language families besides Polynesian in
which an ergative type of case marking has arisen through reanalysis of passive clauses as active transitive. Similar
reanalyses have been proposed by Hale (1970) for certain Australian languages and by Anderson (1977), among others, for
the Indic languages. These parallels raise the possibility
that the passive-to-ergative reanalysis may be one of the
primary routes by which ergative languages are created.

Second, the Polynesian facts discussed here can be viewed
as supporting the principle that linguistic change works generally in the direction of minimizing opacity. In addition,
they suggest that in a given situation, there may be several
different ways of minimizing opacity. In East Polynesian
languages, the opacity of Passive was decreased by eliminating condition (3); in Tongic and Samoic-Outlier languages, it
was decreased by the passive-to-ergative reanalysis, which
did away with Passive altogether. The contrast between these
two changes serves to point out that there may be no single
optimal way to eliminate an opaque situation through change,
just as there may be no unique optimal grammar constructed
by all new speakers of a language from the data presented to
them by the preceding generation.

NOTES

1. C.M. Churchward (1953: 242) attempts to extend the durational suffix to cover the use of -Cia in lexical derivation, but notes that the latter use is not "fundamental".
   The distinction between the two uses of -Cia is drawn

sharply here, and they are treated as distinct suffixes.
2. The discussion has been simplified in two respects. First, no mention is made of the fact that -<u>Cia</u> verbs can differ from their stems in indicating politeness or respect (see C.M. Churchward 1953: 242). Second, few examples are given of -<u>Cia</u> verbs formed from middle verbs; these derivatives have the semantic properties described in 6.3.1.2 but are typically derived canonical transitives. A similar type of derivation is discussed for Samoan in 6.3.3.
3. Clark (1973a: 583-85) notes some of the passive-like characteristics of Tongan -<u>Cia</u>, and concludes from them that Proto-Polynesian *-<u>Cia</u> (more properly, the *-<u>a</u> of *-<u>Ci-a</u>) was a 'stative-durative' suffix, with semantics such that the underlying subject or agent of the clause was frequently omitted. In the absence of further details it is difficult to evaluate such a proposal, but it seems quite close to the proposal that *-<u>Cia</u>, or *-<u>a</u>, was a passive suffix.
4. Cliticization is used here to refer to the fact that the pronoun preceding the verb occurs in clitic rather than independent form. Cliticization in Rennellese seems limited to the first singular pronoun (independent <u>au</u>, clitic <u>kau</u>), and it is unclear to me whether it is the result of a Clitic Placement rule.
5. In addition, <u>i</u> is apparently used to mark proper nouns which are intransitive subjects or canonical transitive direct objects, regardless of their position.
6. As observed by Patrick Hohepa, passive nominalizations exhibiting the passive suffix are allowed in contemporary Maori, though not in the Maori of nineteenth century texts. Nominalizations of this type do not allow the direct ob-

317 The Passive-to-Ergative Reanalysis

ject to be marked with the accusative i. When combined with examples like (78b), this fact argues that Agent Postposing is distinct from Passive in the contemporary language.

7. The facts of Samoan nominalizations are more complicated than suggested by the description in the text, in two respects.

First, there is speaker variation regarding nominalizations of the type (87), which are accepted by some speakers but rejected by others. Still other speakers reject (87) but allow the direct objects of middle nominalizations to undergo Possessor Marking if the subject has been removed by an Agent Postposing rule. This rule marks the subject with e and moves it to the right, leaving the direct object to the immediate right of the nominalized verb:

(a)   'Ua 'ou ofo   i   le agaleaga o a'u e
      prf I surprised Caus the mistreat of me Erg
      'I was surprised that I was mistreated by

      lo'u faiā'oga.
      my   teacher
      my teacher.'

Agent Postposing is distinct from the ergative case assignment rule, since it requires the subject to be moved to the right. It also applies to nominalizations formed from clauses which do not govern ergative case marking:

(b)   *Sā agaleaga a'u e   lo'u faiā'oga.
       past mistreat me Erg my   teacher
       (I was mistreated by my teacher.)

These facts, plus those described in the text, suggest that Possessor Marking originally extended to direct objects of middle nominalizations, although this is not now the case for some speakers of Samoan.

Second, it has been pointed out to me by Dixie Samasoni

that he accepts nominalizations of the type (94b), in which a canonical transitive subject is marked with <u>a</u>. I take this to be an innovation. Although one of my younger Samoan consultants found nominalizations of this type questionable, all others rejected them, and they are not found among the many nominalizations in nineteenth century Samoan texts.

7. Reanalysis & Pukapukan Syntax

In the preceding chapter it was argued that the rise of ergative case marking in Tongic and Samoic-Outlier languages involves a passive-to-ergative reanalysis:

(1)   The Passive-to-Ergative Reanalysis:

Verb-<u>Cia</u>   e Agent   Subj
              (=underlying   (=underlying
                Subj)   DO)

→ reanalyzed as →

Verb-<u>Cia</u>   e Subj   DO

According to one common generative view of linguistic change, this reanalysis should be implemented by (a) loss of Passive, and (b) addition of an ergative case assignment rule. Further, the implementation of these changes should be discrete rather than gradual. This chapter presents evidence from Pukapukan, a Samoic-Outlier language, arguing that the latter assumption should be amended in an interesting way. It is shown that although the Pukapukan version of (1) can be broken down into a series of discrete rule changes, these are being implemented gradually, and in a way that cannot be accounted for within the theory of change as it has been elaborated so far. It is argued further that this gradual realization is governed by the principle:

(2)   A new analysis is actualized first for clauses that are less distorted by syntactic rules, where superficial rules distort the clause less than do major rules.

(2) is one principle governing the differences in output al-

lowed between the grammars of successive generations of speakers of a language. This chapter argues that it should be recognized as part of the theory of change.

7.1 briefly describes how the passive-to-ergative reanalysis would be implemented within a generative framework; 7.2 reviews the case system of Pukapukan. 7.3 examines the surface case patterns of underlyingly transitive clauses and their interaction with a number of rules. It is shown that the 'ergative' and 'passive' types of case marking are more restricted than the 'accusative' type, and the restrictions involved are principled. 7.4 argues that this interaction is not susceptible to a unique synchronic analysis, but instead results from competition between two alternative analyses, one representing the pre-reanalysis, and the other the post-reanalysis, stage. It is proposed that the nondiscrete aspects of the competition are governed by principle (2). Finally, 7.5 discusses two related changes, one from Samoan and the other from Indonesian, which support and suggest refinements of the principle.

7.1. THE PASSIVE-TO-ERGATIVE REANALYSIS

Although there has been little explicit mention of this, generative historical linguistics has tended to view syntactic change as discrete rather than gradual. King (1969: 115), for instance, says in a discussion concerned principally with phonological change:

> Parenthetically, let it be noted that linguistic change other than phonological is clearly not gradual by any stretch of the imagination. If an adult learns to use whom in place of who in the right places, how could this be anything but sudden and abrupt? When a child says foots instead of feet, what is gradual about it?

The assumption of this passage seems to be that nonphonological change could not be gradual, because the elements of those components of grammar are all discrete. Thus, syntax could not change gradually, because it consists entirely of discrete elements such as NP. Although the passage quoted above perhaps comes closest to stating this assumption, the idea of discrete change appears implicitly in a number of works on particular problems of syntactic change (e.g. Klima 1964; Traugott 1965; Bever and Langendoen 1971). These recognize 'trends' of change but treat them as series of distinct stages, related by changes such as rule addition, rule simplification, and reanalysis.

In this framework, the passive-to-ergative reanalysis of (1) would be implemented by two simultaneous changes: (a) loss of Passive, and (b) addition of an ergative case assignment rule:

(3) a. Before the Passive-to-Ergative Reanalysis:
Passive (optional): Promote the direct object to subject, turn the underlying subject into an oblique noun marked with e, and attach the passive suffix -Cia to the verb.

b. After the Passive-to-Ergative Reanalysis:
(no Passive)
Ergative Case Assignment (optional): If there are two direct case NPs in a clause, mark the subject with e and attach the suffix -Cia to the verb.

The subsequent disappearance of -Cia in some languages from the basic transitive case pattern would be viewed as a simplification of ergative case assignment:

(4)   After Simplification of Case Assignment:
        (no Passive)
        Ergative Case Assignment (optional): If there are two direct case NPs in a clause, mark the subject with e.

Now if syntactic change were entirely discrete, we would expect the grammar of every Tongic or Samoic-Outlier language to look like (3b), (4), or some further development of one of these. However, such a prediction is not borne out in at least one Samoic-Outlier language --Pukapukan. The facts of Pukapukan are used below to argue that syntactic change is sometimes gradual, in the sense that stages like those in (3) and (4) may sometimes compete in a nondiscrete fashion within a single synchronic grammar.

7.2. PUKAPUKAN

This section reviews the case system of Pukapukan and then uses the evidence of case marking to predict what the synchronic grammar of this language should be like, given the larger assumptions of 7.1. 7.2.1 describes the case system; 7.2.2 makes the prediction.

7.2.1. Case Marking

Pukapukan has a mixed accusative-ergative case system, described previously in 2.1.6. Intransitive clauses take their subjects in the nominative, which is generally unmarked:

(5)   Na   we-lele te   kau.
        past pl-run   the people
        'The people ran.'

Exceptionally, the nominative marker for proper nouns and the third singular pronoun is i, followed by the pronominal-proper article a:

(6)   Na   wano i   a-na   lā   Victoria Park.
      past go   Nom pro-he across Victoria Park
      'He went across Victoria Park.'

Underlyingly transitive clauses allow three surface case patterns, which are referred to here as 'accusative', 'passive', and 'ergative'. It should be emphasized that these are labels for the morphology only, and are not intended to imply any particular surface syntactic analysis of these clause types. The surface syntax of underlyingly transitive clauses is dealt with in 7.3 and 7.4.

In the 'accusative' pattern, the underlying subject is nominative and the underlying direct object is marked with the accusative i:

(7) a.   Na   patu mātou i   te   tamaiti.
         past hit we   Acc the child
         'We hit the child.'

    b.   Ko   mina i   a-na   i   te   ika.
         prog want Nom pro-he Acc the fish
         'He wants the fish.'

In the 'passive' pattern, the underlying subject is marked with the agentive/ergative e, the underlying direct object is nominative, and some form of the 'passive' suffix -Cia is attached to the verb:

(8) a.   Na   patu-a   te tamaiti e   mātou.
         past hit-Pass the child Agt us
         'We hit the child.'
         'The child was hit by us.'

    b.   Ko   mina-ngia te yua   e-ku.
         prog want-Pass the water Agt-me
         'I want the water.'

Finally, in the 'ergative' pattern, the underlying subject is marked with the agentive/ergative e, the underlying direct object is nominative, and the -Cia suffix does not appear:

(9)a.   Na   patu te tamaiti e   mātou.
        past hit the child   Erg we
        'We hit the child.'

   b.   ?Ko   mina e-ku te   yua.
        prog want Erg-I the water
        'I want the water.'

The three patterns are governed by the large majority of transitive verbs, although the 'ergative' pattern is less acceptable than the 'accusative' or 'passive' for certain middle verbs. The variation among the patterns is determined principally by what other syntactic rules have applied. In clauses to which no other rules have applied (zero-pronominalization excepted), the patterns appear to differ primarily in register and style. In terms of register, the 'accusative' is identified as formal or polite, the 'ergative' as informal or casual, and the 'passive' as neutral. Stylistically, the patterns are sometimes used to organize a narrative in ways described in 2.1.6. The three patterns are distributed along different lines in clauses whose underlying subject or direct object has been removed by certain rules; this is discussed in 7.3.

7.2.2. A Prediction

If syntactic change were entirely discrete, then each individual Polynesian language should have either undergone the passive-to-ergative reanalysis or not. Now the organization of the Pukapukan case system suggests that this language has undergone the reanalysis --a suggestion which is consistent with the claim that all Tongic and Samoic-Outlier languages have undergone this change, and which will be verified below. Therefore, we might expect its grammar to look like (3b), (4), or some further development of one of these. Although the precise form of the Pukapukan rules cannot, obviously, be predicted from the historical proposal of 7.1, one general prediction can be made: the clause types associated with the 'passive' and 'ergative' patterns of (8-9) should be superficially active transitive rather than passive. Consequently, their surface subjects should be subjects, not direct objects, in underlying structure.

7.3. TESTING THE PREDICTION
This section tests the prediction of 7.2.2 by examining the interaction of the 'passive' and 'ergative' case patterns with a number of subject-referring rules. It is shown that the facts are more complex than suggested by 7.2.2, in that clauses with these case patterns allow either the underlying subject or the underlying direct object to undergo the rules. The situation is complicated further by a certain amount of nondiscrete variation.

7.3.1 presents the subject-referring rules; 7.3.2 discusses their interaction with the 'passive' and 'ergative' case patterns.

7.3.1. Subject-Referring Rules
Pukapukan has a number of rules referring to subjects.

Given that the surface subjecthood of NPs associated with the 'passive' and 'ergative' patterns is the topic of investigation, the question arises as to how a rule can be shown independently to be restricted to subjects. It is assumed here that a rule is subject-limited if it affects the subjects of intransitive clauses, the subjects of transitive clauses in the 'accusative' pattern, but not 'accusative' direct objects or --obviously-- oblique NPs. This assumption seems reasonable internal to Pukapukan syntax; within the larger context of Polynesian, it is motivated by the fact that

326   Reanalysis and Pukapukan Syntax

the 'accusative' pattern is not directly affected by the passive-to-ergative reanalysis, whose results are being tested here.

7.3.1.1 deals with Equi; 7.3.1.2, with Raising; 7.3.1.3, with Relativization; 7.3.1.4, with Clefting and Question Movement; and 7.3.1.5, with Subject Preposing.

7.3.1.1. Equi. Pukapukan has an Equi rule which relates sentences like (10) and (11):

(10)   Na wō   te wui tāne yī-ika   i te moana.
       past go=pl the pl man catch-fish in the ocean
       'The men went fishing in the ocean.'

(11)   Na wō   te wui tāne ke yī-ika   lātou i
       past go=pl the pl man sbj catch-fish they in
       'The men went so that they could fish in

       te moana.
       the ocean
       the ocean.'

This rule operates in certain two-clause structures in which one clause contains a verb of motion or position, such as yau 'come' or wano 'go', and the other clause is an adverbial clause of purpose embedded directly under it. Adverbial clauses of this type are typically introduced by the subjunctive tense-aspect-mood particle ke:

(12)   Ke wō   tāua ke yaeleele tūtaka (tāua).
       sbj go=pl we=du sbj walk=pl observe we=du
       '...so that we can go and have a walk around.'

If a target in the embedded clause is coreferential with a controller in the higher clause, it can be deleted by Equi, subject to conditions described below. When this happens, the subjunctive particle is omitted, giving the embedded clause the surface form of a participle:

(13)   Ke wō   tāua yaeleele tūtaka.
       sbj go=pl we=du walk=pl observe
       '...so that we can go walking around.'

Equi can be distinguished from other deletion rules --in particular, zero-pronominalization-- by its deletion of the subjunctive particle and by the other properties described below. Its form is roughly: 'Delete a target in the embedded clause under coreference with a controller in the next higher clause, and delete ke, subject to further conditions (described below)'.

Equi qualifies as a major rule in terms of the rule typology of Chapter 3. It is the counterpart of Equi in English, a cyclic rule. It is governed by verbs of motion or position. It is also bounded, in that it cannot delete a target which is separated from the controller by another clause.

Significantly, Equi exhibits a restriction on the target: it deletes only targets that are both subjects and semantic agents. The rule deletes subjects of intransitive clauses:

(14)   Ka wo   latou koti-lakau, ke yi o latou
       fut go=pl they cut-wood   sbj some pl=their
       'They would go to cut wood, so that they would

       vaka, ke wo   ai wangota.
       canoe sbj go=pl Pro fish
       have some canoes so that (they) could go fishing.' (Beaglehole and Beaglehole 1053)

As well as subjects of transitive clauses in the 'accusative' pattern:

(15)a. Wōmamai te vaka o te kau   Kātorikā kave
        come=pl the boat of the people Catholic take
        'The Catholic boat came to take

        i   a-ku   mai lunga o te payī.
        Acc pro-me from top   of the ship
        me from the ship.'

   b.   Wo   loa te wui tane o te wenua nei patu
        go=pl Emp the pl man of the island this kill
        'The men of the island went to kill

328   Reanalysis and Pukapukan Syntax

```
            i   na    tane o Yangalipule.
            Acc the=pl man of Yangalipule
            the men of Yangalipule.' (Beaglehole and Beagle-
            hole 1157)

       c.   E  kiai au na   wano tuku i  nā     kou.
            uns not I  past go   give Acc the=pl gift
            'I didn't go to give the presents.'
```

But it does not delete 'accusative' direct objects:

```
    (16)    *Na   wōmamai lātou vayi   (ai) te  aliki.
            past come=pl they strike  Pro  the king
            (They came for the king to discipline (them).)
```

Or oblique NPs:

```
    (17)    *Ka  yau  i   a-na    tuku (ki ai) mātou i   te
            fut come Nom pro-he  give  to Pro  we    Acc the
            (He should come so that we could give (him) the

            kou.
            gift
            present.)
```

Further, Equi requires its target to be a semantic agent as well as a subject. It does not delete semantic patients, regardless of their grammatical relations or case marking.

Finally, the rule requires its target to be a subject as well as a semantic agent. It does not delete stative agents, for instance, because these NPs are semantically agentive but syntactically oblique (see 1.3.5):

```
    (18)    *Na   wano te  tamāwine lilo    te  kete.
            past  go   the girl     gotten  the basket
            (The girl went so that the basket could be got-
            ten (by her).)
```

It can be concluded from this that Equi is restricted to targets that are both subjects and semantic agents, and so is a subject-referring rule.

7.3.1.2. <u>Raising</u>. Pukapukan has a Raising rule which relates sentences like (19) and (20):

(19) a. Kiai nā   ika na   maua.
         not the=pl fish past caught
         'The fish were not caught.'

    b.   Auwae au e kake ki lunga o te payī.
         don't I uns climb to top of the ship
         'Let me not climb on the ship!'

(20) a. Kiai na   maua   nā   ika.
         not past caught the=pl fish
         'The fish were not caught.'

    b.   Auwae e kake au ki lunga o te payī.
         don't uns climb I to top of the ship
         'Let me not climb on the ship!'

Raising operates in negative sentences containing the negative verbs *kiai* 'not (past, or for predicate nominals)', or *auwae* 'not (imperative)'. Such sentences are biclausal, the negative acting as the verb of the higher clause and the negated clause, as its sentential subject:

(21)
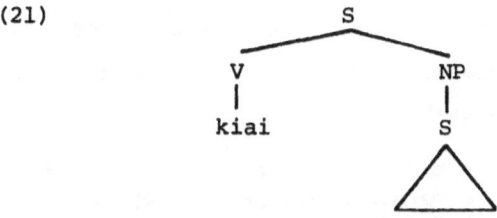

The verbal status of the negative *kiai* is established by several points. First, it can be preceded by the unspecified tense-aspect-mood particle *e*, which is found otherwise only before verbs:

(22) a. E   kiai na   maua   te ika i   a   Turi.
         uns not past caught the fish Caus prop Turi
         'The fish was not caught by Turi.'

    b.   E   kiai i te kino.
         uns not at the bad
         '(It) is not bad.'

Second, it can attract verbal modifiers which are otherwise

attracted only to verbs, including directional particles such as <u>ake</u> 'up', and the pronominal copy <u>ai</u>:

(23) a. Ko   te tamá e tamaiti, kiai ake na
         Pred the boy   a child   not up   past
         'That boy is a child; he has not yet

         wakatāne.
         become=man
         become a man.'

   b. E wea te mea   kiai ai lātou na   wakalale
       a what? the reason not Pro they past speak
       'What is the reason why they don't speak

       i   te talatala Pukapuka?
       Acc the lg   Pukapukan
       the Pukapukan language?'

These characteristics argue that <u>kiai</u> is a verb, and consequently sentences of the type (20) are biclausal on the surface. This and the similar conclusion for <u>auwae</u> are supported further by the facts discussed below.

Raising takes an NP from the negated clause and raises it to the next higher clause, turning it into the derived subject of the negative verb. Consider:

(24) a. Kiai te kovi lewu na   moe   i te wale.
         not the person small past sleep in the house
         'The child did not sleep in the house.'

   b. E   kiai au i te tama kino.
       uns not I at the boy bad
       'I'm not a bad boy.'

The arguments establishing the existence of Raising include the following.

(a) To begin with, the raised NP originates in the lower clause, as can be shown by the usual subcategorization arguments involving a missing NP.

(b) The raised NP is also the derived subject of the higher clause, a point made most clearly by the case marking of pronouns.

The case marking of pronominal subjects of intransitive clauses and transitive clauses in the 'accusative' pattern differs according to whether or not they surface inside the clause. Pronominal subjects that surface inside the clause occur in the nominative. The nominative marker for the third singular pronoun is i, followed by the pronominal-proper article a:

(25)   Koa tunu i   a-na   i   te ika.
       prf cook Nom pro-he Acc the fish
       'He was about to cook the fish.'

The nominative is indicated by lack of marking for the other pronouns:

(26)a. Ka patu au i te kovi lewu.
       fut hit I Acc the person small
       'I am going to hit the child.'

   b. Ka penapena koe i nā   popoa.
       fut prepare you Acc the=pl food
       'You are going to prepare the food.'

(27)a. *Ka patu i a-ku i   te kovi   lewu.
        fut hit Nom pro-I Acc the person small
        (I am going to hit the child.)

   b. *Ka penapena i a   koe i nā   popoa.
        fut prepare Nom pro you Acc the=pl food
        (You are going to prepare the food.)

Pronominal subjects that surface outside the clause are preceded by an overt particle. For instance, pronouns moved to the left by Subject Preposing (see 7.3.1.5) are preceded by the topic particle i, followed by the pronominal-proper article a, regardless of their person and number:

(28)a. I   a-ku ka patu i   te kovi   lewu.
       topic pro-I fut hit Acc the person small
       'I am going to hit the child.'

   b. I   a   koe ka penapena i   nā   popoa.
       topic pro you fut prepare Acc the=pl food
       'You are going to prepare the food.'

This is true even when they are shielded from sentence-initial position by a preposed adverb:

    (29)a.   Tapā   i   a-ku na   lele ki Ākarana.
            perhaps topic pro-I past run to Auckland
            'Perhaps I ran to Auckland.'

       b.   *Tapā   au na   lele ki Ākarana.
            perhaps I past run to Auckland
            (Perhaps I ran to Auckland.)

Pronominal subjects removed from their clause by other rules, such as Clefting, are preceded by other overt particles.

Now when Raising has applied to a pronoun in a negative sentence, the raised pronoun takes the marking appropriate for subjects that surface inside the clause; in other words, it appears in the nominative:

    (30)a.   E   kiai au na   wano tuku i   nā   kou.
            uns not I past go   give Acc the=pl gift
            'I didn't go to give the presents.'

       b.   Auwae kōtou e   manatu i   te   ayo o te
            don't you=pl uns think Acc the day of the
            'Don't you think about Christmas

            Kiritimeti.
            Christmas
            Day!'

    (31)a.   *E   kiai i   a-ku na   wano tuku i   nā
            uns not topic pro-I past go   give Acc the=pl
            (I didn't go to give the

            kou.
            gift
            presents.)

       b.   *Auwae i   a   kōtou e   manatu i   te   ayo
            don't topic pro you=pl uns think Acc the day
            (Don't you think about Christmas

            o te Kiritimeti.
            of the Christmas
            Day!)

This lack of marking argues that it surfaces inside the clause of which it is a subject. Given that the negatives of (30) are verbs, and the raised pronouns are in the linear position appropriate for their subjects, the evidence is fairly strong that the raised pronouns are the surface subjects of the negatives.

(c) Finally, the raised NP does not originate in the higher clause and then trigger deletion of a coreferential target in the negated clause. This can be established by considering the properties of controlled deletion rules in Pukapukan and contrasting them with the properties of Raising.

The raised NP does not control zero-pronominalization in the negated clause, because zero-pronominalization is optional. Raising, however, always leaves a hole in the negated clause:

(32) *Kiai te kovi lewu na moe i a-na i
not the person small past sleep Nom pro-he in
(The child did not sleep in

te wale.
the house
the house.)

Further, the raised NP does not control Equi in the negated clause, for two reasons. It does not result in deletion of the tense-aspect-mood particle of the embedded clause, unlike Equi. It also applies freely to semantic patients, whereas Equi does not:

(33)a. Kiai te palu na maua i a Turi.
not the palu past caught Caus prop Turi
'The palu was not caught by Turi.'

b. Kiai nā kākawu na tuitui-ina e nā
not the=pl clothes past sew-Pass Agt the=pl
'The clothes were not sewn by the

tāne.
man
men.'

In (33a), the raised NP is the subject of a stative verb; in (33b), it is the underlying direct object of a transitive clause in the 'passive' pattern.

It can be concluded from all of this that sentences like (19) do not involve any of the coreferential deletion rules of Pukapukan, but instead are very likely related by Raising. This rule has the form: 'Raise an NP from the embedded clause to become the derived subject of the higher clause, subject to further conditions (described below)'.

Raising in Pukapukan qualifies as a major rule. It is the counterpart of Subject-to-Subject Raising in English, a cyclic rule. It is also bounded: it will raise NPs only from the clause immediately below the higher verb. Finally, Raising is governed by the negative verbs *kiai*, *auwae*, and a a third negative, *kiliai*, which is apparently an alternant of *kiai*; in addition, it is governed by several predicates with the meanings of sentential adverbs in English. But it is not allowed for other higher verbs.

Significantly, Raising is restricted to NPs that are subjects of the negated clause. It affects intransitive subjects, as in (19), as well as transitive subjects in the 'accusative' case pattern:

(34) a. Kiai te tamāwine na patu i te tāne.
not the girl past hit Acc the man
'The girl did not hit the man.'

b. Kiai i a-na na momotu i te wao yī-
not Nom pro-he past break Acc the line catch-
'He didn't break the fishing

ika.
fish
line.'

c. Auwae koe e maka i a-ku.
don't you uns leave Acc pro-me
'Don't you leave me!'

d. Auwae e tangata e   kai i   te kiko niu.
    don't a person uns eat Acc the meat coconut
    'Let no one eat the coconut meat!'
    'Let it not be the case that anyone eats the
    coconut meat!'

However, it does not affect 'accusative' direct objects or oblique NPs. This is demonstrated for 'accusative' direct objects in:

(35)a. *Kiai nā   yakari na   kai (ai) te kurī.
         not the=pl coconut past eat Pro the dog
         (The dog did not eat the coconuts.)

   b. *Auwae te lākau e   yemu ai koe.
        don't the tree uns chop Pro you
        (Don't you chop down the tree!)

It can be concluded from this that Raising is a subject-referring rule.

7.3.1.3. <u>Relativization</u>. Pukapukan has a Relativization rule consisting of two strategies, a deletion strategy and a pronominalization strategy. The deletion strategy simply deletes the relative noun under coreference with the head noun:

(36)   te wui tāngata na   lōmamai mai o lātou
       the pl people [past come=pl from pl=their
       'the people who came from their

       konga mamao
       place distant]
       distant places'

The pronominalization strategy pronominalizes the relative noun to the copy <u>ai</u>:

(37)   te taime na   maka ai au
       the time [past leave Pro I]
       'the time that I left'

The arguments that these strategies are distinct from the normal processes of pronominalization and zero-pronominalization were sketched briefly in 1.4.3; some of them involve facts to be discussed below. Here it is simply asserted that (36) and (37) are not produced by more general processes of anaphora, but instead have resulted from the two strategies of a Relativization rule.

Relativization qualifies as a superficial rule in terms of the rule typology of Chapter 3. It is the counterpart of Relativization by pronominalization or deletion in English (i.e. with the complementizer <u>that</u>), which is postcyclic. It is unbounded, since it allows the relative noun to be separated from its head by any number of intervening clauses:

   (38)   Ko   ta lātou tama tēnei na   pono ka yau
             Pred their   child this [past good fut come
            'This was their child who it was agreed should

             wakatupu i   to lātou manatu-nga.
             increase Acc their   think-Nmlz]
             come to further their purpose.'

It also is not governed and does not exhibit lexical exceptions.

Significantly, the deletion strategy of Relativization is restricted to relative nouns that are subjects. It affects intransitive subjects, as in (36) and (38), as well as transitive subjects in the 'accusative' pattern:

   (39)a.   Ko   te kulī tēnei   na   kakati i   te tāne
            Pred the dog this [past bite   Acc the man
            'This is the dog who bit the fat

            mōmona.
            fat]
            man.'

       b.   Onoono-wia-ake te mea   na   wakangayuayua
            look-Pass-up   the thing [past stir
            'Just look at the thing which stirred the

            i   te taekele tutae.
            Acc the pile   feces]
            pile of feces.' (Beaglehole and Beaglehole 1102)

Reanalysis and Pukapukan Syntax

But it does not affect 'accusative' direct objects or oblique NPs, which must use the pronominalization strategy instead. This is demonstrated for an 'accusative' direct object in:

(40) Oko ki te moana na wakailo ai lua
      reach to the ocean [past name   Pro two
      '(He) reached the sea named by his two

      ona   matutua.
      pl=his parents]
      parents (lit. ...the sea which his two parents
      had named).' (Beaglehole and Beaglehole 1058)

The deletion strategy can thus be identified as subject-referring.

7.3.1.4. <u>Clefting</u> <u>and</u> <u>Question</u> <u>Movement</u>. In addition to Relativization, Pukapukan has two other extraction rules: Clefting and Question Movement. Clefting moves a focused NP to the left and marks it with the predicate particle <u>ko</u>:

(41)a. Ko   Yinaliulu ya   tu   i te uluulu akau.
       Pred Yinaliulu past stand at the outer=reef
       'Yinaliulu was standing on the outer reef.'
       (Beaglehole and Beaglehole 993)

   b. Ko   te moana na   yī-ika   ai lātou.
       Pred the ocean past catch-fish   Pro they
       'It is the ocean that they were fishing in.'

Question Movement moves an interrogative pronoun to the left, either marking it with the predicate particle <u>ko</u> or else, in the case of certain oblique interrogative pronouns, leaving it unmarked:

(42)a. Ko   ai   koa yau nei?
       Pred who? prf come this
       'Who has come here?'

   b. Tiai koe ka ngakaumate ai?
       why? you fut bold   Pro
       'Why are you so bold?' (Beaglehole and Beaglehole 1087)

338   Reanalysis and Pukapukan Syntax

   Each of these rules has a chopping strategy, which simply
leaves behind a hole, and a copying strategy, which leaves behind a pronominal copy of the moved NP. Arguments that these
strategies are distinct from the more general anaphoric processes of Pukapukan are essentially the same as those mentioned for Relativization in 1.4.3.
   Clefting and Question Movement qualify as superficial
rules. They are the counterparts of English Clefting and Wh-
Movement, respectively, which have been shown to be postcyclic
(see Pinkham and Hankamer 1975; Postal 1972). They are also
unbounded, being able to move the focused NP over an unlimit-
ed distance. Finally, they do not exhibit lexical exceptions.
   As might be expected by now, the chopping strategies of
these rules are limited to subjects. They affect intransitive subjects, as in (41a) and (42a), as well as transitive
subjects in the 'accusative' pattern. Consider the Clefting
sentences of (43) and the questions of (44):

   (43)a. Ko-na   na   tuku i   te kou.
           Pred-he past give Acc the gift
           'It is he who gave the present.'

       b. Ko te toa   na   patu i te wawine.
           Pred the warrior past hit Acc the woman
           'It is the warrior who hit the woman.'

   (44)a. Ko ai   na   wakatū i   te wale?
           Pred who? past build Acc the house
           'Who built the house?'

       b. Ko ai   na   aumai i   te puka?
           Pred who? past bring Acc the book
           'Who brought the book?'

But they do not affect 'accusative' direct objects or oblique
NPs, which must undergo the copying strategies instead. This
is demonstrated for several types of oblique NPs in (45):

(45)a. Ko te tāne na maua ai te wua lākau.
       Pred the man past caught Pro the egg tree
       'It is the man by whom/because of whom the
       fruit was gotten.'

   b. Mai wea na wō ai kōtou?
       from where? past go=pl Pro you=pl
       'Where did you come from?'

The chopping strategies of Clefting and Question Movement are therefore subject-referring.

7.3.1.5. <u>Subject Preposing</u>. Finally, Pukapukan has a rule of Subject Preposing, which relates sentences like (46) and (47):

(46)a. Te wui tāne na we-lele.
       the pl man past pl-run
       'The men ran away.'

   b. I   a-ku ka kake ki lunga o te payī.
       topic pro-I fut climb to top of the ship
       'I am going to climb onto the ship.'

(47)a. Na we-lele te wui tāne.
       past pl-run the pl man
       'The men ran away.'

   b. Ka kake au ki lunga o te payī.
       fut climb I to top of the ship
       'I am going to climb onto the ship.'

This rule moves an NP to the left, focusing on it in a mild way and creating a verb-medial word order on the surface. Common nouns that have undergone the rule are unmarked; pronouns and proper nouns are marked with the topic particle <u>i</u>, followed by the pronominal-proper article <u>a</u>.

Although Subject Preposing has no clear counterpart in more familiar languages, cyclic or postcyclic, it has the other properties of a superficial rule. It is unbounded, since it can move an NP over several clauses. It also exhibits no lexical exceptions.

Subject Preposing is restricted to NPs that are subjects. It applies to subjects of intransitive clauses, as in (46), and to transitive subjects in the 'accusative' pattern:

(48) a. Te kurī na kakati i   te tāne mōmona.
         the dog past bite Acc the man fat
         'The dog bit the fat man.'

   b. I   a-ku ka penapena i nā   popoa.
       topic pro-I fut prepare Acc the=pl food
       'I have to prepare the food.'

However, it is marginal at best for 'accusative' direct objects, which require it to leave behind the copy <u>ai</u>:

(49) a. ?Te kete   na   tuku ai au ki te kovi   lewu.
         the basket past give Pro I to the person small
         'The basket, I gave to the child.'

   b. *Te toa   na   kite ai te kovi   lewu.
       the warrior past see Pro the person small
       (The warrior, the child saw.)

   c. *Te toa   na   patu (ai) au.
       the warrior past hit Pro I
       (The warrior, I hit.)

And it is not allowed for oblique NPs, whether or not a pronominal copy <u>ai</u> is left behind:

(50)   *Te moana na   yī-ika   (ai) lātou.
         the ocean past catch-fish Pro they
         (The ocean, they caught fish in.)

Ignoring the complications introduced by (49a), it appears that Subject Preposing is basically a subject-referring rule.

7.3.2. <u>Interaction with the 'Passive' and 'Ergative' Patterns</u>

We now turn to the interaction of these subject-referring rules with the 'passive' and 'ergative' case patterns.

The interaction discussed below is complicated by a certain amount of nondiscrete variation, where variation is understood to mean variation in the judgements of individual speakers. Studies of variation are typically based on data from a large sample of the linguistic community, which, according to Labov (1969), reflects the synchronic and diachronic status of rules more accurately than does data collected from a few speakers. My field research on Pukapukan did not involve a large-scale study of this type; consequently, the facts presented below are not discussed in terms of variation across speakers. It is, however, possible to derive some of the same benefits by examining individual variation in judgements of particular sentence types. When presented with sentences like those below, individual speakers of Pukapukan tended to offer different grammaticality judgements on different occasions. It is assumed here that this variation is principled, and can be brought to bear on the analysis of clauses in the 'passive' or 'ergative' patterns in a way similar to the use of variation across speakers.

This assumption allows fine differences in grammaticality to be discussed on the basis of data from only a small number of speakers. It is motivated in the sense that individual speakers are members of the larger speech community, and so can be expected to reflect some aspects of the community when given a chance. (For quantitative justification of this, see Bickerton (1971, 1973) and Wolfram (1973).) Finally, as far as the facts discussed below are concerned, the assumption is supported by evidence from narrative texts. An examination of Beaglehole and Beaglehole's (1938b) Pukapukan texts reveals that the frequency of sentence types discussed below correlates surprisingly well with the overall grammaticality assigned them by individual speakers. The correlation suggests that individual variation can be as reliable an index of usage, in the long run, as variation across a number of speakers.

7.3.2.1 deals with the effect of subject-referring rules on the unmarked NP (=underlying direct object) of the 'passive' pattern; 7.3.2.2 deals with their effect on the unmarked NP of the 'ergative' pattern. 7.3.2.3 deals with the effect of these rules on the e NP (=underlying subject) of the 'passive' pattern; 7.3.2.4, with their effect on the e NP of the 'ergative' pattern. 7.3.2.5 is a summary.

7.3.2.1. <u>Unmarked NP of the 'Passive' Pattern</u>. Because Equi is restricted to targets that are both subjects and semantic agents, this rule cannot be used to test for the subjecthood of the unmarked NP of the 'passive' case pattern, which is never a semantic agent. The other rules of 7.3.1 do provide tests, however, and indicate that the unmarked NP of this pattern can always serve as a subject.

The unmarked NP of the 'passive' pattern is always eligible for Raising:

```
(51)a.  Kiai i   a-na   na   patu-a    e   Yina.
        not  Nom pro-he past hit-Pass Agt Yina
        'He was not hit by Yina.'

    b.  Kiai te lā  na   liaki-na    e   te wui
        not  the sail past raise-Pass Agt the pl
        'The sail was not raised by the

        tāngata.
        men
        men.'

    c.  Auwae nā     yakari  e   vayi-a     e  koe.
        don't the=pl coconut uns split-Pass Agt you
        'Don't you split the coconuts!'

    d.  Auwae te wāwā e   yemu-ina    e   te tama.
        don't the taro uns chop-Pass Agt the boy
        'Let the boy not chop the taro!'
```

It can always undergo the deletion strategy of Relativization:

(52) a. Na   kai au i   te yakari   na   a-u
        past eat I Acc the coconut [past pro-you
        'I ate the coconut that you

        aumai-a   ki a-ku.
        bring-Pass to pro-me]
        brought to me.'

   b. ...ma te manu tao pipiko   na   patu-a
          and the bird beak crooked [past kill-Pass
       '...and the birds with crooked beaks which were

        mai e   Malangatiale.
        here Agt Malangatiale]
        killed by Malangatiale.' (Beaglehole and Beaglehole 1036)

It can always undergo the chopping strategies of Clefting and Question Movement:

(53) a. Ko   te wāwā ka tunu-a   e   te tama.
        Pred the taro fut cook-Pass Agt the boy
        'It is the taro that the boy is about to cook.'

   b. Ko   na   tama la   a Palakula ma Kutikuti
        Pred the=pl boy that of Palakula and Kutikuti
        'The children of Palakula and Kutikuti were

        ya   vayi-a   e   Uila.
        past whip-Pass Agt Uila
        whipped by Uila.' (Beaglehole and Beaglehole 1138)

(54) a. Ko   ai   na   welāvei-ngia e   lāua?
        Pred who? past visit-Pass Agt them=du
        'Who did they visit?'

   b. Ko   ai   na   wakautunga-ina e   te pūāpī?
        Pred who? past punish-Pass Agt the teacher
        'Who was punished by the teacher?'

And it always undergoes Subject Preposing:

(55)   Te tāne mōmona na   kakati-a   e   te kurī.
        the man fat   past bite-Pass Agt the dog
        'The fat man was bitten by the dog.'

344   Reanalysis and Pukapukan Syntax

These facts argue that the unmarked NP of the 'passive' pattern can always serve as the subject for the purposes of these rules. Since the unmarked NP is an underlying direct object, a natural hypothesis would be that it has been promoted to subject --presumably by Passive-- before any of the subject-referring rules applied.

7.3.2.2. <u>Unmarked NP of the 'Ergative' Pattern</u>. The situation as regards the unmarked NP of the 'ergative' pattern is more complicated, in that this NP appears to act as the subject more consistently for some rules than for others. Again, the evidence of Equi is not considered, for the reason given in 7.3.2.1.

The unmarked NP of the 'ergative' pattern is eligible for Raising only occasionally. Consider the following:

(56) a. ?Kiai i   a-na   na   patu e   Yina.
         not Nom pro-he past hit   Erg Yina
         'He was not hit by Yina.'

     b. ?Kiai te lā   na   liaki e   te wui tāngata.
         not the sail past raise Erg the pl men
         'The sail was not raised by the men.'

     c. ?Auwae te lākau e   yemu e   koe.
         don't the tree uns chop Erg you
         'Don't you chop down the tree!'

     d. ?Auwae nā   manú e   patu e   kōlua.
         don't the=pl bird uns kill Erg you=du
         'Don't you two kill the birds!'

However, this NP can always undergo the deletion strategy for Relativization:

(57) a. Ko   i wea   te lākau e   yemu e   lāua?
         Pred at where? the tree [uns chop Erg they=du]
         'Where is the tree that they are going to chop down?'

b. Ko   yuluyulu ai na   pa e   avatu e
    prog fasten   Pro the=pl hook [uns bring Erg
    '(He) fastened the fishhooks brought by

    ana   ipo matakula.
    pl=his love red-eyed]
    his red-eyed sweethearts.' (Beaglehole and
    Beaglehole 1027)

It can always undergo the chopping strategies for Clefting or Question Movement:

(58) a. Ko   te wāwā ka tunu e   te tama.
         Pred the taro fut cook Erg the boy
         'It is the taro that the boy is about to cook.'

     b. Ko   Uyo lā   kiai lā   na   maua ete patu
         Pred Uyo that not that past able Comp kill
         'It was Uyo who the people were unable

         e   te wenua.
         Erg the island
         to kill.'

(59) a. Ko   ai   na   turituri e   koe?
         Pred who? past chase   Erg you
         'Who did you chase?'

     b. Ko   ai   na   wakautunga e   te pūāpī?
         Pred who? past punish   Erg the teacher
         'Who was punished by the teacher?'

And, finally, it can always undergo Subject Preposing:

(60) I   a   matou na   vayi loa e   Uila.
      topic pro we   past whip Emp Erg Uila
      'We have been whipped by Uila.' (Beaglehole and
      Beaglehole 1139)

This suggests that the unmarked NP of the 'ergative' pattern can always serve as the subject for the purposes of superficial rules, but can do so only occasionally for Raising. Given that the unmarked NP originates as a direct object, the former fact appears to argue that it has been promoted to subject, presumably by Passive; the significance of the latter fact is dealt with in 7.4.

7.3.2.3. <u>e</u> <u>NP</u> <u>of</u> <u>the</u> <u>'Passive'</u> <u>Pattern</u>. Rather surprisingly, the rules of 7.3.1 also indicate that the <u>e</u> NP of the 'passive' pattern can serve as a subject, although the evidence is complicated by a certain amount of nondiscrete variation.

The <u>e</u> NP of the 'passive' pattern can serve occasionally as the target for Equi, as shown by:

(61) a. ?Na lōmamai lātou patu-a   te toa.
        past come=pl they kill-Pass the warrior
        'They came to kill the warrior.'

    b. ?Na   wakapono te   wenua ke   wō   lātou
        past decide   the island sbj go=pl they
        'The people decided that they would go

        vayi-a   nā   yakari.
        split-Pass the=pl coconut
        split coconuts.'

    c. ...ke yau ake tokotoko-na-ake te   langi.
            sbj come up raise-Pass-up   the sky
        '...that (he) should come to raise up the sky.'
        (Beaglehole and Beaglehole 977)

The <u>e</u> NP can also occasionally undergo Raising:

(62) a. ?Kiai i   a   Te Malo na   tiaki-na te wenua.
        not Nom prop Te Malo past lead-Pass the island
        'Te Malo did not lead the island.'

    b. ?Kiai i   a   Uyo na   onoono-wia te tāne.
        not Nom prop Uyo past see-Pass   the man
        'Uyo did not see the man.'

    c. ?Auwae koe e   yemu-ina te wāwā.
        don't you uns chop-Pass the taro
        'Don't you chop the taro!'

    d. ?Auwae kōtou e   kai-ina nā   wua moa.
        don't you=pl uns eat-Pass the=pl egg chicken
        'Don't you eat the eggs!'

In contrast, the <u>e</u> NP is almost always eligible for the deletion strategy of Relativization. This near perfect acceptability is indicated with †:

(63) a. †Ko   te   kulī tēnei na   kāti-a   te tāne
       Pred the dog this [past bite-Pass the man
       'This is the dog which bit the fat

       mōmoná.
       fat]
       man.'

   b. Kai wo   kolua wakawiti-a   mai i   te
       lest go=pl you=du return-Pass here Acc the
       'Let you not bring back the person

       tangata na   maka-tia   au i te moana na.
       person [past leave-Pass I   in the ocean that]
       who threw me into the sea.' (Beaglehole and
       Beaglehole 1069)

It is almost always eligible for the chopping strategies of Clefting or Question Movement:[1]

(64) a. †Ko   te toa   koa patu-a   te tamaiti.
       Pred the warrior prf hit-Pass the child
       'It is the warrior who has hit the child.'

   b. Ko to latou tangata wolo na   wakatupu-lia
       Pred their   person big past conceive-Pass
       'Their head man conceived

       te manako ia.
       the desire that
       the idea.' (Beaglehole and Beaglehole 1124)

(65) a. †Ko ai   na   kalo-wia i a   Te Malo?
       Pred who? past see-Pass Nom prop Te Malo
       'Who saw Te Malo?'

   b. Ko ai   na   kave-a   i a   Vakayala?
       Pred who? past take-Pass Nom prop Vakayala
       'Who has removed Vakayala?' (Beaglehole and
       Beaglehole 1134)

Finally, the e NP can always undergo Subject Preposing, as shown by:

348   Reanalysis and Pukapukan Syntax

(66) a. Te manu totolo na   kāti-a   tāua.
         the bird crawl past bite-Pass we=du
         'The animal bit us.'

    b.   I   a   koe na   wakatū-ngia te   wale   āpī.
         topic pro you past build-Pass the house school
         'You built the schoolhouse.'

It thus appears that the e NP of the 'passive' pattern can serve as a subject almost always for the purposes of superficial rules, but only occasionally for the purposes of Equi and Raising. This conclusion is curious, both because of the nondiscrete variation involved and because the unmarked NP of this case pattern can serve as a subject itself.

7.3.2.4. <u>e</u> <u>NP</u> <u>of</u> <u>the</u> <u>'Ergative'</u> <u>Pattern</u>. Finally, the evidence suggests that the e NP of the 'ergative' pattern can serve as a subject, though with less success than the other NPs discussed so far.

The e NP of the 'ergative' pattern is rarely, if ever, able to serve as the target for Equi. Consider the following:

(67) a. ?*Ka yau i   a   Uyo tiaki te wenua.
         fut come Nom prop Uyo lead the island
         (Uyo will come to lead the island.)

    b.   ?*Na yau i   a-na   wakalā nā   wāwā.
         past come Nom pro-he dry   the=pl   taro
         (He came to put the taro out to dry.)

    c.   ?*Yau koe onoono te   tala o toku wale.
         come you look   the side of my   house
         (You come look on the roof of my house.)

The e NP is also rarely, if ever, able to undergo Raising, as shown by:

(68) a. ?*Kiai te tamāwine na   patu te tāne.
         not the girl   past hit the man
         (The girl did not hit the man.)

b. ?*Kiai i a   Te Malo na pepelu te
   not Nom prop Te Malo past don   the
   (Te Malo did not don the loin-

   malo.
   loincloth
   cloth.)

c. ?*Auwae koe e   yuyuke te pū.
   don't you uns open   the door
   (Don't you open the door!)

The e NP can occasionally undergo the deletion strategy of Relativization and the chopping strategy of Clefting, as shown by sentences like:

(69)a. ?Ko i wea   te tāne na kai te ika?
       Pred at where? the man [past eat the fish]
       'Where is the man who ate the fish?'

   b. Ko ai   te kau   e   langa a tatou ui
       Pred who? the people [uns pull pl=our taro
       'Who is the group who pulls up our

       nei?
       this]
       talo?' (Beaglehole and Beaglehole 1128)

(70)a. ?Ko te toa   na patu te tamaiti.
       Pred the warrior past hit the child
       'It is the warrior who hit the child.'

   b. ?Ko Te Malo kiai na pepelu te malo.
      Pred Te Malo not past don   the loincloth
      'It is Te Malo who did not don the loincloth.'

However, this NP can rarely, if ever, undergo the chopping strategy of Question Movement:

(71)a. ?*Ko ai   na   wakatū te wale nei?
       Pred who? past build the house this
       (Who built this house?)

   b. ?*Ko ai   na   aumai te puka?
      Pred who? past bring the book
      (Who brought the book?)

350   Reanalysis and Pukapukan Syntax

Finally, the e NP is always eligible for Subject Preposing:

(72) a. Te tāne na   yoka te yakari.
         the man past husk the coconut
         'The man husked the coconut.'

   b. I   a matou ya   wai te yau ma   na
       topic pro we   past make the come with the=pl
       'We have made a copulating place with the

       kakai i   te loto   alai.
       people in the inside reef
       kakai in the middle reef.' (Beaglehole and
       Beaglehole 1024)

It thus appears that the e NP of the 'ergative' pattern can always act as a subject for the purposes of Subject Preposing, but can do so only occasionally for Relativization and Clefting, and rarely --if ever-- for Equi, Raising, and Question Movement. The significance of this rather complex result is discussed further in 7.4.

7.3.2.5. Summary. In short, either the underlying direct object or the underlying subject of the 'passive' and 'ergative' case patterns can serve as the subject for the purposes of subject-referring rules. The ability of the underlying direct object to serve as subject appears to argue that the clause has undergone Passive; the ability of the underlying subject to serve as subject suggests that the clause is active transitive. Further, although the unmarked NP (=underlying direct object) of the 'passive' pattern can always act as subject, the behavior of the other NPs is complicated by nondiscrete variation. Table 2 summarizes the overall grammaticality judgements for all types of NPs with respect to their eligibility for subject-referring rules.[2]

Although the facts of Table 2 could be described as a squish of subjecthood (see Ross 1974), it is ultimately more

Availability of Different NPs for Subject-Referring Rules:

	Unmarked NP		e NP	
	'passive'	'ergative'	'passive'	'ergative'
Equi	−	−	?	?*
Raising	✓	?	?	?*
Question Movement	✓	✓	†	?*
Relativization	✓	✓	†	?
Clefting	✓	✓	†	?
Subject Preposing	✓	✓	✓	✓

Table 2

352   Reanalysis and Pukapukan Syntax

revealing to treat them as the product of several intersecting generalizations, which can be stated as follows:

(73) a. The unmarked NPs of 'passive' and 'ergative' patterns undergo subject-referring rules more successfully than do the e NPs.

b. In general, the NPs of the 'passive' pattern undergo subject-referring rules more successfully than do the NPs of the 'ergative' pattern.

c. The e NPs of 'passive' and 'ergative' patterns undergo superficial rules referring to subjects more successfully than they do major rules.

The synchronic description of these facts is taken up in 7.4. For the moment, all that is important is that the historical prediction of 7.2.2, in its most straightforward form, is contradicted: the surface subjects of clauses in the 'passive' and 'ergative' patterns are not always subjects in underlying structure. This suggests that, if the passive-to-ergative reanalysis has occurred in Pukapukan, it has not been actualized in the discrete fashion described in 7.1.

7.4. AN ACCOUNT OF THE FACTS

This section attempts to provide a synchronic account of the interaction of the 'passive' and 'ergative' case patterns with subject-referring rules. It is suggested that no single synchronic analysis of these case patterns can account for all aspects of the interaction; in particular, for the non-discrete facts of Table 2. It is proposed instead that these facts result from competition between two analyses and a substantive principle governing it. The two analyses correspond to stages preceding and following the passive-to-ergative reanalysis, and the principle is one of the principles

governing syntactic change. In other words, Pukapukan is in
the middle of actualizing the passive-to-ergative reanalysis.

7.4.1 argues that the 'passive' and 'ergative' case patterns do not have a unique synchronic analysis; instead, the
clauses associated with each pattern have two analyses, one
involving Passive and the other involving an ergative case
assignment rule. 7.4.2 and 7.4.3 then attempt to account for
the generalizations of (73) by invoking the principle of the
cycle and variable rules, as described by Labov (1969, 1972).
7.4.4 suggests that the facts are better dealt with if Pukapukan is viewed as actualizing the passive-to-ergative reanalysis in a gradual, but principled, fashion. 7.4.5 discusses
some implications of the proposal.

7.4.1. <u>Two Analyses</u>

The argument that 'passive' and 'ergative' case patterns do
not have a unique synchronic analysis rests on two assumptions, whose status is discussed further below. First, it is
assumed that the subject-referring rules of 7.3.1 pick out
the NP that is subject at that level of derivation. Second,
it is assumed that at any level of derivation, a clause contains at most one subject.

Adopting these assumptions, we consider the facts of Table
2, ignoring their nondiscrete aspects for the moment and simply considering the absolute possibilities. On the one hand,
the underlying subjects of 'passive' and 'ergative' patterns
can undergo the rules of 7.3.1; this argues that they are
still subjects, and their clauses are still active transitive,
at the time when the rules apply. But if clauses in the 'passive' and 'ergative' patterns were invariably active transitive at this point, then there would be no way to account for
the ability of their underlying direct objects to undergo the
rules.

On the other hand, the underlying direct objects of 'passive' and 'ergative' patterns can undergo the rules of 7.3.1; this argues that they have been promoted to subject before the rules apply, presumably by Passive. But if clauses in the 'passive' and 'ergative' patterns had invariably undergone Passive at this point, then there would be no way to account for the ability of their underlying subjects to undergo the rules.

It appears from this that clauses in the 'passive' or 'ergative' patterns can have their morphology assigned in two ways. They can undergo Passive and have their morphology assigned by that rule. This is illustrated for the 'passive' pattern by:

(74)   Passive (optional): Promote the direct object to subject, turn the underlying subject into an oblique noun marked with e, and attach the passive suffix -Cia to the verb.

Or they can remain active transitive and have their morphology assigned by an ergative case assignment rule which may or may not insert the -Cia suffix. This is illustrated for the 'passive' pattern by:

(75)   Ergative Case Assignment (optional): If there are two direct case NPs in a clause, mark the subject with e and attach the suffix -Cia to the verb.

In other words, each case pattern is associated with two synchronic analyses of the clause.

The two assumptions on which this conclusion is based could, of course, be questioned. However, the conclusion has the advantage of distinguishing between clauses whose underlying direct objects have undergone the subject-referring rules of 7.3.1 and those whose underlying subjects have: the former are derived by Passive, and the latter, by ergative case assignment. The distinction between the two types of clauses turns out to be crucial in accounting for the facts of Table 2. A unique synchronic analysis of the case patterns could not make this distinction in as principled a way: therefore, the possibility of such an analysis is rejected here.

Having asserted the existence of the two analyses in (74) and (75), we now turn to the nondiscrete aspects of the facts --in particular, the generalizations of (73)-- and their description.

7.4.2. The Principle of the Cycle
Given that transformational grammar is not particularly concerned with describing nondiscrete variation, it is not immediately clear how a transformational analysis would deal with generalizations (73a) or (73b). However, since (73c) mentions the contrast of major vs. superficial rules, one might attempt to account for it by appealing to the principle of the cycle, which provided the original model for the major vs. superficial distinction (see 3.1.3).

For instance, it might be proposed that the *e* NP of the 'passive' pattern did not undergo major rules very successfully because the ergative case assignment rule of (75) was postcyclic. Such a proposal would assume that the subject-referring rules of 7.3.1 would be identified as cyclic or postcyclic in the straightforward way: the major rules, Equi and Raising, would be cyclic, whereas the superficial rules, Relativization, Clefting, Question Movement, and Subject Preposing, would be postcyclic.

The postcyclic character of ergative case assignment would prevent it from applying until after Equi or Raising had applied. Since the case assignment rule requires the clause to contain two direct case NPs, it would never be able to affect clauses whose underlying subjects had been removed by Equi or Raising. However, assuming that postcyclic rules were freely ordered with one another, it would be able to apply before rules like Relativization, Clefting, and so forth. As a result, relative clauses and other clause types whose underlying subjects had been extracted by superficial rules would be able to surface in the 'passive' pattern. A similar proposal could perhaps be made for the e NP of the 'ergative' pattern.

Such a proposal gives a fair description of the idea behind generalization (73c), and could perhaps be extended to describe other aspects of the generalizations as well. For instance, it might account for the effect of subject-referring rules on the unmarked NP of the 'passive' pattern by claiming that the Passive of (74) was cyclic. Derived subjects created by this rule would then be eligible for cyclic or postcyclic rules referring to subjects, thereby capturing one aspect of generalization (73a).

The proposal is, however, deficient in several respects. In claiming that clauses whose underlying subjects have undergone Equi or Raising could never occur in the 'passive' pattern, it fails to allow for the occasional occurrence of sentences like (61) or (62), in which exactly this happens. It does not describe the total range of possibilities, in other words. The proposal also fails to deal with other aspects of the generalizations --for instance, (73b), and the ability of the unmarked NP of the 'passive' pattern to undergo superficial rules more successfully than the e NP of this pattern. This suggests that the full range of facts cannot be accounted for by an appeal to the cycle alone.

7.4.3. Variable Rules

The failure of the proposal of 7.4.2 suggests that we might try to appeal instead to a theory which is explicitly concerned with describing variation. Perhaps the best known theory of this sort is the version of generative grammar developed by Labov (1969, 1972). According to Labov, rules may be accompanied by variables indicating the probability with which they apply under various conditions. Elements whose presence or absence affects this probability are assumed to be part of the statement of the rule, and are written into its structural description or structural change inside angled brackets. Such a theory is essentially a notational elaboration of transformational grammar, differing from the latter primarily in its attempt to account for nondiscrete facts.

In a framework of this type, a description of the Pukapukan facts might look like this. The Passive of (74) and the ergative case assignment rule of (75) would be ordered before the subject-referring rules, either by virtue of being cyclic or else via some explicit ordering statement. In addition, each subject-referring rule would include conditions causing it to apply less frequently to subjects marked with e, and even less frequently to such subjects when the verb is not suffixed with -Cia. The actual probabilities involved would be coded into the variables attached to each rule. To take a hypothetical example:

(76)   Relativization:

NP_i [X V <-Cia> <e> NP_i Y]
 1   2 3   4   5   6   7 → 1 2 3 4 ∅ ∅ 7

Probability of Applying:

$\phi = 1 - m$

$m = (1-k_0)$ if 5, but not 4, is present

$= (1-k_0)(1-k_1)$ if 4 and 5 are present

$= (1-k_0)(1-k_1)(1-k_2)$ otherwise

(This rule is stated in transformational formalism for convenience. Observe that the elements inside angled brackets inhibit, rather than facilitate, application of the rule.)

Such a system is capable of describing all of the variation in Table 2; however, it provides no explanation of why the rules should vary as they do. In particular, it seems unable to capture the unified behavior of the major rules --or of the superficial rules-- in their interaction with ergative case assignment. This behavior could not be described in any general fashion, but would have to be coded separately into the statement of each rule. This suggests that the account of the facts involving variable rules should be rejected as well.

7.4.4. Actualizing the Reanalysis

It thus appears that neither the cycle nor variable rules are able to provide a complete account of the generalizations of (73). And while other attempts could conceivably be made to describe these generalizations within current linguistic theory, it seems unlikely that these would be any more successful. Accordingly, this subsection provides an account of (73) by looking beyond linguistic theory to the theory of language change.

The two analyses proposed in 7.4.1 for 'passive' and 'ergative' case patterns are remarkably similar to the pre- and post-reanalysis grammars posited in the historical discussion of 7.1. This suggests that Pukapukan may well be in the process of actualizing the passive-to-ergative reanalysis, and so some or all of the facts of Table 2 may reflect the actualization of change.

359   Reanalysis and Pukapukan Syntax

This proposal is borne out by a closer examination of the three generalizations of (73). In almost every case, the NPs identified in these as undergoing subject-referring rules more successfully are the products of the <u>earlier</u> analysis, in terms of the historical discussion of 7.1. Thus, the unmarked NPs of 'passive' and 'ergative' case patterns undergo subject-referring rules more successfully than the <u>e</u> NPs, according to (73a). The unmarked NPs have acquired their subjecthood through Passive, a rule posited for the pre-reanalysis grammar (see (3a)); the <u>e</u> NPs are underlying subjects that have undergone ergative case assignment, a rule posited for the post-reanalysis grammar (see (3b) and (4)). Further, the NPs of the 'passive' pattern undergo subject-referring rules more successfully than the NPs of the 'ergative' pattern, according to (73b). The former NPs have undergone a Passive or an ergative case assignment rule which inserts -<u>Cia</u> (see (3)); the latter have undergone a rule which does not insert -<u>Cia</u> and is hypothesized to be the result of later change (see (4), for instance).

In general, the more recent the analysis, in terms of the historical discussion of 7.1, the less successful its interaction with the subject-referring rules of the grammar. This suggests that Pukapukan <u>has</u> undergone the passive-to-ergative reanalysis, but the new grammar fragments resulting from this change have not been implemented full-blown; instead, they are being introduced as less frequent, or less successful, alternatives to the older grammar fragments, which they will eventually replace completely. The general principle behind this type of introduction can be stated as follows:

(77)   Syntactic change is actualized gradually.

This principle accounts for the coexistence of the two analyses of 7.4.1, and for generalizations (73a) and (73b), assuming that Pukapukan has undergone the passive-to-ergative reanalysis.

The larger motivation of (77), presumably, is that it constrains the degree to which the outputs of successive grammars of a language can differ from each other. In other words, it contributes to mutual intelligibility among successive generations of speakers of a language. This can be seen by comparing Pukapukan to a hypothetical language in which the passive-to-ergative reanalysis was actualized abruptly and completely. In such a language, the grammars of older (pre-reanalysis) speakers and younger (post-reanalysis) speakers would produce identical outputs as far as clauses that had undergone no rules were concerned. But they would produce totally different outputs for clauses that had undergone subject-referring rules. Grammars of older speakers would allow only the unmarked NPs of 'passive' or 'ergative' patterns to be affected; grammars of younger speakers would allow only the e NPs to be affected. In requiring change to be actualized gradually, (77) prevents such abrupt transitions in output and so contributes to continuity of the surface data.

This same line of thought can be used to account for the remaining generalization, (73c), which states that the e NPs of 'passive' and 'ergative' patterns undergo superficial rules referring to subjects more successfully than they do major rules.

In general, major rules have a more serious effect on the syntax of the clause than do superficial rules. This difference is revealed most clearly by grammatical relations: major rules typically create or destroy grammatical relations, whereas superficial rules do not (see 3.1.3). It is also revealed by other properties. Major rules are 'deeper' than superficial rules in the sense that they often apply first (see 3.1.3 and 4.4). They have a more radical effect on morphology, in that they tend to result in infinitives or participles, whereas superficial rules do not.

These contrasts suggest that the continuity of the surface data may be contributed to if change is introduced first for clauses that exhibit the least syntactic distortion, and only later for other types of clauses. In this way the strangeness of the new analysis --a rather different type of distortion-- will be less apparent. The specific version of this that accounts for (73c) can be stated as follows:

(78) A new analysis is actualized first for clauses that are less distorted by syntactic rules, where superficial rules distort the clause less than do major rules.

(78) insures that ergative case assignment will interact with rules like Relativization, Clefting, Question Movement, and Subject Preposing before it interacts with rules like Equi or Raising. It can be viewed as a particular implementation of (77), since it describes one parameter along which change can be actualized gradually.

In summary, it is proposed that Pukapukan is actualizing the passive-to-ergative reanalysis, and the nondiscrete variation of Table 2 is the product of competition between two synchronic analyses, governed by principle (77) and the more specific (78). These principles constrain the range of differences allowed between the outputs of successive grammars of a language, and so belong to the theory of linguistic change.[3]

7.4.5. Implications

In claiming that change is actualized gradually, (77) contradicts the view that syntactic change is entirely discrete. Some remarks are required about the precise sense in which this view is contradicted.

Because (77) is limited to the actualization of change, it does not claim that all aspects of syntactic change are gradual, and is consistent with a theory in which some of them are abrupt or discrete. For instance, (77) does not rule out the passive-to-ergative reanalysis of (1), which is discrete in the sense that the grammars preceding and following it employ (partially) distinct sets of rules. It says only that the effects of the reanalysis must spread through the grammar in gradual fashion.

In constraining the actualization but not the form or ultimate outcome of changes, (77) allows syntactic change to be discrete in one sense, but gradual in another. It therefore is consistent with the larger model of change proposed by Andersen (1973) for phonology and Timberlake (1977) for syntax.[4] According to Andersen and Timberlake, change originates primarily in the discontinuous transmission of language from one generation to the next. Because speakers do not inherit the grammar of a language but instead recreate it on the basis of surface data, there is no guarantee that their grammars will be the same as those of the preceding generation. All that is required is that the grammars of the two generations produce the same, or highly similar, outputs. This situation allows for the possibility that new speakers may give a particular output an analysis different from the analysis of the preceding generation. This type of change --termed abductive change by Andersen-- is discrete, since it occurs in the gap between grammars of successive linguistic generations.

Andersen and Timberlake point out that a new analysis may
account for a set of data slightly different from that presented by the older generation. To correct for this, the new
generation may modify its analysis by adding extra rules to
produce output similar to that of the older generation. However, if the new analysis gains currency, subsequent generations will simplify the grammar by failing to formulate the
extra rules and allowing the analysis to emerge in its true
form. This type of change --termed deductive change by Ander-
sen-- is gradual, and so insures the continuity of surface
data from one generation to the next.

This model makes two claims about the nature of linguistic
change, both of which are consistent with the Pukapukan facts.
First, it claims that change can be decomposed into an initial
decision to change, followed by the surfacing of this decision in the outputs of successive generations of speakers.
This is basically the distinction that can be made in Pukapukan between the passive-to-ergative reanalysis and the nondiscrete variation of Table 2. Second, it claims that the initial decision to change is discrete, whereas its subsequent
realization is not. This is consistent with principle (77),
which states that syntactic change is actualized gradually.

At this point it might conceivably be suggested that (77)
was also consistent with the view of change outlined in 7.1.
Such a suggestion would have to start from the premise that
the end results of change are always discrete, and so could
be described within the assumptions outlined in 7.1. Assuming that the theory of change were restricted to describing
changes in terms of their outcomes, it would not have to account for any aspects of the Pukapukan facts aside from the
passive-to-ergative reanalysis itself. The nondiscrete variation of Table 2 and the principles governing it could be at-

tributed to performance factors.

The problem with such a suggestion is that generative historical linguistics is not restricted to describing the results of change. Instead, it attempts to account for the ways in which languages can change by constraining the possible differences, in rules and in outputs, between grammars of successive generations of speakers of a language. A theory with this goal obligates itself to account for the grammar of Pukapukan and its differences from grammars of previous stages of the language. But this cannot be done without appealing to (77). Therefore, in order to deal with Pukapukan, either the theory should be restricted to describing the end results of change, or else the claim that syntactic change is entirely discrete should be given up. It is in this sense that (77) is incompatible with the position outlined in 7.1.

7.5. TWO FURTHER EXAMPLES

Principle (78) claims further that syntactic change is actualized in _systematic_ fashion. According to it, the relative chronology with which a change will intersect with different clause types is determined by the rules that they have undergone. Clauses that are less distorted by syntactic rules will be affected first; those that are more distorted will be affected later. This section discusses two further examples of change that support the basic claim and suggest refinements of (78). These are the extension of ergative case marking to some middle clauses in Samoan, and the reanalysis of several rules of Indonesian, a Western Austronesian language, as affecting subjects and direct objects.

7.5.1. Samoan

Samoan has an ergative case system, described previously in

2.1.4. Canonical transitive verbs govern the ergative type of case marking; middle verbs govern a type of case marking resembling that for intransitive clauses containing an oblique NP.

Recently, ergative case marking has been extended to a number of middle verbs. This change had begun by the end of the nineteenth century, judging from texts (e.g. Stuebel 1896; Sierich 1900-02), and has certainly gained ground since then. Today ergative case marking is governed by a wide range of middle verbs in the speech of many Samoans -- particularly younger speakers-- who allow it as an alternative to the older middle pattern:

>
(79) a. Sā   va'ai e   le tama manu e   lima.
         past see Erg the boy bird uns five
         'The boy saw five birds.'

   b. Sā   leoleo e   la'u maile lo'u fale anapō.
         past watch Erg my   dog   my   house last=night
         'My dog guarded my house last night.'

   c. Sā   vala'au e   Toma lana uō   e   sau
         past call   Erg Toma his friend uns come

         lā   te tāfafao.
         they=du uns play=pl
         so that they could play.'

   d. Na   tofo e   ia le kuka.
         past taste Erg he the cooking
         'He tasted the cooking.'

Compare the middle pattern:

>
(80) a. Sā   va'ai le tama 'i manu e   lima.
         past see the boy to bird uns five
         'The boy saw five birds.'

   b. Sā   leoleo la'u maile i lo'u fale anapō.
         past watch my   dog   at my   house last=night
         'My dog guarded my house last night.'

c. Sā   vala'au Toma 'i lana uō   e   sau
    past call   Toma to his friend uns come
    'Toma called his friend to come

    lā   te tāfafao.
    they=du uns play=pl
    so that they could play.'

d. Na   tofo 'oia 'i le kuka.
    past taste he   to the cooking
    'He tasted the cooking.'

The extension of ergative case marking seems to have affected verbs of perception and communication before other subtypes of middle verbs. Alternations of the type (79-80) are regular for verbs such as <u>va'ai</u> 'see', <u>matamata</u> 'watch', and <u>fa'afetai</u> 'thank', but not for <u>alofa</u> 'love', <u>asiasi</u> 'visit', or <u>māsani</u> 'be acquainted with'. Further, within the class of perception and communication verbs, the change appears to have progressed farther for some lexical items than others --a point which can be seen from the semantic/stylistic value associated with choice of the ergative pattern. For verbs such as <u>va'ai</u> 'see' and <u>vala'au</u> 'call', choice of the ergative pattern is frequent and associated with no special semantic/stylistic value. For verbs such as <u>tofo</u> 'taste', choice of this pattern is less frequent and implies more focus on the subject. Finally, for verbs such as <u>fa'alogo</u> 'hear' or <u>tago</u> 'touch', which few speakers allow to govern ergative case marking, use of the ergative pattern is restricted to special semantic or pragmatic circumstances:

(81) a. Sā   fa'alogo a'u e   le fōma'i.
         past hear   me Erg the doctor
         'The doctor examined me with a stethoscope
         (lit. The doctor heard me).'

     b. Sā   tago e   a'u le nofoa.
         past touch Erg I   the chair
         'I touched the chair (when I was blindfolded).'

Compare the middle pattern:

(82) a. 'Ua 'ou fa'alogo 'i le agi o le matagi.
         prf I hear   to the blow of the wind
         'I heard the blowing of the wind.'

   b.   Sā tago a'u 'i le nofoa.
         past touch I to the chair
         'I touched the chair.'

The extension of ergative case marking could be viewed as part of a larger change to eliminate the middle case pattern for some (or all) middle verbs in Samoan --a change which has evidently been in progress for some time. For instance, there is evidence suggesting that verbs of contact, such as <u>sasa</u> 'beat', <u>fasi</u> 'hit', and <u>toso</u> 'rape', were treated as middle verbs at an earlier stage of Samoan. In the language recorded by Stuebel (1896), these verbs governed the middle or the ergative case patterns, and a few still retain this characteristic in the language of written documents and the Bible; most, however, have been reanalyzed as canonical transitives and allow only the ergative pattern in contemporary Samoan.

It may be that the same fate is in store for the verbs of perception and communication of (79-80). The ultimate fate of these verbs is not of immediate interest, however. What is important is that, for a number of them, the ergative case pattern has not been extended across the board. For instance, the verbs <u>tofo</u> 'taste' and <u>leoleo</u> 'watch' govern either the ergative or middle pattern in clauses to which no syntactic rules have applied (zero-pronominalization excepted). But when their subjects have been relativized, clefted, or cliticized, only the middle pattern is allowed:[5]

(83) a. *'O fea   le maile sā   leoleo lo'u fale
         Pred where? the dog [past watch my   house
         (Where is the dog that was guarding my house

```
         anapō?
         last=night]
         last night?) (Relativization)

    b. *'O   ia na   tofo le kuka.
         Pred he past taste the cooking
         (It was he that tasted the cooking.) (Clefting)

    c. *Sā   'ou tofo  lau kuka.
         past I   taste your cooking
         (I tasted your cooking.) (Clitic Placement)
```

Compare the middle pattern:

```
(84)a.   'O  fea    le maile  sā    leoleo i lo'u
         Pred where? the dog  [past watch  at my
         'Where is the dog that was guarding my

         fale  anapō?
         house last=night]
         house last night?' (Relativization)

    b.   'O  ia na   tofo 'i le kuka.
         Pred he past taste to the cooking
         'It was he that tasted the cooking.' (Clefting)

    c.   Sā   'ou tofo 'i lau kuka.
         past I   taste to your cooking
         'I tasted your cooking.' (Clitic Placement)
```

In general, the subjects of canonical transitive clauses in the ergative pattern can undergo these rules, as shown by:

```
(85)a.   'O  ia lenā sā    iloa le gaoi.
         Pred he that [past know the burglar]
         'He is the one who recognized the burglar.'
         (Relativization)

    b.   'O  a'u sā   togi le tusi i le maile.
         Pred I   past throw the book at the dog
         'It was I who threw the book at the dog.'
         (Clefting)

    c.   Sā   ia 'aumai se meaalofa o  le Easter 'i-āte
         past he bring  a  gift     of the Easter to-pro
         'He brought an Easter present to

         a'u.
         me
         me.' (Clitic Placement)
```

369   Reanalysis and Pukapukan Syntax

In short, it seems that the ergative pattern has been extended to verbs such as *tofo* and *leoleo* only in restricted fashion; it is allowed in clauses to which no rules have applied, but not in clauses that have undergone Relativization, Clefting, or Clitic Placement. There is a clear sense in which clauses that have undergone no rules are less syntactically distorted than clauses that have undergone superficial rules. This suggests that the change in case pattern is being actualized gradually, in conformity with principle (77): it is affecting the least distorted clause type, clauses that have undergone no rules, before it affects clauses that have undergone any rules at all.

7.5.2. *Indonesian*

Indonesian belongs to the Western branch of the Austronesian family, a branch that includes Malagasy, most of the ethnic languages of Indonesia and the Malay Peninsula, and the Philippine languages (Pawley 1974). Although comparative work on the syntax of these languages has not progressed very far, it is reasonably clear that they originally had verb-initial word order (see Pawley and Reid 1976). In addition, it seems likely that extraction rules in these languages were originally restricted to subjects. These characteristics are found synchronically in a number of Western Austronesian languages (Keenan 1972).

Along with several other Western Austronesian languages, Indonesian has innovated SVO word order. This change may (or may not) be related to the fact that this language has begun to extend some of its extraction rules to direct objects as well as subjects. Since the Indonesian grammatical tradition is extremely prescriptive, it is possible to observe two stages of the change by examining the formal language, as described in Indonesian grammars, and comparing it with the more colloquial versions volunteered by native speakers.[6] This is done briefly below.

In formal Indonesian, transitive clauses are distinguished by the appearance of the transitive prefix <u>meng</u>- on the verb. This prefix has a number of phonologically conditioned variants:

(86) a. Orang itu me-masak   daging.
         man the Trans-cook meat
         'The man cooked the meat.'

     b. Dokter itu me-meriksa   saya.
         doctor the Trans-examine me
         'The doctor examined me.'

     c. Saya me-lihat diri saya dalam air.
         I   Trans-see self my   in   water
         'I saw myself in the water.'

Rules such as Relativization, Clefting, and Question Movement are restricted to subjects in the formal language. These rules extract the focused NP, either deleting it (in the case of Relativization) or moving it to the left (in the case of Clefting and Question Movement), and insert the complementizer <u>yang</u> at the beginning of the clause:

(87) a. Orang yang me-masak   daging, nama-nya Achmad.
         man   [Comp Trans-cook meat]   name-his Achmad
         'The man who cooked the meat, his name is
         Achmad.' (Relativization)

     b. Dokter itu yang me-meriksa   saya.
         doctor the Comp Trans-examine me
         'It was the doctor that examined me.' (Clefting)

     c. Siapa-kah yang me-lihat kejadian itu?
         who?-Q   Comp Trans-see accident the
         'Who saw the accident?' (Question Movement)

Given that the rules are subject-limited, they affect direct objects only if these have been first turned into derived subjects. This can be accomplished by one of two methods, depending essentially on whether the underlying subject of the clause is a common noun or a pronoun (see Chung 1978). If the underlying subject is a common noun, the clause undergoes a Passive rule which is not of immediate interest. If, however, the underlying subject is a pronoun or (for some speakers) a proper noun, the clause undergoes a rule of Object Preposing which promotes the direct object to subject and cliticizes the underlying subject to the left of the verb (Chung 1976b). Because the resulting clause is superficially intransitive, the transitive prefix meng- does not appear; no new morphology is added elsewhere:

(88) a. Mobil itu kita perbaiki.
car the we repair
'We repaired the car.'
'The car was repaired by us.'

b. Dokter itu saya periksa.
doctor the I examine
'I examined the doctor.'
'The doctor was examined by me.'

c. Perempuan itu kamu lihat.
girl   the you see
'You saw the girl.'
'The girl was seen by you.'

The derived subject (=underlying direct object) is then eligible for Relativization, Clefting, and Question Movement:

(89) a. Mobil yang kita perbaiki adalah Mercedes.
car [Comp we repair] be   Mercedes
'The car that we repaired was a Mercedes.'
(Relativization)

b. Dokter itu yang saya periksa.
doctor the Comp I examine
'It was the doctor that I examined.' (Clefting)

c. Perempuan yang mana yang kamu lihat?
girl   [Comp which?] Comp you see
'Which girl did you see?' (Question Movement)

Although informal Indonesian differs from formal Indonesian in several respects (see Dyen 1964), the crucial difference for this discussion is that the transitive prefix need not be inserted in superficially transitive clauses (Chung 1978). Thus, alongside (86), we have the superficially transitive clauses of (90), in which the verb appears in its stem form:

(90)a. Orang itu masak daging.
        man   the cook meat
        'The man cooked the meat.'

   b.   Anak lakilaki itu kasih saya payung.
        child man   the give me   umbrella
        'The boy gave me an umbrella.'

   c.   Saya lihat diri saya dalam air.
        I   see   self my   in   water
        'I saw myself in the water.' (Dyen 1964: 17a.12)

The absence of the prefix makes the clauses of (90) morphologically similar to the Object Preposing clauses of (88), with the principal surface difference being that the underlying direct object occupies a different position relative to the verb. This surface difference is not apparent in constructions like those of (89), in which the direct object has been removed by an extraction rule. And it suggests the following possibility. Since the clause remnants following yang in (89) look like remnants of superficially transitive clauses in the informal language, it might be possible to reanalyze them as being derived directly by extraction of the direct object, without an intermediate stage involving Object Preposing. As a consequence of the reanalysis, the extraction rules would be extended to direct objects as well as subjects.

In fact, reanalyses of this sort appear to have occurred in informal Indonesian. This can be seen from the fact that constructions like (89) now involve clause remnants which could not have undergone Object Preposing, either because their underlying subjects are not pronouns/proper nouns, or because their verbs do not govern Object Preposing to begin with. In constructions of this type the direct object must have been relativized, clefted, or questioned directly as a direct object.

The reanalyses have progressed farther for some extraction rules than for others. For instance, Clefting and Question Movement apply regularly to direct objects for most speakers, and are even found this way in some grammars:

(91) a. Saya-lah yang dokter itu periksa.
I-Emp   Comp doctor the examine
'It was me that the doctor examined.' (Clefting)

b. Hanya nama itu saja yang tukang beca   tahu.
only name the just Comp worker pedicab know
'It is only this name that the pedicab driver knows.' (Dyen 1964: 19a.14; Clefting)

c. Apa   yang anak itu masak?
what? Comp child the cook
'What did the child cook?' (Question Movement)

d. Apa   yang lakilaki itu kerjakan?
what? Comp man   the do
'What did the man do?' (Question Movement)

In contrast, Relativization seems to lag slightly behind in the actualization of this change. This rule applies regularly to direct objects for some speakers; for others, it is allowed to do so only when the underlying subject is a short noun. A few speakers comment that constructions like those in (92) are common in everyday speech, but extremely colloquial:

(92) a. Bunga   yang ibu   saya beri-kan sudah mati.
flower [Comp mother my   give-Ben] prf   die
'The flowers that my mother gave (me) have already died.'

374   Reanalysis and Pukapukan Syntax

> b. Kamu me-lihat   ikan yang anak itu masak?
>   you Trans-see fish [Comp child the cook]
>   'Have you seen the fish that the child cooked?'
>
> c. Dia mem-baca   surat   yang pak guru   tulis.
>   he Trans-read letter [Comp Mr. teacher write]
>   'He read the letter that the teacher wrote.'

The contrast between Clefting and Question Movement on the one hand and Relativization on the other may seem unusual, given that all three rules are usually classified as superficial. But closer examination suggests that Clefting and Question Movement have more properties typical of superficial rules than Relativization. For instance, Clefting and Question Movement are unbounded, but Relativization must operate in the clause immediately under the head noun; i.e. it is downward-bounded:

> (93)a. Apa-kah yang Achmad sedang men-coba
>   what?-Q Comp Achmad prog   Trans-try
>   'What was Achmad trying
>
>   meny-impankan di bawah ranjang-nya?
>   Trans-hide   at under bed-his
>   to hide underneath his bed?' (Question Movement)
>
> b. ??Apa-kah kejadian buku itu yang kamu
>   what?-Q   fate   book the [Comp you
>   (What was the fate of the book that you
>
>   (men)-coba (meny)-sembunyikan?
>   Trans-try Trans-hide]
>   tried to hide?) (Relativization)
>
> c. *Apa   yang terjadi terhadap orang tua yang
>   what? Comp happen about   man   old [Comp
>   (What happened to the old man who
>
>   kami ber-setuju harus meng-atur
>   we   Intr-agree must Trans-organize
>   we agreed should organize the
>
>   parapekerja?
>   worker]
>   workers?) (Relativization)

375 Reanalysis and Pukapukan Syntax

Clefting and Question Movement also obey the no-ambiguity condition (Hankamer 1973), whereas Relativization does not. Finally, Clefting and Question Movement have productive strategies for prepositional phrases, whereas Relativization is restricted to subjects and direct objects. Since lack of bounding, blindness to grammatical relations, and the no-ambiguity condition are characteristics common of superficial rules in the languages of the world, it appears that Clefting and Question Movement are more superficial than Relativization. This correlates nicely with the fact that the actualization of the reanalysis has progressed farther for the former two rules.

Indonesian, then, provides a third example of the gradual actualization of syntactic change. The reanalysis described above is implemented faster for Clefting and Question Movement than for Relativization, whose status as a superficial rule is somewhat less secure. It is instructive to compare all three rules with the rule of Tough Movement, or Derived Subject Raising, which in Indonesian is restricted to direct objects that have first undergone Passive or Object Preposing (Chung 1976b). The fact that this rule is limited to subjects that were formerly direct objects would seem to make it a good candidate for a reanalysis of the sort described above; however, such a change seems not to have occurred. We can connect this (somewhat speculatively) to the fact that Tough Movement has the properties of a major rule, and so can be expected to undergo such a change later than Clefting or Relativization, if it undergoes it at all.

7.6. CONCLUSION

This chapter has used one example of change in progress to argue against the position that syntactic change is entirely

376   Reanalysis and Pukapukan Syntax

discrete. The example was taken from Pukapukan, a Samoic-Outlier language which is in the process of actualizing the passive-to-ergative reanalysis. The synchronic facts of Pukapukan were used to argue that syntactic change is actualized gradually. A general principle and a specific principle were formulated to account for this, and were then shown to be supported in spirit by facts from two other languages.

The specific changes discussed above provide evidence for the following. First, syntactic change affects clauses that have undergone superficial rules before it affects clauses that have undergone major rules. Second, it affects 'untouched' clauses before it affects clauses that have undergone any rules at all. Third and finally, it may distinguish between clause types that are distorted by more or less superficial rules, interacting with the former before it interacts with the latter. Combining these conclusions, we can say that the actualization of change is governed by the principle:

(94)   A new analysis is actualized first for clauses that are less distorted by syntactic rules, where the degree of distortion is determined by the following hierarchy:

Less Distorted
    Clauses that have undergone no rules
    Clauses that have undergone superficial rules
        Clefting/Question Movement
        Relativization
    Clauses that have undergone major rules
More Distorted

Such a hierarchy is natural in the sense that it corresponds to what we already know about these clause types and the rules that they involve. Synchronically, it is possible to classify rules as more or less superficial, depending on their various properties; it is also possible to classify clause types as more or less distorted, depending on the types of rules that they have undergone. The fact that these classifications also figure in syntactic change is striking, and suggests that linguistic synchrony and diachrony may not be as separate as some have proposed.

It can be concluded, then, that the synchronic properties of syntactic rules can be used in constraining the actualization of syntactic change. This conclusion is satisfying for several reasons. First, assuming that linguistic change is change in grammars, we would expect to find instances in which the structure of grammar has some specific consequences for the structure of linguistic change. The hierarchy of (94) provides one such instance. Second, in showing that the contrast between major and superficial rules is relevant for change, we produce more evidence for the reality of this contrast in synchronic grammar. Hence we confirm many of the conclusions of the preceding chapters, which take the reality of this contrast as their starting point.

NOTES

1. Given that the *e* NPs of these clause types are not always eligible for the deletion strategy of Relativization, or the chopping strategies of Clefting or Question Movement, the question arises as to whether they can act like oblique NPs and undergo the pronominalization strategy of Relativization, or the copying strategies of Clefting or Question Movement, instead. The answer to this is no. It appears that underlying subjects must be extracted by the deletion or chopping strategies where possible. If these

strategies are not felt to be possible for the e NPs of
(63-65), speakers will simply use the 'accusative' pattern,
thereby avoiding the problem.

2. The overall grammaticality judgements reflect the rough
percentages of times that speakers approved each of the
sentence types in question. As noted at the beginning of
this subsection, the judgements correlate surprisingly
well with the frequency of these sentence types in Beaglehole and Beaglehole (1938b). Statistics from approximate-
ly one hundred pages of texts are given in Table 3. These
statistics are more comprehensive than those reported in
Chung (1976a).

Two comments are in order about these statistics.
First, it may be that the number of e NPs of the 'ergative'
pattern serving as targets for Equi is actually lower than
the number given in Table 3. Of the ten instances counted,
seven involve embedded verbs ending in /i/ and followed by
a common noun direct object. Since adjacent like vowels
are often written as a single vowel in the texts, the
final /i/ of these verbs may well conceal an accusative
marker; if so, the sentences in question would illustrate
deletion of the unmarked NP (=underlying subject) of the
'accusative' pattern.

Second, the figures for Raising include only one instance of Raising governed by a negative verb; in this
instance, the raised NP is the underlying subject of the
'accusative' pattern. All other instances of Raising involve higher predicates with the meaning of English sentential adverbs. I have no explanation for the rather
low frequency of Raising to negatives in the texts, although it should be noted that (contrary to Chung 1976a)
Raising to negatives occurs several times for subjects

Availability of Different NPs for Subject-Referring Rules:

	Unmarked NP			e NP	
	'passive'	'ergative'	'accusative'	'passive'	'ergative'
Equi	-	-	36	7	10
Raising	1	1	9	-	1
Question Movement	-	-	-	1	-
Relativization	16	15	7	11	3
Clefting	2	2	1	3	1
Subject Preposing	4	6	2	-	1

NOTE: The unmarked NP of the 'passive' and 'ergative' patterns is an underlying direct object.

The unmarked NP of the 'accusative' pattern and the e NP of the 'passive' and 'ergative' patterns are underlying subjects.

Table 3

of intransitive clauses.
3. Although (77) and (78) account for almost all of the non-discrete variation of Table 2, two facts remain unaccounted for: first, the fact that the e NPs of the 'ergative' pattern are less eligible for Question Movement than for Relativization or Clefting; and second, the fact that the e NPs of 'passive' and 'ergative' patterns undergo Subject Preposing more successfully than any of the other rules.
4. The proposal of 7.4.4 differs from the model developed by Andersen in recognizing a pre-reanalysis grammar that competes with the post-reanalysis grammar, in a fashion governed by (77-78). Following Andersen's model strictly, there would be no such competing analyses; instead, adaptive rules would be added to the post-reanalysis grammar allowing certain direct objects --the unmarked NPs of 'passive' and 'ergative' patterns-- to undergo subject-referring rules.
5. Sentences like (83) are grammatical if the -Cia suffix is attached to the verb; however, it is difficult to tell whether the -Cia suffix in question is the flag for missing transitive subjects or the derivational suffix of 6.3.3. Because of this ambiguity, such sentences are not considered here. In any case, sentences like (83) should be grammatical if ergative case marking had been extended across the board to tofo 'taste' and leoleo 'watch'.
6. As is well known, there is considerable linguistic and sociolinguistic variation in Indonesian, due to the fact that the language has been a national language only since 1945 and is still a second language for the large majority of speakers. The facts discussed here hold for all of my Indonesian consultants, who were chosen deliberately to reflect a small segment of the population. All are young,

well-educated, upper or upper-middle class Indonesians from Jakarta; all speak Indonesian as their first language, and only one speaks any of the other languages of Indonesia. By and large, the description here agrees with that of Dyen (1964).

Appendix A. Orthography

Orthography is generally unchanged from the original sources, except that glottal stop is written ', and vowel length is indicated with a macron. The orthography distinguishes long vowels (e.g. ā) from rearticulated like vowels (e.g. aa).

The following conventions deserve note:

Maori ng is a velar nasal; wh is a voiceless bilabial continuant.

Tongan ng is a velar nasal.

Samoan g is a velar nasal; t and n are realized as dentals in formal speech and as velars in informal speech.

Kapingamarangi stops written with a following h are aspirated, and sonorants written with a following h are voiceless. Many instances of these segments recorded in Elbert's (1948) high-level phonetic transcription appear not to be underlying, but rather to arise via phonological rules of vowel syncope and consonant contraction.

Kapingamarangi ng is a velar nasal; ' indicates an elided vowel rather than glottal stop.

Pukapukan ng is a velar nasal; y is a voiceless interdental continuant.

Finally, the acute accent (´) is used to indicate a morphophonemic shift in stress from normal position (penultimate mora) to final mora. This stress shift, which goes by the name of the definitive accent, is productive in Tongan and occurs sporadically in Samoan and Pukapukan.

Appendix B. Sources

Examples from published sources are cited by author or editor, date of publication, and page number. Examples from collections of narrative texts referred to often are cited by author or editor and page number only. These are:

> Beaglehole and Beaglehole = Beaglehole and Beaglehole (1938b)
> Biggs, Hohepa, and Mead = Biggs, Hohepa, and Mead (1967)
> Elbert = Elbert (1948)
> Elbert and Monberg = Elbert and Monberg (1965)
> Fanua = Fanua (1975)
> Gifford = Gifford (1924)
> Grey = Grey (1971[1928])
> Orbell = Orbell (1968)
> Stuebel = Stuebel (1896)

One of the stories in Fanua (1975) was created by the author; the others are her versions of traditional tales. The selections in Biggs, Hohepa, and Mead (1967) include a wide range of material from early and modern, written and oral literature. With these exceptions, the other sources listed above are records of oral literature.

Bibliography

Andersen, Henning (1973) "Abductive and Deductive Change." *Language* 49: 765-93.

Anderson, Stephen R. (1976) "On the Notion of Subject in Ergative Languages." In Li (1976), pp. 1-23.

------ (1977) "On Mechanisms by which Languages Become Ergative." In Li (1977), pp. 317-63.

Anderson, Stephen R. and Sandra Chung (1977) "On Grammatical Relations and Clause Structure in Verb-Initial Languages." In *Syntax and Semantics 8: Grammatical Relations*, ed. by Peter Cole and Jerrold M. Sadock, pp. 1-25. New York: Academic Press.

Andrews, Avery D. (1971) "Case Agreement of Predicate Modifiers in Ancient Greek." *Linguistic Inquiry* 2: 127-51.

------ (1973) "Agreement and Deletion." In *Papers from the Ninth Regional Meeting*, ed. by C. Corum, T. Smith-Stark, and A. Weiser, pp. 23-33. Chicago: Chicago Linguistic Society.

Bach, Emmon (1971) "Questions." *Linguistic Inquiry* 2: 153-66.

Bailey, Charles-James N. and Roger W. Shuy, eds. (1973) *New Ways of Analyzing Variation in English*. Washington, D.C.: Georgetown University Press.

Beaglehole, Ernest and Pearl Beaglehole (1938a) *Ethnology of Pukapuka*. Honolulu: Bernice P. Bishop Museum Bulletin 150.

------ (1938b) "Myths, Stories, and Chants from Pukapuka." MS. Bernice P. Bishop Museum, Honolulu.

Bever, T.G. and D.T. Langendoen (1971) "A Dynamic Model of the Evolution of Language." *Linguistic Inquiry* 2: 433-63.

Bickerton, Derek (1971) "Inherent Variability and Variable

Rules." *Foundations of Language* 7: 457-92.

------ (1973) "Quantitative Versus Dynamic Paradigms: the case of Montreal *que*." In Bailey and Shuy (1973), pp. 23-43.

Biggs, Bruce (1961) "The Structure of New Zealand Maaori." *Anthropological Linguistics* 3. 3: 1-54.

------ (1969) *Let's Learn Maori*. Wellington, N.Z.: A.H. and A.W. Reed.

------ (1971) "The Languages of Polynesia." In *Current Trends in Linguistics 8: Linguistics in Oceania*, ed. by Thomas A. Sebeok, pp. 466-505. The Hague: Mouton.

------ (1974) "Some Problems of Polynesian Grammar." *Journal of the Polynesian Society* 83: 401-26.

Biggs, Bruce, P. Hohepa, and S.M. Mead, eds. (1967) *Selected Readings in Maori*. Wellington, N.Z.: A.H. and A.W. Reed.

Brathwaite, K. (1973) *Case Shift and Verb Concord in Georgian*. Ph.D. dissertation, University of Texas.

Chapin, Paul (1974) "Proto-Polynesian *ai*." *Journal of the Polynesian Society* 83: 259-307.

Chomsky, Noam (1965) *Aspects of the Theory of Syntax*. Cambridge, MA: MIT Press.

------ (1970) "Remarks on Nominalization." In *Readings in English Transformational Grammar*, ed. by Roderick W. Jacobs and Peter S. Rosenbaum, pp. 184-221. Waltham, MA: Ginn and Co.

------ (1973) "Conditions on Transformations." In *A Festschrift for Morris Halle*, ed. by Stephen R. Anderson and Paul Kiparsky, pp. 232-86. New York: Holt, Rinehart and Winston.

------ (1975) "Conditions on Rules of Grammar." In *Essays on Form and Interpretation*, by Noam Chomsky, pp. 161-210. New York: North-Holland.

------ (1977) "On Wh-Movement." In *Formal Syntax*, ed. by Peter W. Culicover, Thomas Wasow, and Adrian Akmajian, pp. 71-132. New York: Academic Press.

Chung, Sandra (1970) *Negative Verbs in Polynesian*. Senior honors thesis, Harvard University.

------ (1973a) "The Syntax of Nominalizations in Polynesian." *Oceanic Linguistics* 12: 641-86.

------ (1973b) "The Semantics of *i* in Samoan." MS.

------ (1976a) *Case Marking and Grammatical Relations in Polynesian*. Ph.D. dissertation, Harvard University.

------ (1976b) "On the Subject of Two Passives in Indonesian." In Li (1976), pp. 57-98.

------ (1977a) "On the Gradual Nature of Syntactic Change." In Li (1977), pp. 3-55.

------ (1977b) "Maori as an Accusative Language." To appear in *Journal of the Polynesian Society*.

------ (1978) "Stem Sentences in Indonesian." Paper delivered at the Second International Conference on Austronesian Linguistics, Canberra, Australia, in January 1978.

Chung, Sandra and William Seiter (1977) "On the History of Raising and Relativization in Polynesian." Paper delivered at the Austronesian Symposium, Honolulu, in August 1977.

Chung, Sandra and Alan Timberlake (1974) "Passive and Grammatical Relations in Maori." Paper delivered at the Winter LSA Meeting, New York, in December 1974.

------ (1978) "Tense, Aspect, and Mood." To appear in *Language Typology and Syntactic Fieldwork*, ed. by Timothy Shopen.

Churchward, C. Maxwell (1953) *Tongan Grammar*. London: Oxford University Press.

------ (1959) *Tongan Dictionary*. London: Oxford University Press.

Churchward, Spencer (1928) "On the Origin of the Polynesian Passive." *Journal of the Polynesian Society* 37: 300-05.

------ (1951) *A Samoan Grammar*, 2d ed. Melbourne, Australia: Spectator.

Clark, Ross (1973a) "Transitivity and Case in Eastern Oceanic Languages." *Oceanic Linguistics* 12: 559-605.

------ (1973b) "Passive and Surface Subject in Maori." Paper delivered at the Winter LSA Meeting, San Diego, CA, in December 1973.

------ (1976) *Aspects of Proto-Polynesian Syntax*. Auckland, N.Z.: Linguistic Society of New Zealand.

Comrie, Bernard (1976) *Aspect*. Cambridge: Cambridge University Press.

Cook, Kenneth William (1978) "The Mysterious Samoan Transitive Suffix." To appear in *Proceedings of the Fourth Annual Meeting of the Berkeley Linguistics Society*.

Dyen, Isidore (1964) *Beginning Indonesian, Lessons 1-24*. 4 vols. Office of Education, U.S. Department of Health, Education, and Welfare.

Elbert, Samuel H. (1948) *Grammar and Comparative Study of the Language of Kapingamarangi, Texts, and Word Lists*. Pacific Science Board, National Research Council.

Elbert, Samuel H. and Torben Monberg (1965) *From the Two Canoes*. Honolulu: University of Hawaii Press.

Fanua, Tupou Posesi (1975) *Po Fananga*. San Diego, CA: Tofua Press.

Fox, C.E. (1950) "Some Notes on Nggela Grammar." *Journal of the Polynesian Society* 59: 135-69.

Gifford, Edward W. (1924) *Tongan Myths and Tales*. Honolulu: Bernice P. Bishop Museum Bulletin 8.

Gonda, J. (1952) "Indonesian Linguistics and General Linguistics 2." *Lingua* 3: 17-51.

Bibliography

Green, Georgia M. (1974) *Semantics and Syntactic Regularity*. Bloomington: Indiana University Press.

Grey, Sir George (1971[1928]) *Nga Mahi a Nga Tupuna*, 3d ed. Wellington, N.Z.: A.H. and A.W. Reed (1st ed., 1854).

Gruber, Jeffrey S. (1970) *Studies in Lexical Relations*. Bloomington: Indiana University Linguistics Club.

Hale, Kenneth (1968) "Review of Hohepa (1967)." *Journal of the Polynesian Society* 77: 83-99.

------ (1970) "The Passive and Ergative in Language Change: the Australian Case." In *Pacific Linguistic Studies in Honor of Arthur Capell*, ed. by S.A. Wurm and D.C. Laycock, pp. 757-81. Pacific Linguistics, Series C, 13.

Hankamer, Jorge (1973) "Unacceptable Ambiguity." *Linguistic Inquiry* 4: 17-68.

------ (1974) "On the Noncyclic Nature of WH Clefting." In Lagaly, Fox, and Bruck (1974), pp. 221-33.

------ (1977) "Multiple Analyses." In Li (1977), pp. 583-607.

Hankamer, Jorge and Ivan Sag (1976) "Deep and Surface Anaphora." *Linguistic Inquiry* 7: 391-426.

Hohepa, Patrick W. (1967) *A Profile Generative Grammar of Maori*. Indiana University Publications in Anthropology and Linguistics, Memoir 20.

------ (1969a) "The Accusative-to-Ergative Drift in Polynesian Languages." *Journal of the Polynesian Society* 78: 295-329.

------ (1969b) "*Not* in English and *Kore* and *Ēhara* in Maori." *Te Reo* 12: 1-34.

Jackendoff, Ray (1972) *Semantic Interpretation in Generative Grammar*. Cambridge, MA: MIT Press.

Jespersen, Otto (1924) *The Philosophy of Grammar*. London: Allen and Unwin.

------ (1970[1931]) *A Modern English Grammar on Historical*

Principles, Part 4. London: George Allen and Unwin.

Kayne, Richard S. (1975) *French Syntax*. Cambridge, MA: MIT Press.

Keenan, Edward L. (1972) "Relative Clause Formation in Malagasy." In *The Chicago Which Hunt: Papers from the Relative Clause Festival*, ed. by P.M. Peranteau, J.N. Levi, and G.C. Phares, pp. 169-89. Chicago: Chicago Linguistic Society.

Keenan, Edward L. and Bernard Comrie (1977) "Noun Phrase Accessibility and Universal Grammar." *Linguistic Inquiry* 8: 63-99.

King, Robert D. (1969) *Historical Linguistics and Generative Grammar*. Englewood Cliffs, NJ: Prentice-Hall.

Kiparsky, Paul (1971) "Historical Linguistics." In *A Survey of Linguistic Science*, ed. by William O. Dingwall, pp. 576-649. College Park, MD: University of Maryland Linguistics Program.

------ (1973) "Phonological Representations." In *Three Dimensions of Linguistic Theory*, ed. by Osamu Fujimura, pp. 1-136. Tokyo: Institute for Advanced Studies of Language.

Klima, Edward S. (1964) *Studies in Diachronic Transformational Syntax*. Ph.D. dissertation, Harvard University.

Labov, William (1969) "Contraction, Deletion, and Inherent Variability of the English Copula." *Language* 45: 715-62.

------ (1972) *Sociolinguistic Patterns*. Philadelphia: University of Pennsylvania Press.

Lagaly, M.W., R.A. Fox, and A. Bruck, eds. (1974) *Papers from the Tenth Regional Meeting*. Chicago: Chicago Linguistic Society.

Lakoff, George (1965) "Deep and Surface Grammar." Mimeo.

Li, Charles N., ed. (1976) *Subject and Topic*. New York: Academic Press.

------, ed. (1977) *Mechanisms of Syntactic Change*. Austin, TX: University of Texas Press.

Mark, Ann (1970) "The Use of *ki* and *i* in New Zealand Maaori." MS.

McCawley, James D. (1970) "English as a VSO Language." *Language* 46: 286-99.

McEwen, J.M. (1970) *Niue Dictionary*. Wellington, N.Z.: Department of Maori and Island Affairs.

Meillet, Antoine (1966[1925]) *La méthode comparative en linguistique historique*. Instituttet for Sammenlignende Kulturforskning, Series A, 2. Paris: Honoré Champion.

Milner, G.B. (1962) "Active, Passive, or Perfective in Samoan: a Fresh Appraisal of the Problem." *Journal of the Polynesian Society* 71: 151-61.

------ (1966) *Samoan Dictionary*. London: Oxford University Press.

------ (1973) "It is Aspect (not Voice) which is Marked in Samoan." *Oceanic Linguistics* 12: 621-39.

Neffgen, H. (1903) *Grammatik der samoanischen Sprache nebst Lesestücken und Wörterbuch*. Vienna: A. Hartleben.

Ngata, Sir Apirana (1953) *Maori Grammar and Conversation*. Christchurch, N.Z.: Whitcombe and Tombs.

Orbell, Margaret, ed. (1968) *Maori Folktales in Maori and English*. Auckland, N.Z.: Blackwood and Janet Paul.

Pawley, Andrew K. (1966) "Polynesian Languages: a Subgrouping Based on Shared Innovations in Morphology." *Journal of the Polynesian Society* 75: 39-64.

------ (1967) "The Relationships of Polynesian Outlier Languages." *Journal of the Polynesian Society* 76: 259-96.

------ (1972) "On the Internal Relationships of Eastern Oceanic Languages." *Studies in Oceanic Culture History* 3, ed. by R.C. Green and M. Kelly. Pacific Anthropological

Records 13. Honolulu: Bernice P. Bishop Museum.

------ (1973a) "On the Origins of the Polynesian Active, Passive, and Stative Constructions." MS.

------ (1973b) "Some Problems in Proto-Oceanic Grammar." *Oceanic Linguistics* 12: 103-88.

------ (1974) "Austronesian Languages." In *Encyclopaedia Brittanica*, 15th ed., *Macropaedia* 2, pp. 484-94. Chicago: Encyclopaedia Brittanica.

------ (1975) "A Reanalysis of Fijian Transitive Sentences, or Why Change a Structure that has Lasted 5,000 Years?" MS.

Pawley, Andrew K. and Lawrence A. Reid (1976) "The Evolution of Transitive Constructions in Austronesian." *University of Hawaii Working Papers in Linguistics* 8. 2: 51-74.

Perlmutter, David M. (1973) "Evidence for the Cycle." Paper delivered at the Fourth Meeting of the Northeastern Linguistic Society, Providence, RI, in Fall 1973.

------ (forthcoming) "Possessor Ascension and the Laws Governing Ascensions." In *Studies in Relational Grammar*, ed. by David M. Perlmutter.

Perlmutter, David M. and Paul M. Postal (1974) "Some General Laws of Grammar." Mimeo.

------ (1977) "Toward a Universal Characterization of Passivization." In *Proceedings of the Third Annual Meeting of the Berkeley Linguistics Society*, ed. by Kenneth Whistler et al., pp. 394-417. Berkeley, CA: Berkeley Linguistics Society.

Perlmutter, David M. and Scott Soames (forthcoming) *Syntactic Argumentation and the Structure of English*.

Pinkham, Jessie and Jorge Hankamer (1975) "Deep and Shallow Clefts." In *Papers from the Eleventh Regional Meeting*, ed. by R.E. Grossman, L.J. San, and T.J. Vance, pp. 429-50.

Chicago: Chicago Linguistic Society.

Postal, Paul M. (1972) "On Some Rules that are not Successive Cyclic." <u>Linguistic Inquiry</u> 3: 211-22.

------ (1974) <u>On Raising: One Rule of English Grammar and its Theoretical Implications</u>. Cambridge, MA: MIT Press.

------ (forthcoming) "Antipassive in French." To appear in <u>Studies in Relational Grammar</u>, ed. by David M. Perlmutter.

Pratt, Reverend George (1960[1911]) <u>Grammar and Dictionary of the Samoan Language</u>, 4th ed. Malua, Western Samoa: Malua Printing Press.

Pullum, Geoffrey and Deirdre Wilson (1977) "Autonomous Syntax and the Analysis of Auxiliaries." <u>Language</u> 53: 741-88.

Reedy, Tamati (1977) "<u>he</u>-Phrases in Maori." To appear in <u>University of Hawaii Working Papers in Linguistics</u>.

Ross, John Robert (1967) <u>Constraints on Variables in Syntax</u>. Bloomington: Indiana University Linguistics Club.

------ (1969) "Auxiliaries as Main Verbs." In <u>Studies in Philosophical Linguistics</u>, Series One, ed. by W. Todd, pp. 77-102. Evanston, IL: Great Expectations.

------ (1974) "There, there, (there, (there, (there...)))." In Lagaly, Fox, and Bruck (1974), pp. 569-98.

Sapir, Edward (1917) "Review of Uhlenbeck (1916)." <u>International Journal of American Linguistics</u> 1: 82-86.

Schmidt, Johannes (1872) <u>Die Verwantschaftverhältnisse der indogermanischen Sprachen</u>. Weimar: H. Böhlau.

Schuchardt, Hugo (1895) "Über den passiven Charakter des Transitivs in den kaukasischen Sprachen." <u>Sitzungsberichte der Philosophisch-Historischen Classe der Kaiserlichen Akademie der Wissenschaften</u> 133: 1-90.

Seiter, William (1977) "Instrumental Advancement in Niuean." MS.

Shumway, Eric B. (1971) <u>Intensive Course in Tongan</u>. Honolulu:

University of Hawaii Press.

Sierich, O. (1900-02) "Samoanische Märchen." *Internationales Archiv für Ethnographie* 13: 223-37; 14: 15-23; 15: 167-200.

Sinclair, M.B.W. (1976) "Is Maori an Ergative Language?" *Journal of the Polynesian Society* 85: 9-26.

Stuebel, O. (1896) *Samoanische Texte*. Berlin: Veröffentlichungen aus dem Königlichen Museum für Völkerkunde.

Timberlake, Alan (1977) "Reanalysis and Actualization in Syntactic Change." In Li (1977), pp. 141-77.

------ (1979) "Reflexivization and the Cycle in Russian." To appear in *Linguistic Inquiry*.

Traugott, Elizabeth Closs (1965) "Diachronic Syntax and Generative Grammar." *Language* 41: 402-15.

Uhlenbeck, C.C. (1916) "Het Passieve Karakter van het Verbum Transitivum of van het Verbum Actionis in Talen van Noord-Amerika." *Verslagen en Mededeelingen der Koninklijke Akademie van Wetenschappen*, Afdeeling Letterkunde 5. 2: 187-216.

Waititi, Hoani R. (1962) *Te Rangatahi 1*. Wellington, N.Z.: R.E. Owen, Government Printer.

------ (1969) *Te Rangatahi 2*. Wellington, N.Z.: A.R. Shearer, Government Printer.

Watkins, Calvert (1976) "Towards Proto-Indo-European Syntax: Problems and Pseudo-Problems." In *Papers from the Parasession on Diachronic Syntax*, ed. by S.B. Steever, C.A. Walker, and S.S. Mufwene, pp. 305-26. Chicago: Chicago Linguistic Society.

Williams, H.W. (1928) "Some Observations on Polynesian Verbs." *Journal of the Polynesian Society* 37: 306-17.

------ (1971) *A Dictionary of the Maori Language*, 7th ed. Wellington, N.Z.: A.R. Shearer, Government Printer (1st ed., 1844).

Williams, W.L. and H.W. Williams (1950[1862]) <u>First Lessons in Maori</u>. Christchurch, N.Z.: Whitcombe and Tombs.

Wolfram, W. (1973) "On What Basis Variable Rules?" In Bailey and Shuy (1973), pp. 1-12.

Index

active 66-67, 68-69, 76-79
agent-emphatic 175-77
agents
   generic 85-86, 88, 275, 292
   semantic 13, 113-14, 116, 128-29, 130-31, 138-39, 198, 327-28
   stative 28-30
Agreement
   -Cia 83, 302-03
   Verb 147-48, 158
Antipassive 219-20, 232-33, 233-34
articles
   pronominal-proper 24, 52, 61, 289, 295, 322, 339
   specificity-number 23-24, 25; (Maori) 73-75, 135-37, 172, 179
aspect 75-81, 89-92
canonical transitive 47, 48-49, 49-50, 55, 67, 76, 79-80, 81, 88, 162, 213, 239, 240, 260, 278-79, 284, 307-08, 309-10, 367
case assignment 211-13, 214, 215-16, 218, 219, 242; (Pukapukan) 354, 355-56, 357, 359; (Samoan) 213, 214, 218-19, 233-34; (Tongan) 213, 214, 218-19, 233-34
case marking 26, 46-50, 97-99, 215, 241-42; (Kapingamarangi) 57-61; (Maori) 50-52, 135, 178, 300; (Proto-Polynesian) 244-45, 246-47, 250-51, 257, 258-59, 261-62, 264, 297, 310-11, 311-12; (Pukapukan) 61-65, 322-24, 330-33; (Rennellese) 287-93; (Samoan) 54-57, 160, 164-65, 184, 217-18, 237-38, 238-40, 306, 309-10, 364-69; (Tokelauan) 294-96; (Tongan) 52-54, 150-52, 217-18, 237-38
case marking, history of 246-47, 250-51, 262-63, 312-14
-Cia 65-66, 257-58; see also derivational suffix, Passive, transitive suffix
-Cia Insertion (Samoan) 88, 162-63, 240
Clefting 23; (Indonesian) 370-71, 372-75; (Maori) 69, 71, 76, 139-41, 178, 210; (Puka-

pukan) 337-39, 343, 345, 347, 349; (Rennellese) 289-91; (Samoan) 86, 87, 235-38, 367-68; (Tongan) 226-29, 230-33, 235, 237-38

Clitic Placement 31; (Samoan) 34-37, 82, 85, 101, 126-28, 157, 159, 162-63, 220-23, 367-68; (Tongan) 32-34, 101, 149, 208, 277

definitive accent 10-11, 38, 189-90

derivational suffix (Niuean) 283-84; (Samoan) 56-57, 284-86; (Tongan) 269-83

distribution of he: see articles

Eastern Oceanic 8, 256-59

Equi 106, 202; (Maori) 68-69, 71, 76, 106-16, 138-40, 172; (Pukapukan) 326-28, 333, 342, 346, 348; (Samoan) 82-83, 84-85, 124-31, 162, 163; (Tongan) 116-24, 197-99, 277, 278-80

extraction, constraints on 118-19, 139-41

government 104, 110-11, 121, 126-28, 141, 153-54, 160, 166-67, 171-72, 180-81, 181-82, 185-86, 191, 327, 334

grammatical relations 95-96, 97-101, 104, 202-04, 212, 213, 214, 215-16, 360

imperatives 17, 21, 44-45, 67, 70, 91

Indonesian: see Clefting, Passive, Question Movement, Relativization

Kapingamarangi: see case marking, transitive suffix, word order

linear order 83, 100, 101, 195, 196, 212-13, 215-16, 307-08

locatives, affected 169-70, 174, 181, 183, 188, 195

Maori: see articles, case marking, Clefting, Equi, Object Incorporation, Passive, Possessor Marking, Promotion, Raising, Relativization

middle 47-48, 49, 64, 78, 79, 181, 183, 195, 216-18, 222-23, 225-26, 229, 234, 236, 284-86, 307-08, 324, 365-69

modifiers
nominal 25-26, 189-90
verbal 21, 22, 133-34, 184, 190, 329-30

negatives 90-91, 92, 110, 132-34, 176-77, 329-30
Niuean: see derivational suffix
nominalizations 108, 298-300
Object Incorporation 203; (Maori) 188; (Samoan) 183-88; (Tongan) 45, 151-52, 188-89
Passive 48, 49-50, 203, 246, 247-48, 282; (Indonesian) 370-71, 372; (Maori) 51-52, 66-81, 137, 170-74, 180-81, 246, 260, 302-03; (Proto-Polynesian) 262-63, 264, 286-87, 294, 312; (Pukapukan) 344, 345, 354, 356, 357, 359
passive-to-ergative reanalysis 263, 264-66, 312, 314, 321-22, 324-25, 358-61
Polynesian
 classification of 7-10
 subgrouping of 8-9
Possessor Marking 25, 299, 300; (Maori) 108, 300-04; (Samoan) 238-39, 304-10; (Tongan) 149, 277
Possessor Preposing 25, 299
predicate nominals 22-23, 33, 176
predicate PPs 22, 32, 175, 176, 177
prepositions, oblique 26-28, 28-30, 42-43, 48, 49, 51, 53-54, 56, 59, 183, 195, 217, 218, 258-59, 289-93
Promotion 203; (Maori) 174-83
Pronoun Preposing (Samoan) 159-160, 238, 304-05, 307
pronouns 11, 13, 16, 26, 30-44, 56, 61, 135, 288-89, 293-94, 295, 296, 330-33, 339
Proto-Polynesian: see case marking, Passive
Pukapukan: see case assignment, case marking, Clefting, Equi, Passive, Question Movement, Raising, Relativization, Subject Preposing
Quantifier Float 203; (Samoan) 83, 158, 159, 196; (Tongan) 149, 189-96
Question Movement (Indonesian) 370-71, 372-75; (Pukapukan) 337-39, 343, 345, 347, 349
Raising 132, 202-03; (Maori) 132-45, 179-80; (Pukapukan) 328-35, 342, 344, 346, 348-49; (Samoan) 83, 84-85, 156-

69, 199-202; (Tongan) 145-56
reflexive 78-79, 157, 180, 279
Relativization 26, 37-38, 44; (Indonesian) 370-71, 372-75; (Maori) 69, 71-73, 76, 140, 144, 171-72, 178; (Pukapukan) 335-37, 343, 344-45, 346-47, 349; (Samoan) 85-86, 87, 235-38, 367-68; (Tongan) 38-44, 223-26, 230-33, 235, 237-38, 277
Rennellese: see case marking, Clefting, transitive suffix
rule ordering 103, 229-33, 242
rule typology 101-05
rules
  anaphora 104-05, 209-10
  cyclic vs. postcyclic 101-04, 355-56
  direct object-referring 83, 169-70, 173-74, 182-83, 186-88, 191, 192-95, 202-04, 302, 303-04, 306-07, 308-09
  major 104-05, 109-11, 120-21, 126-28, 141, 153-54, 166-67, 171-73, 181-82, 184-86, 191, 198, 200, 219, 241-42, 327, 334, 360-61
  morphology 104-05, 238, 240, 241-42
  subject-referring 33-34, 36-37, 71, 73-74, 106, 111-14, 116, 121-23, 128-31, 132, 141-45, 147-48, 154-56, 158, 167-69, 191-92, 202-04, 300-01, 303-04, 305-06, 308-09, 325-26, 327-28, 334-35, 336-37, 338-39, 340, 352, 353, 370
  superficial 88, 104-05, 221, 224, 227, 241-42, 336, 338, 339, 360-61, 369, 374-75
Samoan: see case assignment, case marking, -Cia Insertion, Clefting, Clitic Placement, derivational suffix, Equi, Object Incorporation, Possessor Marking, Pronoun Preposing, Quantifier Float, Raising, Relativization, transitive suffix
Subject Preposing (Pukapukan) 331-32, 339-40, 343, 345, 347-48, 350
tense-aspect-mood 20-21, 22,

31, 32-33, 35-36, 110, 133, 134, 177, 329
third singular restrictions 33, 36, 40, 221-22, 223, 224-25, 227-28
Tokelauan: see case marking
Tongan: see case assignment, case marking, Clefting, Clitic Placement, derivational suffix, Equi, Object Incorporation, Possessor Marking, Quantifier Float, Raising, Relativization, Topicalization, transitive suffix, zero-pronominalization
Topicalization (Tongan) 189, 226-29
transitive suffix (Kapingamarangi) 60; (Rennellese) 291-93; (Samoan) 55-56, 81-93, 284, 286; (Tongan) 268-69, 281
transitivity restrictions 36, 40, 73-74, 126-28, 135-36, 221-22, 223, 224-25, 227-28, 278-79
verbs
    classification of 47
    stative 29, 113, 143-44
word order 12-15, 55, 62, 135, 256, 296, 369; (Kapingamarangi) 15-20
zero-pronominalization 17, 30-31, 37-38, 70, 71, 84, 104, 109, 125-26, 137-38, 157-58, 200, 205-06, 292, 327, 333, 335-36; (Tongan) 32, 39, 41-44, 120, 197-98, 204-05, 206-07

www.ingramcontent.com/pod-product-compliance
Lightning Source LLC
Chambersburg PA
CBHW021937240426
43668CB00036B/77